WIN THE VALUE REVOLUTION

WIN THE VALUE REVOLUTION

How to Give Your Customers a Quality Product, Excellent Service, and Still Make Money

BY

ROBERT B. TUCKER

Career Press
3 Tice Road
P.O. Box 687
Franklin Lakes, NJ 07417
1-800-Career-1
201-848-0310 (outside U.S.)

Win the Value Revolution
ISBN 1-56414-174-8, $21.99
Cover design by Dean Johnson Design, Inc.
Text design by A Good Thing Inc.
Printed in the U.S.A. by Book-mart Press

To order this title by mail, please include price as noted above, $2.50 handling per order, and $1.00 for each book ordered. Send to: Career Press, Inc., 3 Tice Road, P.O. Box 687, Franklin Lakes, NJ 07417

Or call toll-free 1-800-CAREER-1 (Canada: 201-848-0310) to order using VISA or MasterCard, or for further information on books from Career Press.

Library of Congress Cataloging-in-Publication Data
Tucker, Robert B., 1953-
  Win the value revolution/ by Robert B. Tucker.
  p. cm.
  Includes index.
  ISBN 1-56414-174-8 : $21.99
  1. Industrial management. 2. Consumer satisfaction. 3. Value
I. Title.
HD31.T785   1995
658.8'.12--dc20
                                                                95-6953
                                                                CIP

To my daughter, Cara Rose Tucker

TABLE OF CONTENTS

PREFACE

Are your customers demanding more from you, yet looking for ways to pay less? Are you facing a host of new competitors, some of whom you're not even familiar with? Are your customers noticeably more sophisticated in making purchases from you than ever before?

If your answer is Yes to such questions, you're hardly alone. The new reality is that buyers—both individual consumers and business-to-business purchasers alike—can have it all: high quality, excellent service, and a competitive price. Across North America, and spreading rapidly throughout Europe, South America, and Japan, a seismic shakeup is altering the relationship between buyers and sellers. In industry after industry, buyers have become more demanding and less loyal. They are refusing to pay prices inflated by layers of middlemen; turning up their noses at sellers' dictates previously taken for granted; questioning everything from price to terms to warranties; substituting private-label, "no load," or clone products for brand names; negotiating harder for the absolute best deal at the absolute lowest price. What is occurring, as *Win the Value Revolution* makes clear, is nothing less than a global Value Revolution.

From Madison Avenue to Main Street, from retail to manufacturing to the service sector, the "game" is changing fast. But what are the new rules? How does a firm turn the customer's quest for greater value into an opportunity rather than a stumbling block? *Win the Value Revolution* is designed to lay out the new rules for competing successfully in a new and rapidly changing business environment. It will serve as a primer in giving your business—and your leadership skills—an all-points checkup: your positioning in the marketplace and how you "go to market," your marketing and sales operations, the extra services you offer, how you engender customer loyalty and employee loyalty, and how you add value to your offerings.

Win the Value Revolution will give you the practical guidelines for translating your customer's demand for greater value into powerful new sources of competitive advantage. Here is a step-by-step guide for rethinking, repositioning, and reengineering your firm for success in this exciting but volatile new era. *Win the Value Revolution* urges that every aspect of your firm's offerings, from your products and services to your people, must be analyzed from the standpoint of how each either adds or subtracts from your overall ability to deliver more for less.

Using dozens of real-life examples and case studies, *Win the Value Revolution* will guide you through the three R's essential to turning this "driving force of change" into a powerful competitive weapon: *Rethinking* (your Value Proposition), *Repositioning*, (products and services, marketing and selling methods), and *Reengineering* (departments, job functions, distribution methods).

Win the Value Revolution will guide you in developing critical new strategic skills and will cause you to think about your competitive challenges and new opportunities in entirely new ways. Here is a brief summary of what each chapter provides:

In Chapter 1 you'll discover why neither excellent quality, terrific service, nor low price may be enough in the value era, and you'll learn:

- The four critical forces driving the value revolution
- What the revolution means to your firm

In Chapter 2, "Rethinking Your Value Proposition," you'll:

- Audit the unique "equation" of quality, service, and price that form your firm's Value Proposition
- See first hand how companies are getting slammed because they stopped innovating improvements in the Q Factor, S Factor, and P Factor
- Learn eight essential pricing strategies

In Chapter 3, you'll discover why Value Innovators don't play by the old rules but instead invent new ones. This chapter will guide you in becoming a Value Innovator, and show you:

- How to hone in on what your various customers truly value and are willing to pay for (and pay extra for)
- How to fight back with a value strategy in your market, region, industry, or market niche

In Chapter 4, you'll learn how to gain unique competitive advantage by taking on your customers' problems, by out-customizing the competition, and empowering customers through knowledge and four other proven strategies for adding value.

In Chapter 5, "Adding Value Profitably," you'll be issued an essential checklist to guide your launch of any new service offer, from the simplest to the most complex. You'll master:

- How to "think through" new value-adding services to see if they make sense in the longer run
- Eight innovative ways of listening to customers
- Nine steps to creating successful value-added programs

Chapter 6 will probably blast away a few of your paradigms regarding customer loyalty. You'll see how a Dallas car dealer estimates the value of "lifetime loyalty" and how he and other firms actually achieve it. In this chapter you'll learn the five critical factors you can put to use right away to dramatically increase customer loyalty to your firm.

In Chapter 7, we'll take a fresh look at marketing to today's sophisticated, jaded consumer. You'll see why marketing must move from a paradigm of manipulation and gimmickry to one of building trust, educating the customer, discovering new markets, and challenging "commodity thinking."

In Chapter 8, "Value-Added Selling," you'll master five factors that are critical for adding value to your offerings, regardless of what business you're in. One of these is innovation, as you might expect. The other four may surprise you!

In Chapter 9, "Adding Value to Products," you'll learn why the most successful sales organizations and individual salespersons in the value era will be those who can effectively deliver value at the point of sale. You'll be ready to guide your sales team toward out-innovating and out-thinking the competition when you master:

- The seven essential strategies for reinventing your sales organization
- How to "tangibalize" your value added and get more marketing mileage out of the services and extras you already provide
- How to rethink your sales methods and ways of creating and delivering value at the front lines of customer contact

In Chapter 10, "Delivering Customer Value Through People," you'll see that the biggest factor in winning the Value Revolution is your people. You'll go with the CEO of Southwest Airlines as he hands out donuts and coffee to line workers, and you'll hear from Levi Strauss CEO Robert Haas what he means when he says, "We're not [spelling out our values] because it makes us feel good but because we believe in the interconnection between liberating the talents of our people and business success." In this important chapter, you'll learn:

- How to establish a continuous value improvement process
- How to communicate to your people the urgent requirements of the value era
- How to define and communicate your core company values to your associates so they can genuinely add value to the end customer

In Chapter 11, you'll gain specific new insights into how to champion the value vision, and how to lead the charge in keeping the focus on this constantly moving target in your firm. You'll learn to master the five imperatives of the value-adding leader.

Win the Value Revolution is based on my 12-year experience as a consultant to, and researcher of, businesses that are profiting from change through innovation. The book also taps my exclusive, behind-the-scenes interviews with dozens of CEOs and leaders of companies who are indeed winning the Value Revolution. Some, like Home Depot,

McDonald's, Southwest Airlines, and Charles Schwab, are widely known to business persons. Others, like Babush Corporation, a distributor of conveyor systems, and F. D. Titus, a fast-growing purveyor of health care products, you will read about in these pages for the first time.

How to Get the Most Value from this Book

You'll get the most value from this book if you :

1. *Read the book during a creative time in your schedule.* Take it along on your next cross-country flight or when you've set aside some time for strategic planning. When your mind is fresh and you're feeling relaxed, you'll generate powerful profit-producing ideas as you move through the many examples and ideas in this book.

2. *Read actively, rather than passively.* In other words, answer the questions that are designed to get you thinking about your firm's future. It will take a little longer but will definitely be worth it. Keep your favorite tool for "downloading" your ideas ready at hand, whether that be a tape recorder, laptop computer, or simple but effective idea notebook. Record your ideas and future possibilities as soon as they come to mind.

3. *Think of this book as a tool.* Mark up the text as you read, highlight passages that are especially meaningful to you, and write notes to yourself right in the margins.

4. *Share the information with others.* One of the most powerful things you can do to fully integrate the message of this book is to make a presentation on it to others—your associates or your management team, for example, but also at your regional or national trade association meetings, service clubs, or chamber of commerce, Toastmasters club, or other groups. In so doing, you'll discover the secret that every teacher knows: In the act of instructing others, we truly learn.

5. *Form a study group in your company.* You may want to give each of your key people a copy of this book and make it required reading. What better way to put the imperative of adding value in the forefront of people's thoughts.

6. *Take action*. Nolan Bushnell, founder of Atari Corporation, once said: "Anyone who's ever taken a shower has had a good idea. But it's the person who gets out, dries off, and does something with those ideas who makes a difference in this world." Bushnell's right. Plan to sort through the ideas you glean from reading this book and take action on those that seem most feasible and appropriate.

7. *Review your notes frequently on the book.* Keep *Win the Value Revolution* in your office after you've read it through the first time, and skim back through marked passages from time to time. Are you on track? What's the next thing you want to tackle?

With that, let's get started!

ACKNOWLEDGMENTS

I would like to extend my thanks and sincere appreciation to a number of people who helped make *Win the Value Revolution* possible:

- To my wife and partner, Carolyn, whose love and encouragement during the dark days of this project helped sustain me

- To my daughter, Cara Rose, who has, in her 5 years of life, taught me many lessons about value . . . and values

- To Steve Diamond, an author in his own right, who came on board this project and assisted greatly at a time when he was needed the most

- To my colleagues who read and commented on the proposal and/or manuscript: Dale Achabal, Steven Broydrick, Eldon Edwards, Joani Flynn, Michael LeBoeuf, Jack Opet, Edwin Rigsbee, Tom Justin and my dad, Charles Tucker

- To my pals at "Gold Coast" whose support and eagerness to "think outside the box" kept me going

- To my research team: Jason Cary, Nancy Marriott, Sandra Jewell, and Eva Anda for their valuable assistance

- To Ron Fry and the entire team at Career Press, who truly understand what it means to win the Value Revolution in the field of publishing and are doing so every day

CHAPTER

THE VALUE REVOLUTION

FALL IN SOUTHERN CALIFORNIA IS "FIRE SEASON." The chaparral on the hillsides turns brown and parched from months of rainless days, and the boots of hikers hit the ground with little poofs of dust. A careless match tossed into the brush can begin an horrific firestorm.

Just as the northern states have their killer winter storms, and the Midwest its floods and tornadoes, Southern California must endure these uncontrollable wildfires. During one particularly devastating firestorm, fire officials were quoted as saying that hot cinders were being driven far and wide only to start still more fires. As soon as firefighters thought they had "the fire" contained, wind-whipped cinders would zoom across vast distances of sky, igniting new fires miles away.

Today, with much the same force as these wildfires, there is a revolution spreading across the economic landscape. It is, at root, a change

1

in the relationship between buyers and sellers. In industry after industry, buyers have increasingly become more demanding and less loyal. They are refusing to pay prices inflated by layers of middlemen whom they do not perceive as adding value; turning up their noses at sellers' dictates previously taken for granted; questioning everything from price to terms to warranties; substituting generic, "no load," or clone products for brand names; and negotiating harder for the absolute best deal. In short, it is a revolutionary call for greater value, and it affects firms large and small in every economic sector. Consider:

- For years, American Express based much of its appeal on the perception of prestige and status its charge card imbued. The strategy worked, and throughout the 60s, 70s, and 80s, AmEx's card business grew. Then came the 90s. AmEx stayed with the same strategy, but membership began to drop. Suddenly status and prestige weren't working as well in the face of a torrent of new cards touting more benefits for less money.

- In 1986, the Business Products Industry Association had 4,563 dealer-members, mostly independent, family-owned stationery stores across the U.S., many of which enjoyed lofty profit margins on such items as legal pads, pens, Post-It Notes, tape, and hundreds of other items. By the mid- 90s, BPIA had only 2,853 dealers, the rest having exited the business.

What changed? To be sure, the stationers hadn't. Their prices hadn't changed. Their service, ranging from very good at some to lackluster at most, was the same as it had always been. No, these businesses hadn't changed, but their customers had been given a new choice, a new way of satisfying a need that many apparently found more appealing. And they had voted with their feet, electing to shop at the growing number of new office products superstores that sprouted up across the land during this period.

- Warehouse clubs, which hardly existed in 1980, had grown to a $25 billion industry by the mid-90s, having decimated untold thousands of companies in their wake.

- After peaking in 1991, sales of Mercedes Benz automobiles and trucks tumbled so steeply that they pushed the parent company into the red.

In 1993, Mercedes lost money for the first time. From its preeminent position as the world's oldest carmaker, the pride of German engineering could no longer ignore a fundamental precept of the "Value Revolution": that quality alone was not enough. Mercedes ignored signs that its relatively more costly, anachronistic methods of coming to market would not work in the new world order. Other luxury car manufacturers had entered its turf sensing better value, which was made possible through advantages in costs and productivity.

- In early 1995, major U.S. airlines suddenly abandoned the decades-old tradition of paying travel agents 10 percent commissions on all fares, markedly reducing the revenues of the nation's 33,000 agencies. Citing the excess costs (about $30 of every $100 spent on airline travel), the airlines hope to steer more passengers to their direct reservations centers; meanwhile, widespread bankruptcies among agencies were expected.

- For decades, Bayer was so identified with aspirin that it practically became the generic word for the drug in the minds of consumers. But today, if consumers want aspirin at all, they increasingly reach for a store brand. Bayer has been attacked on two sides: from the left are less pricey private-label "brands," and from the right, non-aspirin pain relievers such as Tylenol. While private-label aspirin continues to gain market share, Bayer lost 17 percent in a recent year.

Whether the product is as simple as aspirin or as complex as luxury automobiles, and whether the service is brokering tickets or merchandising pens and paper clips, what such disparate examples point to is this:

There is a sea change occurring in terms of what satisfies customers, and what keeps them coming back for more. What worked yesterday cannot be presumed to work today, and what satisfies well today almost assuredly will not satisfy tomorrow.

But this brave new world of change need not unsettle us, so long as we are willing to understand its demands, and to rethink our products and services and ways of coming to market. Indeed, if we do that, it is quite possible, as the many companies we will examine in these pages have done, that we can turn this force to our advantage.

Just What Is Value, Anyway?

Today, the operative word in business is value, which *Webster's New World Dictionary* defines as "a fair or proper equivalent in money, for something sold." If a firm's products or services meet a buyer's needs and are offered at a price that buyer considers fair, we can say that that business has created value for that buyer, and its "Value Proposition" works for that buyer. For the purposes of this book, we'll look at value as a combination of three important factors: quality, service, and price. Let's take these one by one:

- *Quality.* Let's call this one the "Q Factor," by which we mean the tangible, physical aspects of a product, or, in the case of a service, the quality of the actual work, the physical amenities offered or not offered.

- *Service.* We'll call this one the "S Factor," by which we'll be referring to both the perceived level of customer service (how attentive were those doing the attending?), and the amount of *services* that were purchased or offered along with the "product."

- *Price.* We'll call this one the "P Factor," and it is perhaps the most straightforward of the three. What did you pay for what you got? That's the price.

Pretty straightforward, right? It's when we combine these three factors together that things get interesting. Taken together, these three factors form the "Value Proposition" offered to customers. The challenge comes in trying to decide what your customers value, what they consider "fair and proper treatment," what they are willing to pay for, what they are willing to pay extra for, and what you can realistically provide them.

Today, as this book will explore, various forces of change are at work that are causing more customers to question what is best for them when they purchase your product or service. Offering the same Value Proposition today to your customers that you did yesterday may not cut it. Traditional office product stores watched as customers voted for a different Value Proposition proffered by the cavernous office products superstores. These outlets, with names like Office Depot, Staples, Office Max, and others, offer many of the same products (the Q Factor is the same), a lowered S-factor (less selection, less customer service, fewer services, etc.), but at less cost (a lower P Factor). American Express watched as its well-heeled customers voted against the superhigh Q and S Factors (along with a higher P Factor annual membership fee) it had successfully used to attract customers for years.

"Value" Is a Moving Target

Perhaps you've seen the effects of changing priorities in your own life with regards to the goods and services you choose. As I've researched and lectured on and consulted with companies about their Value Proposition in a world of change, these experiences have made me acutely aware of how one consumer makes different choices today than in the past.

For example, I'm the president of a small research and executive development company based in Santa Barbara, California. Until recently, we used a local answering service that we chose because it "sounded like your secretary." Mostly for after-hours callers, the service also provided a backup receptionist for times during the day when we were all out of the office, or were otherwise unable to answer the phones.

The system was imperfect, to say the least. When I asked friends and customers to comment on the customer service of the answering service, many were less than enthusiastic (the S Factor wasn't cutting it). So when the local phone company introduced a low-cost version of voice mail, I began to rethink the value of the service, versus the price. (I was paying around $200 a month for the service). I looked into voicemail and discovered it would cost less than $10 a month for unlimited use! So despite the fact that I had some concerns with voicemail, much preferring that our clients reach a "human-being" receptionist rather than a recording, the value equation was simply too weighted against the answering service. We discontinued the answering service and went electronic.

If you pause a moment to consider your own recent buying decisions, you'll probably discover similar switches you've made having to do with changes in what you perceive as the best value as you personally define it. And this process of assessing the value of things extends beyond just products and services; it involves the very essence of how we choose to spend our time, how we vote, and how we look at what we are getting from government services versus what we pay in taxes, and the associations we choose to take part in.

As I interview business leaders and consumers during the course of my work, I often hear value questions coming up. For example, a colleague and I were talking about a professional sales organization to which he formerly belonged. After dropping out of the group several years ago, he recently attended a dinner meeting and was not inclined to renew his membership. He explained that 15 years ago, there weren't national training companies teaching sales techniques. Yet this organization still has an attitude that it is exclusive; that becoming a member is difficult. Meanwhile, its membership has continued to dwindle!

The Spreading Search for Value

And the value wildfires continue to jump to new industries, and new sectors of the economy. Let's take a look at specific sectors:

Retailing. The late Sam Walton did more than found what has become the nation's largest merchant: He brought the Value Revolution to the retail sector. Today an overstored, look-alike retail environment has produced cutthroat competition, constant sales, and chastened operators. Major department store chains with names like Gimbels and Fairstore and Robesons did not survive the brutal competition. The new threat comes from interactive merchandising, where the consumer bypasses the local store altogether. While today shopping via television, through catalogs, over the Information Highway, and other direct-marketing methods comprises only 2.8 percent of the overall retail pie, such "nonstore shopping" will capture an estimated 15 percent of total sales in the next 10 years, according to research by Management Horizons, the retail arm of Price Waterhouse.

Wholesaler-Distributors. This sector of the economy is experiencing growing upheaval that will inevitably spread over the next decade. Increasingly, customers are questioning the efficiency of a four-step distribution system that adds no value for the end customer, only costs. One example of such inefficiency is the pattern of major players in the wholesale grocery business, who make much of their profits, not from moving grocery products from manufacturers to grocery stores but through *forward buying*, an industry term for the practice of stocking up on merchandise that manufacturers discount during certain periods of the year. The practice artificially inflates demand and adds costs to manufacturers who then must work overtime to meet the inflated demand. One $13-billion food wholesaler reportedly made a third of its profits through such contrivances in a recent year. And while grocery wholesalers are loathe to give up such profits, the big discount deals are being challenged by manufacturers and retailers responding to consumers who are hungry for lower prices.

Of course, each of the 300,000 wholesaler-distributors in the U.S. is facing the Value Revolution in its own unique way. But studies by the National Association of Wholesaler-Distributors indicate clearly that many wholesaler-distributor's market share is likely to decrease in coming years because of the emergence of new competitors and pressure from customers to buy direct from manufacturers. The reality for many is the loss of market share to so-called "alternate channels of distribution."

Sam's Clubs, just one of these new competitors, enjoys buying clout and economies of scale that enable it to offer products at prices 40 to 50 percent lower than some wholesalers it competes against. In recent years, the Wal-Mart division has begun targeting an ever-widening number of businesses including health care providers, janitorial companies, and hotel and motel operators, while seeking ways to gain schools, government agencies, and even corporations as customers. In a growing number of commodity lines, as wholesalers refer to their products, these alternative channels of distribution are growing faster than middlemen in the same sector, while severe margin pressure is requiring dramatic changes in the cost structure of the industry.

For middlemen, the implications of the Value Revolution are increasingly obvious: *They must bring more to their manufacturing partners and down-chain customers than in the past or risk being bypassed.* Customers will not buy when they believe that the manufacturer or they themselves can perform the wholesaler-distributor's functions more effectively. Thus, middlemen must look for ways to remove inefficiencies across the entire channel and add value in the form of creative, impactful new services that benefit both manufacturers and down-chain customers.

Manufacturers. In Canada, private-label soft-drink makers quadrupled their market share in less than 5 years. In and of itself, such a dramatic change might seem insignificant. But across North America, soft drink bottlers and packaged-goods manufacturers are facing stronger, higher-quality store brands. *Advertising Age* predicts private-label products will nab up to a fourth of U.S. supermarket volume before the year 2000—and eventually as much as half. "Private label is here," comments David Glass, Wal-Mart's CEO, "It's going to be a growing factor in the future."

From packaged-goods producers to automakers, manufacturers are daily feeling the effects of the Value Revolution. And manufacturers will continue to be challenged by the growing necessity to provide more for less to customers, or less for much less if they cannot. In this sector, the driving imperative is to change the way firms do business: how they design, manufacture, and bring products to market; how they partner with suppliers for the benefit of the end-use customer who has choices and is more discerning than ever. They will be forced to offer products that are better designed, of the highest quality, with full support services before, during, and after the sale, at continuously lowered prices. Reengineering costs out of operations becomes not a one-time event but a way of doing business. As is the case with distributors, manufacturers will increasingly be under pressure to sell their products direct to end customers where such an arrangement makes sense, much as some personal-computermakers have done in the recent past.

Service Firms and Professional Service Providers. The Value Revolution has come to this previous "above the competitive fray" sector of the economy, whether the service is health care or satellite transmission from the latest war-torn nation, or billable hours from a company's outside law firm.

The health care "reform" of the early 90s was assumed to be in response to impending legislative changes from Washington. Yet the real reform was that of an out-of-touch industry "reforming" the processes and costs and structures involved in the way it delivered its "product."

Or consider what has happened to leading law firms. Until only a few years ago, corporations commonly "rubber-stamped" their lawyers' bills. No more. A prolonged revenue slump at *American Lawyer 100* firms in the first half of the 90s, in addition to a general trend of corporate belt-tightening, triggered greater scrutiny of legal expenses.

"We have become enlightened consumers," says Robert C. Weinbaum, head of General Motors' legal staff, who reports that such closer examination reduced the carmaker's legal costs by more than $40 million in a recent

2-year period alone. General Motors is merely following the trend. "This market [corporations purchasing legal services] is getting to be much pickier and smarter about what it's buying," observes Steven Brill, editor in chief of the *American Lawyer*. And law firms are hardly alone.

If any industry should be booming as a result of market opportunities, it would seem to be outplacement, the profession of counseling managers and executives who've been downsized by companies as they attempt to respond to the Value Revolution's demands. Since its birth as an industry in the 70s, the profession charged for its services based on a percentage of the dismissed-executive's salary. Outplacement services typically include post-termination counseling sessions, skills assessment, résumé preparation, and interview skills training, along with temporary office space during a candidate's job search.

Yet, after enjoying annual growth rates of as much as 40 percent and equally heady profit margins throughout the 80s, the cinders of a spreading Value Revolution have ignited a wildfire of customer revolt. "We're fighting for our existence as an industry," the head of one of the nation's largest outplacement firms told *The Wall Street Journal*. Business failures were widespread among smaller outplacement firms in the first half of the 90s, and even the largest ones were forced to cut staff—and staff salaries—in order to stay in business.

Today, the pricing trend is clearly toward flat fees, negotiated for whole groups of departing employees at much lower rates. U.S. companies spent an average of $2,000 per outplaced employee in the 80s. Now they commonly spend less than $500, according to *Consultants News*, an industry publication.

What happened to this once-thriving industry? The underlying explanation can be coupled under the heading of a *growing demand for better value*. The outplacement profession's experience provides a lesson for all professional service firms and providers who might be tempted to believe that they are immune from this powerful force.

In hindsight, when things are always much clearer, the likelihood that the Value Revolution would not be kind to this industry should have been obvious. At odds was an increasing need for the outplacement service on the part of downsizing corporations, coupled with an urgent need to cut costs.

Reexamining the buyer-seller relationship in much closer detail, corporate decision-makers inevitably looked at what they were *getting* for what they were *paying*. Sensing they could gain concessions, they set off a competitive war among formerly friendly rivals that further diluted the service's perceived value. Some companies did away with the perk altogether, figuring that termination in a "temporary society" was now the norm, and that workers should develop transition skills on their own. Still other companies responded by creating internal career-transition departments, taking the function in-house at reduced costs.

In pre-value revolutionary times, a company contemplating a mass discharge might have asked for proposals from two or three firms. But sensing the advantages of negotiating price, a major firm today might commission bids from a dozen competitors or more. Another issue is that the very attractiveness of the industry's profitability caused overexpansion in a profession with few barriers to entry.

As the Value Revolution continues to affect the fate and fortune of entire industries, businesses, and workers across North America, it would be easy to assume that it's "business as usual" in other countries. Such a conclusion, however, would be wrong.

The Value Revolution Goes Global

From Tokyo to São Paulo to Paris, what is occurring is nothing short of a *global* Value Revolution. The emerging reality is that buyers—both individual consumers and business-to-business purchasers alike—can have it all: high quality, excellent service, and competitive prices, because firms are arising to meet these new demands.

- In Japan, wholesale clubs and factory outlets are springing up outside Tokyo, as support builds for deregulation of the cumbersome distribution system that keeps prices artificially high for domestic consumers. On weekends in Tokyo, full-color newspaper ads advertise up to 90 percent off men's suits.

- All over Europe, the spread of deep discounting has become the rage. Discount chains in Britain are challenging traditional full-price supermarkets, while German discounters are expanding into France. Private-label goods, which represent a threat to manufacturers of branded products, now account for a growing percentage of super-market sales volume in Switzerland and Italy, and as much as 32 percent of supermarket sales in Britain and 24 percent in France.

- Increasing numbers of U.S. firms are venturing abroad, and are, in the process, redefining "best value" for millions of consumers wherever they set up operations. Toys R Us doesn't sell its toys at the same steep discounts in Tokyo as it does in the United States. But that's only because it doesn't yet have to. For the most part, the toy retailer is still competing against full-margin retailers in Japan. But as the Value Revolution spreads, the firm may face stiffer price competition in the future.

- In bargain-hungry Britain, Price-Costco stores generate average sales of $150 million a year, about 50 percent more than Price-Costco outlets in the U.S.

In short, the Value Revolution isn't confined to any single country, nor is it being fomented globally exclusively by U.S. firms. Instead, this is a transnational force of change. Add to this an aging population in Japan, the U.S., and Europe, and the net result is a highly strategic consumer who is constantly searching for value and is less swayed by marketing gimmickry. Today's consumers, regardless of where they reside, can get what they want, when they want it, have it customized to their individual taste, and expect to pay less for it than in the past.

Forces Driving the Revolution

That customers of all stripes are demanding greater value is hardly breaking news. What is new is the extent to which they can get it. And these days, customers can get it by buying direct from the manufacturer, by shopping by computer or 800 number, and in a myriad of other ways that bypass the traditional distribution chain. Today's buyer can choose, not just among competing traditional sellers, or competing sellers in one's own country, but also among new ways of solving the problem at hand from a panoply of global solution-providers.

These are but a few of the forces driving the Value Revolution that it will pay us to take a closer look at.

Driving Force 1: The New Consumer

The 90s consumer has gone from a mindset of invincibility and affluence to a feeling of permanent caution and vulnerability. The new consumer demands to be more involved in what your product is, how it functions, and how much you charge for it. The new consumer is better informed, more demanding, and has vastly greater choices in what and where he or she purchases. Consider:

- A national poll by Warwick Baker & Fiore found that 9 out of 10 consumers go shopping for frequently purchased items armed with a specific strategy for saving money.

- In New Hampshire, a home builder may have been the first to design in a new lifestyle addition: a warehouse club room, where all the bulk items purchased at local warehouse clubs can be stored.

- Says Dale Achabal, director of the Retail Management Institute at Santa Clara University, "We Americans have gotten into the discount mindset. It used to be that people bragged about the brand and *how much* they spent on a particular item. But now, it's almost a reverse; we brag about the great buys we've discovered."

What these and other indicators point to is a vastly different kind of consumer, dramatically more sophisticated than even a few years ago. "You are already sharply aware of the phenomenon of the new consumer, because you are one," ventured *Fortune* magazine in a cover story on the "Tough New Consumer." "On behalf of yourself and your company, you are almost certainly a better informed, more demanding, shrewder, and busier buyer than ever before. Now multiply yourself by billions worldwide and you begin to see the scope of what is happening and how it changes the game for every business on earth."

This tough new consumer doesn't just shop differently. He or she is much more apt to probe the built-in value of the product or service itself, aside from the millions spent to add a perception of value through advertising. "Consumers in the 90s are taking the time to decide what a product is really worth," points out a major attitudinal study by Grey Advertising. And even historically normal economic growth and unemployment rates fail to unleash a return to the profligate spending patterns of the past.

The fact is, American wages, benefits, and living standards are flat and have been for over two decades. Meanwhile almost 40 million Americans, or 15 percent of the population according to the Census Bureau, are living below the official poverty level. (The poverty level for a family of four is $14,763.) Most of the rewards of the 90s growth are going to a relatively narrow slice of the populous—highly educated, affluent households—while the typical American family continues to tread water.

Even among families with good-paying jobs, there is what some researchers call a "quiet but pervasive economic malaise." While the 1990s have witnessed the creation of millions of new jobs, there is no longer the illusion that employment is secure, much less lifelong, and this too affects the attitudinal bent of today's consumer. Moreover, at least half of these new jobs are what economists call *soft* jobs, part-time or temporary, paying low wages and offering limited or no benefits. Indeed, employment at temporary service agencies as a percentage of the work force is at its highest level ever, while the number of Americans with employer-provided health insurance continues to decline.

For nearly two decades, DDB Needham Worldwide, a leading New York City-based advertising agency, has conducted an annual survey of 4,000 adult heads of households in the United States. There is, in recent surveys, a growing pattern of skepticism and frustration among Americans. The number of people who feel their family income is high enough to satisfy all their important desires continues to slide. And in yet another telling characteristic of today's consumer, the number of adults who report feeling their families are "too heavily in debt today" has increased steadily as well, from 24 percent in 1976 to 37 percent in 1993.

There is yet another factor driving the attitudinal reshaping of today's value-conscious consumer: the aging of the Baby Boom generation.

"Baby Boomers who had a long run at youth are looking age in the face and saying, 'Holy cow, I'm not going to live forever and I've been living like I would,' " says marketing expert John Parikhal, author of *The Baby Boom: Making Sense of Our Generation at 40*. Seventy-six million Americans, born between 1946 and 1964, are now in their prime earning years — and what should be prime saving years as well.

Yet Boomer consumers are saving only 36 percent to 55 percent of what they will need to fund a comfortable retirement, according to economist B.

Douglas Bernheim of Stanford University in a major study on the subject for Merrill Lynch. In a worst-case scenario—in which Social Security is cut and taxes are raised—they are saving only 10 percent of what they will need.

The result: A generation defined by excess, one that questioned authority and parental values, is finally having to come to terms with limits, with the concept of responsibility. Hence the sudden search is on for value. Rather than purchases that will impress others, they are increasingly looking for offerings that will bring lasting satisfaction, that are efficient, durable and simple to maintain, and above all demonstrate their prowess as "smart" consumers.

Brought together, these trends mean that greater numbers of American consumers are destined to become more discerning, more sophisticated, more savvy, and more demanding shoppers as they move through the life span. Partly out of necessity and partly out of choice, millions of Americans have become, and will continue to become, more rational decision-makers in selecting the products and firms they will or will not do business with.

It's an age-old truism to say that people buy for emotional reasons, then justify with logic. And this will not change, for it is part of deeply ingrained cultural mores. But what has changed and is likely to continue to change is the amount of logic that presses against the emotion. Asked why they bought the fully loaded new Volvo station wagon, the couple responds in unison, "We wanted a safe car for the family." Okay, right, but the unarticulated reason was also the *status* conferred by the make and model.

The Boomer, when purchasing his or her first car, might have been guided solely by emotion. But having purchased any number of vehicles since and having observed performance variations, the Boomer now considers a whole range of rational factors in addition to emotional affinity. These include warranties, trade-in value, operating costs, quality ratings by independent agencies, and word-of-mouth feedback from friends who've owned similar models.

It's the same with other product purchases as well. Experience tends to rationalize buying decisions, but it seldom takes the emotional aspect completely out of the equation. And as the consumer improves on his or her skills of reading labels, of deciphering the "fine print" of ingredients, contracts, warranties, and guarantees, of comparing prices and features, of waiting for sales, of clipping coupons, of asking for and getting discounts, the consumer becomes more and more capable of discovering what constitutes value as he or she defines it.

Driving Force 2: Bypass Competition

In addition to its immediate woes, the outplacement industry suffers from a broader challenge. It is a challenge that increasingly affects many full-service stock brokerages, accounting, legal, real estate, consulting, and other service firms: The knowledge they sell, because it is more widely available through alternate channels, becomes less esoteric, and thus is perceived to have less value.

In the case of outplacement services, how-to-books, computer programs, public seminars, videotapes, and walk-in job-counseling outlets encroach on its formerly exclusive turf. Collectively, these other means of the customer solving his or her problem can be referred to as *bypass competition*. And today, more than ever, consumers demanding value can bypass traditional "only game in town" suppliers.

Take banks for example. Banks used to be the only source of money in town. No longer. These days, businesses and individuals can obtain loans from a host of alternative sources. They can deposit paychecks in a money market account with a brokerage firm. They can write checks on their insurance company policies. "It is possible for banks to die and still have a vibrant economy," concludes Edward Furash, a Washington bank consultant.

Banks are not alone in the threat of being bypassed by consumers armed with new options. Consider the growing number of ways consumers can bypass local retailers in their communities altogether by the growing use of the computer, television, and telephone.

Stamford, Connecticut-based Shoppers Advantage is a "retailer" that has not a single store. It has no salespeople and no warehouses. What it does have is an 800 number and a growing legion of members all over North America who are hell-bent on paying less and getting more for their money. Shoppers Advantage customers pay an annual membership fee to be able to purchase such products as camcorders, stereos, and TVs at greatly reduced prices.

Shoppers Advantage operators search a database full of offerings from competing manufacturers to find a product with the desired features and price. Then, instead of shipping the product from its own warehouse, the firm passes the order on to say, Toshiba, who then ships the television to the customer's home. With such an arrangement, Shoppers Advantage is able to sell thousands of products at prices that are one-third to one-half what even local discounters charge.

Shoppers Advantage is but one example of a "just-in-time retailer," a bold new alternative that could provide us with a glimpse of how products might be transferred from maker to user in completely different ways in the future.

Walter Forbes, chairman and CEO of CUC, parent company of Shoppers Advantage, describes the sources of his advantage over traditional retailers: We have no inventory," he told *Forbes*. "Our [firm] is made up of computers, databases, and telecommunications, all of whose costs are going down. All [our] competitors' bricks, mortar, costs of people, health care, are going up. We have 30 million members, and that's volume. We're doing it already. We're already on-line all over the country, so we're experienced."

Forbes looks ahead to the day when customers won't even need to talk with an operator; they will be able to shop electronically via computer. As Forbes sees it, video-on-demand will be the standard of the future, and everything else is merely "interim technology."

Shoppers Advantage is hardly alone in pioneering new methods of moving the merchandise. Take Indelible Blue, a firm based in Raleigh, North Carolina. It's software products are selling unexpectedly well in cyberspace, which is to say, they are sold entirely over the Internet. The rapidly growing company did not exist until 1993, yet has since made millions.

Until recently, the Internet was a decidedly commercial-free zone. But these days, new firms are crowding as fast as they can onto a special section of the Internet called the World Wide Web, each trying to outdo the others with splashy multimedia graphics and deep databases containing buyer information on everything from selecting the perfect Club Med vacation to ordering flowers from FTD. And almost daily, new ventures are announced to make interactive shopping a reality for more and more people. Increasing numbers of consumers are steering their fingers onto the Information Superhighway to shop for the best bargains on products ranging from housewares and apparel to airplane parts and restaurant supplies. The implications are enormous.

"If these new interactive [shopping] systems just take away 5 percent or 10 percent of sales, it takes away the margin of profit from most retailers," argues Walter Forbes. From just-in-time retailing and cyberspace stores to home television shopping and even the somewhat passé warehouse clubs, new forms of putting products into the hands of customers are springing up across the landscape. Their collective impact is anything but minor.

Driving Force 3: Value Innovators

In a growing number of industries, aggressive new competitors are chain sawing the ties that have traditionally bound sellers with their customers. These "Value Innovators" are giving customers new choices of quality and service up and down the price spectrum—both more-for-less, and in some cases less-for-less, and in others more-for-more. In the process they are leaving laggard competitors in the lurch. Increasingly, firms that are merely "in business," yet offer no unique value advantage, will struggle with thinner and thinner profit margins—if they survive at all.

Value Innovators raise consumer awareness and expectations about what good value is in a particular product line or service offering. If a consumer living, let us say, in LaCrosse, Wisconsin, has never shopped at Home Depot, that consumer doesn't miss or compare Home Depot's unique Value Proposition; he shops the local home improvement or hardware store.

Similarly, if consumers in Brazil have never experienced the Value Proposition of a Sam's Club, then after they do, they'll have that option and that perception of value to consider in future purchase decisions.

What is happening, and happening at an increasingly rapid rate, is what we might call the *wildfire effect*: Since products no longer need be purchased locally, consumers' perception of value is not based on, nor limited to, local players. For example, if I need a new, higher baud rate modem, I can drive over to the computer store, which is only three blocks away, and buy one, or I can call any number of catalog vendors, and they'll have it here tomorrow morning. Ditto for a growing number of items that I might need.

This ability to shop nationally is not new, for indeed the arrival of the Sears Roebuck catalog gave farmers such a choice 50 years ago. What is different today is the increased *pervasiveness* of choice, and its impact on national and international markets.

As U.S. firms like Wal-Mart, Toys R Us, and McDonald's continue to expand globally, they are merely symbolic of the larger trend, that of Value Innovators upsetting the status quo with a new and improved value equation. But U.S. firms are hardly alone in spreading the Value Revolution. Japanese cars exported to all corners of the globe raised the bar with respect to quality and price. Ikea, the Swedish furniture maker, has recently expanded across the United States, dominates western Europe's furniture business, and is opening stores in the former Russian satellites. Value Innovators make the impossible possible by looking at the existing Value Propositions of other players in a particular market and asking, "What does the customer *really* want?" Then they set to work to provide such value by their overall strategies and the way they do business.

DRIVING FORCE 4: BUYER INFORMATION POWER

Consumers and buyers today approach the bargaining table with more information sources than in the past. They have more ways to discover the lowest price and the best overall value, and doing so is getting easier all the time.

- Publications such as *Consumer Reports* and *Car & Driver* have long published price guides and quality ratings on various makes, models, and brands of products ranging from microwave ovens to golf clubs. Today, they are joined by an explosion of local, regional, and national ratings services.

- J. D. Power, the Agoura Hills, California-based research firm, began in 1968 by rating the quality of automobiles based on customer satisfaction. Today, Power rates not only cars but also computers, airlines, cellular service providers, medium-duty trucks, tires (both original and replacement), and releases on audio components. The firm is actively looking for additional products to rate, having changed the very definition of the value equation for car buyers.

- Best-selling books and magazine and newspaper feature articles on personal finance are heavily oriented towards cutting through the clutter of advertising claims to provide more objective information.

- In health care, employers now prepare "report cards" for their employees that compare the cost and quality of competing health insurers. Which hospitals in town have the best outcomes—and the best prices—for heart surgery? How do members of Acme Health Plan rate its doctors and hospitals? Which facilities have the lowest and highest rates of Cesarean-section births?

When one *Fortune 500* company wanted to find out how well its health care dollars were being spent, it surveyed 18,000 workers nationwide and asked them to rate their medical plans. It then used the results to create a satisfaction index that ranked 52 health maintenance organizations from best to worse, then discounted the cost to employees who joined the best plans and increased it for those who joined plans low on the index. Result: One highly rated HMO saw its enrollment among the company's employees jump 30 percent, even though it was more expensive than rival plans in its area.

In addition to independently sourced information, firms increasingly volunteer information that helps consumers more accurately compare and contrast competing claims. Long-distance carriers, credit card companies, and others spend billions each year to compare their Value Proposition with those of their competitors. While such negative ads often have no substance, they have the effect of educating the consumer and of elevating the consumer's awareness of the criteria of the overall Value Proposition. Does your carrier grant instant credit on misdials? Is the discount your carrier touts really much of a discount? Does contacting your friends and family about your savings plan constitute poor taste or smart savings?

Ever more shrill and intrusive on the psyche, such advertising becomes the model, and others follow. What it does is to raise the ante, raise the consumer's awareness that not only do they have choices but they also become more skeptical about accepting *anyone's* claims about anything.

For years, local sellers (both retail and wholesale) did well because they were the only places buyers could go to gain information and to comparison shop. On any nonroutine purchase of a product such as a major appliance, computer, or automobile, most consumers ask around, talk to friends, then get in their car, drive around, kick tires, talk to salespeople, look at price tags, and finally make a purchase. Often, this is a frustrating and time-consuming process, and the *flow of information*—on prices and an item's attributes—is imperfect. Local sellers benefited from this condition and were reluctant to change it. They wanted to keep it that way and erected barriers to prevent information from flowing freely.

But, as we have seen, the local seller's lock on the information flow, as well as being the "only game in town," is quickly coming to an end and is creating a massive restructuring of the consumer-seller relationship. Dozens of fax, on-line, and other high-tech services are springing up on an almost daily basis which offer price information at the touch of a button. Thanks to the proliferation of such sources, local sellers no longer control the flow of information. What is more, the buyer of the near future will be able to do the comparisons and information gathering with an ease that makes "let your fingers do the walking" seem as antiquated as rotary dial telephones. And that impact can be measured in a variety of ways:

- Department and specialty store shares of the apparel market have declined since the late 80s.

- The number of consumers shopping by catalog has doubled in the last decade. Each year, over half the American population makes at least one purchase from a catalog.

- Mail-order drug sales totaled $100 million annually in 1981. A decade later, such sales had grown to $4 billion, according to the Managed Care Pharmacy Association.

- On-line computer services have more than quintupled since 1987. These numbers will continue to explode as more Americans become computer literate.

The two greatest advantages the local seller traditionally had were that the consumer could see, touch, and smell the product he or she was interested in buying, and also could take immediate delivery. Indeed, these are advantages that savvy retailers will continue to exploit and will never allow to be neutralized entirely by the other forms of acquisition. But today, the local store is in danger of becoming a mere showroom where customers come in, handle the merchandise, learn about various products, and then return to their electronic cottages to order the same item at substantial discounts, only to have it delivered the next day.

While the technology is still in flux, most experts agree that any system to accommodate this demand will have three basic features:

Quick locate: where you know the item you are seeking and use the television-computer to locate it, get details and price consistency, and then make a tele-direct purchase.

Feature shop: a system in which you select components, or design combinations for your selections, say, a travel package or an automobile.

Browse: a catalog or showroom type of experience, where you've told the system what general types of things you're looking for, and the television brings them to you in rapid succession for you to browse and sample before making your choice.

The impact of buyers having far greater amounts of information at their disposal will not only affect retailers selling to consumers. Businesses selling to businesses must now compete, not just with the competitor down the street or across town but across the country as well. One boundaryless company is W.W. Grainger, a rapidly growing $2.6-billion national distributor of products ranging from nuts and bolts to lighting fans to electrical generators. Grainger gives commercial, industrial, institutional, and contractor customers the choice of whether they'll purchase from one of over 337 branch outlets or through an ever expanding array of catalogs. And Grainger is certainly not alone.

From Madison Avenue to Main Street, from retail to distribution to manufacturing to the service sector, the "game" is changing fast. But what are the new rules? If indeed "value" is what buyers seek, how does a firm "add value" in ways that both create loyal customers, improve the bottom line, and insulate against competitive inroads?

To answer these questions, it is necessary first to understand some of the implications of this new, more demanding, buy-from-anywhere consumer, who has more information at his or her disposal, and who is being courted by competing firms constantly improving their Value Propositions.

What the Value Revolution Means to Your Firm

While the implications of the Value Revolution are complex and far-reaching, the only ones that matter are those that will impact your firm.

Let's look at four overarching implications, however, that apply to virtually any business:

Implication 1: Excellent Quality Is No Longer Enough. As we saw earlier, a reputation for quality did not protect Mercedes from suffering losses when new, equally high-quality luxury cars came to market at substantially lower cost. The message is clear: Today's customer doesn't care how good your Q Factor *was*, only how good it is today, compared to the other guy's offering.

This is a legacy of the "total quality management" (TQM) movement. And while some of the fervor of the TQM movement has dissipated, its lasting impact can be assessed. Conclusion: Quality is expected by today's consumer like never before. The tolerance for a product or service not working immediately and working all the time is quickly approaching zero.

And yet, as important as it is, quality alone has not helped companies to thrive, and, in a few cases, even to survive. Wallace Company, a Texas-based oil equipment purveyor, spent 3 years implementing a program aimed at improving the firm's quality and was awarded the Malcolm Baldridge National Quality Award for its efforts. But 2 years later, as the cost of its quality programs soared and oil prices sank, the company was forced to file for Chapter 11.

Wallace is hardly alone as a "quality" company that had everything but a quality bottom line. The point is, you can be the best company, quality-wise, on the block, and your people can all be in work teams and recite the buzzwords of quality-speak. But if your products or your people are not meeting the needs of your customers, and if your costs (and therefore your P Factor) are out of line, quality alone won't pull you through.

Implication 2: Low Prices Alone Are Not Enough. "If low prices were what everybody wanted, we'd all be driving Hyundais," is the way one wag put it. It's true. Despite the clamor for lower prices, merely lowering your prices won't necessarily bring in many more customers, and it may bankrupt you. The "low price leader" is always vulnerable to somebody else somewhere offering the product for a few pennies less. Moreover, the Value Revolution does not mean that customers focus solely on the price tag alone. In today's environment, where every player is matching everyone's lowest prices ("our low prices are guaranteed"), it's become more of a necessity merely to stay in the game, but not necessarily a viable differentiator over the longer term. There has to be something more, some other point of differentiation, to get customers to consistently and loyally choose you. As complexity increases, customers will rely on people—and crave the value they add to the transaction—more than ever. Value-added services that make the customer feel special, that meet and anticipate the customer's needs, become important.

Implication 3. Excellent Service Is Not Enough. As we saw with traditional office products dealers, if the customer does not perceive that you provide extra value in your S Factor, that customer will veto your Value Proposition and go elsewhere for less service but lower prices. The reality is that excellent service is harder to deliver on a consistent basis than even product quality, which can be standardized and objectively measured. But service, while valued, is more difficult to measure and make tangible, so the customer tends to take it for granted. In a seminar I led, I asked the group if anyone had recently purchased a personal computer. Several hands shot up. I then asked each person how they had chosen to purchase: from a traditional dealer, a catalog, via the Internet, from a superstore, direct from the manufacturer. One man said he'd just purchased from the manufacturer using a credit card and an 800 number. "So you were willing to forgo the service of a local dealer for the lower price of that particular value equation," I suggested. "Not at all," he responded. "I got excellent service from this firm, better than my local dealer ever provided." Excellent service is, as this man clearly demonstrated, in the eyes of the beholder.

Implication 4. Even Customer Satisfaction Is Not Enough. At first glance, customer satisfaction and value might seem to be the same thing. If you are satisfying your customers, they are getting good value, case closed. But according to research by Bain & Company, on average 65 percent to 85 percent of customers who abandon a business report that they were "satisfied" or "very satisfied" with their former supplier. The new reality of the Value Revolution is more complicated than that, as the case of AT&T demonstrates.

In the late 80s, AT&T was losing market share all the while surveys of its customers showed that they reported being satisfied. How could that be? On further analysis, the company made an important discovery.

What AT&T found out was that deserting customers felt that AT&T's higher prices, compared to those of new competitors like MCI and Sprint, simply weren't justified. In essence they were saying, "AT&T, I know you're top quality, but I'm willing to put up with a little more hiss and a little more static because I want to save a bundle of money."

The biggest eye opener of all was that customers perceived AT&T's price premium to be higher than it really was. And that was just the good news. The bad news was that AT&T's competition was gaining on it in terms of perceived quality. With commercials that showed how clearly the sound of a pin dropping could be heard over its fiber optic lines, Sprint emphasized its state-of-the-art transmission quality. Meanwhile, MCI continued to pound away on its lower P Factor.

By 1988, AT&T's customer erosion became a flood. That May, the company's own surveys showed that its price disadvantage reached a new peak. By October, customers were reporting that they didn't perceive that AT&T had any advantage over the other players in terms of its Q Factor, a perception that quickly made its way to the bottom line. For the fiscal year, AT&T reported its first loss ever.

To its credit, AT&T management used its new insights to think outside the box. It began to rethink long-held assumptions. It realized that quality alone is not enough and that customers can be satisfied and still desert you. Rather than trying to match competitors on price, the top team thought through its Value Proposition and those of its competitors and emerged with a brilliant offensive. It elected to improve customer-perceived quality across the board. It began spending heavily to improve technical quality, pouring billions into equipment improvements, and writing off billions more in obsolete equipment years ahead of schedule. It formed teams of internal experts to further improve billing and installation processes. And, through its media advertising, AT&T fought back against price competitors with its hard hitting "I Came Back" ads, featuring customers who had returned to AT&T after being disappointed with savings they'd gotten elsewhere. By 1989, AT&T's market share began to stabilize, and the erosion abated.

AT&T's wake-up call is one that firms big and small would do well to understand and heed. The message is clear:

- Quality alone is not enough.
- Nor is excellent customer service enough to keep customers coming back.
- Nor is a super low price enough to ensure long-term success. No, not even customer satisfaction is enough.

So, what is enough? What is enough is what we might call *your* winning formula, the right combination of quality, service, and price your customers want to meet their unique and individual needs. And that's what we'll explore in the next chapter, "Rethinking Your Value Proposition."

2

C H A P T E R

RETHINKING YOUR VALUE PROPOSITION

"We have to become single-minded in our quest to deliver better value."

Edwin Artzt, CEO
Procter & Gamble

NOW THAT WE'VE EXAMINED WHAT THE VALUE Revolution is about and looked at some of its implications, it's time to shift our attention to turning this driving force of change into a driving force of profit for your firm. In this chapter, you'll learn how to begin turning value from a timeworn slogan into a powerful, profit-boosting tool. We'll begin with a series of six questions designed to help you objectively evaluate the strengths and weaknesses of your current Value Proposition. Next, we'll take an in-depth look at your Q Factor, S Factor, and P Factor with an eye towards what you might do to deliver better value and vanquish the competition in the process.

Let's begin with a key statement. It's so important I've set it apart from the rest of the text.

To win the Value Revolution, you must out-think and out-value your competition.

Now let's examine the key words in this statement:

To Win: By this we mean to create a market for your business, to attract customers to your business, and to keep customers loyal to your business, and indeed to your *way* of doing business.

Out-think: Go with me in your mind inside a business that you are familiar with. Walk the corridors, poke around, talk to people. The entire place, the people, how they relate to you, it's all the sum total of the ideas and the thinking of that business.

Out-value: Value becomes tangible when you convince the buyer that your offering is worth more in terms of its *payoff* (however the customer defines it) than you are charging in dollars. That's what the customer calls a *good deal.* Obviously, if you charge less, the customer expects less from your Value Proposition. If you charge more, your customer expects more in the way of product quality, service, and services. Wherever you are up (more-for-more) or down (less-for-less) the value ladder, to *out-value* means to add more perceived value at that rung than does your competition.

The Competition: By this we mean anybody or anything that takes business away from you. Today, it is necessary to understand profoundly your value relative to what value your competition brings to the customer. And because of the threat of bypass competition, you must examine carefully how else your customers might solve their problem, including, as we saw with the outplacement industry, not solving it at all (doing away with the perk for employees) or providing your service in-house. Understanding what your customers value, and how they experience your value, is becoming increasingly essential to survival.

Recall the office products superstore invasion we talked about in Chapter 1. A consultant colleague who specializes in that industry described a visit to several small dealers in Las Vegas not long after six new superstores opened there. At one store, the dealer stood talking to this consultant on the sales floor, bemoaning the competitive situation and berating the local chamber of commerce for allowing superstores to join. And if you had asked this manager why someone should shop at his store rather than a superstore, he would have quickly answered, "Our customer service, of course."

Here's the irony. While the manager loudly aired his grievances for all to hear, *his customers were wandering around the store completely ignored.* So here's the lesson from this battleground of the Value Revolution for the rest of us: If you're facing new competition, if there is tumult in your market, don't let yourself be lulled into thinking you're delivering quality or service that is unique if you really aren't. To survive the Value Revolution, you must deliver value superior to that of your competition, or lower your prices accordingly. So now let's turn our attention to specific ways to help you do just that.

AudiTiNG YOUR VALUE PROPOSiTiON

Auditing your Value Proposition doesn't have to be complicated. You don't need an army of consultants. You just need to think about your business in an objective, critical fashion. That's what the following questions are designed to help you do.

Question 1: Are You Competing Primarily on Price or Competing on Value? There's nothing wrong with competing on price, but if being the "low price leader" in your market isn't your full-bore, dead-on strategy, flirting with price competition could become your firm's eventual death certificate. What are the signs that you've unintentionally headed down the path of price competition? If your salespeople are telling you that they lost out because of price or are continually asking for extra discounts and price concessions, this can be an obvious tip off. If conversations and meetings of your management team increasingly revolve around discussions of price rather than of ways to add additional value, this can be another signal that you're headed down price competition boulevard.

The more you've allowed your firm and the products or services you sell (let's call them *offerings* for short) to be thought of as commodities, the greater the likelihood that without consciously intending it, you've already begun to consider price-based competition as your only alternative. If this is not your intention, take heed. Look for ideas and strategies in this book and elsewhere that will dramatically change your course, strategies that will help you in repositioning your firm and communicating your value (rather than your price) advantages to your market.

Question 2: How Have You Added Value to Your Customers of Late? In other words, what new services have you introduced for the benefit of your customer in the past 12 months? These don't have to have been big things; often it's the new programs that use creativity, rather than cost a lot of money, that are the most effective. In what new ways do you attempt to create loyalty in your customers today versus a year ago? How much in the way of training your staff in delivering front-line value have you invested? How much have you communicated to your sales force about the importance of selling your firm's value-added services? How have you encouraged your staff to look for new ways to add value to customers?

If you're going to compete primarily on value , you're inevitably going to need to think up new ways to add value at every opportunity.

Question 3: What Is Unique About Your Value Proposition? As we've seen, every business and indeed every offering has a Value Proposition. The question your customer wants to know is: What's unique about yours? If you carry the same products that your competition does, you've got nothing unique to offer in that respect. The customer cancels out Q Factor comparisons and looks entirely to your P and S Factors in making comparative decisions. If you're a lot more convenient locationally to your customer, he might be willing to pay more; the convenience (an S Factor value) you offer is "worth it" to him. If you're easier to do business with, willing to customize some aspect of your product or service, or provide a meaningful degree of informed, knowledgeable customer assistance, each of these are part of your unique Value Proposition.

Question 4: Who Is Your Customer? If this is an easy exercise for you, you're either very lucky or else you've done a lot of market research. Confusion over this question can be damaging because it creates a lack of focus and action. Yet confusion, and diluted focus, are common.

Ask a U.S. distributor of machine tools, many of which are manufactured in Japan, who his customer is, and chances are he will say it's the builder (manufacturer) of the products he sells, and, yes, the end-use customer also.

The person he buys product from is his customer? Strange but true. Thus, keeping the builder happy is part of his reality, and therefore value must be added to this relationship if it is to flourish over time.

Or ask the folks at Saskatchewan Wheat Pool, based in Regina, Saskatchewan, who their customer is, and they will, to a manager, never tell you it is the people who buy their wheat. Instead it's the farmers who voluntarily select to move their raw wheat to market and to use the services of this giant cooperative. The grain gets bought, at fixed prices set by the Canadian government according to its quality grade, and shipped out of the province on huge cargo ships. There's almost no incentive to add value to those doing the buying. But the farmers, on the other hand, have choices and must be cajoled by the Pool to recognize that the Pool's services bring additional value to them compared to alternative channels of moving their grain to market.

It's difficult to generalize about who the customer really is. The question of whom to "aim" at, of whom to add value to, can easily become muddled and messy, leading to a breakdown in focus. If you have multiple customer groups, start by making a list of all of them. Rank them in their order of importance to your firm. Then use the ideas in this book to decide how you'll deliver unique value to those that you rank as most important.

Question 5: How Does Your Customer Experience Value? Companies that guess at what the customer values often miss. Even those that do lots of formal research can find that they missed something major in their analysis. Just ask Coca-Cola.

Before Coke introduced New Coke, they hired a top agency to help them listen to cola drinkers. In countless taste tests, blindfolded consumers swore up and down that they preferred New Coke over the older version. So it must have seemed pretty simple what to do: Introduce New Coke with a huge ad budget and lots of fanfare.

But something strange happened on the way to successfully launching the new beverage. A few diehards didn't take to the new concoction, and they went out and bought up cases of the old Coke before stores ran out. Then the media picked up on the "story," and it developed a life of its own. In a matter of weeks, it became an issue of renegade, vigilante customers pitted in battle against the monolithic Corporate Coke that was forcing them to go for the new drink when they wanted the old, the traditional, the unchanging, thank you very much! Finally, the protests grew so loud and so many people started stocking up on old Coke that Coca-Cola brought back the old Coke and renamed it Coca-Cola Classic. These days you'll be hard pressed to find a can of New Coke anywhere.

The moral of the story: Sometimes what customers value isn't so obvious. Sometimes it doesn't show up in perfunctory taste tests or in yes/no questions asked by indifferent survey researchers. What the customer values about your business may be consciously unknown to your customers. What the customer values about your business may be realized only when it gets taken away.

In Coke's case, these values might be described as a desire for tradition, for a touchstone of constancy in a changing world. The rejection of New Coke may have had something to do with the need of consumers to talk back to a giant corporation, to feel they could have a say in that company's decisions.

At times, what the customer values gets lost because the firm has a "we know what is best for them" attitude. Singer Corporation, to cite one manufacturer, did not realize its customers valued a simple sewing machine. So its engineers kept adding more complex features. Singer's sales organization wanted these features because they thought they would add value for the home seamstress. But the sales force wasn't really in touch with the real customer. They were listening to selected retailers. By adding more bells and whistles, Singer was innovating for the wrong people.

Singer is hardly alone. I regularly lead senior management sessions designed to elicit new thinking and innovative ideas that organizations might implement to increase their value. One of the purposes of these sessions is to help leaders spot mismatches between what their customers value and what the company *assumes* their customers value.

To make this point, I sometimes do an exercise that uses the hotel in which we are holding the meeting as an example. During the morning break, I'll go out to the lobby and take a quick survey of the hotel's catering people. I ask them: "What do seminar attendees really want in morning coffee service?" They will tell me different things. At a recent program, the banquet managers said people wanted quality coffee, freshly brewed, served with danish on a clean, attractively set serving table.

After the break, I then had the managers list what *they* valued, in order of importance, from this service. Two items at the top of their list were, "coffee located near the restrooms and phones" and "alternative snacks to those high in calories and fat." Nothing whatsoever about the coffee or the setup.

In discussing the two lists, we made several observations. One was that these managers *expected* that coffee would be freshly brewed and of high quality. They also expected to find the usual breakfast muffins and Danish. But to exceed their expectations, the hotel staff needed to look beyond the obvious to less tangible S Factors.

The extent to which these two lists diverged is not uncommon. Most businesses, and the people who run them, *assume* they know what their customers value, when in fact they have never really made finding out a matter of top priority. This leaves firms vulnerable. Companies that do not determine—and then regularly take the blinders off and *redetermine*—what their customers value, often miss fundamental changes.

What customers value changes; it is not static. It changes with demographic trends, such as the Boomer consumer, the Baby Bust generation, and the aging of the American population. It shifts in response to regulatory and legislative changes (the luxury tax, combined with a recession in the early 90s, wiped out over a third of all boat dealers in the U.S. and numerous boat manufacturers), environmental changes, social changes (the rise of working women and the foresight to design more feminine, expressive workplace attire gave rise to Liz Claiborne, Inc., one of the fastest growing companies in the 80s), economics, lifestyle, safety issues, and research reports into the health effects of certain products.

To determine how your customers experience value requires more than mere objective, quantitative research. It also requires fresh, unfettered thinking—and listening. It means taking a hard look at your Q Factor, your S Factor, and your P Factor as the customer looks at them. It means identifying how you *think* your customer realizes value from your firm. And then it means going out and finding out what your customers tell you they actually value about what you do.

Start by inventorying how your customer realizes value from your business as a whole. Make a list of all the no-extra-charge services you now provide that you assume the customer values: your hassle-free return policy, convenient hours, your wide selection of offerings, your in-stock record, your speed of satisfaction, etc. Add to this a list of the extras that you do in fact charge extra for: your inventory management system, your ability to customize to their exact specifications, etc.—and assigning these a priority based on how important you believe your customers rank them.

Question 6: What Are You Willing to Do to Deliver Better Value? Whether or not you decide to do anything different with your Value Proposition, remember this: Your customer is constantly if quietly asking, Who's got the better value? Who's bringing better value to the table now? Not yesterday. Today! So the future-focused leader continues to look at the overall value equation through the eyes of the dispassionate, self-centered customer. Because in doing so, he's got his eye on what Adam Smith called the "invisible hand of the market. "

Sam Walton probably wasn't thinking about Value Propositions and P Factors and such when he opened his first Wal-Mart in the small hamlets of Arkansas 30 years ago. Walton, in countless interviews, never claimed to have had a grand strategy to take over retailing in America. But he did have the horse sense to notice that when he came across a good deal from a supplier, if he turned around and sold that item at a price that his customer considered a good deal, everybody benefited. As obvious as all of this may seem today, it wasn't obvious to the other merchants in small towns as they watched the Wal-Mart juggernaut grow.

Asking how can we win by creating a better deal for our customers is a radical question. Radical because, invariably, that question leads to a second question, which is: How can we deliver greater customer value at the end of the line by what we do all the way back up the line and internally in our business processes? Yet, if you're willing to ask this question of yourself, your team, your suppliers, and down-chain partners, you could very well start a process that could transform your company's prospects. From the answers you get by asking these questions, you might just create a juggernaut of your own.

The history of innovation and economic progress is grounded in such rethinkings. Just as the technology of fire once spread, and just as the Industrial Revolution once spread, the rethinking process is spreading from a limited number of industries to all industries; and from innovative companies to firms that would prefer to run their businesses without changing a single thing until hell freezes over, and from a few countries to many countries.

Winning the Value Revolution doesn't necessarily mean that you make revolutionary changes in your business. But it does require that you become aware of and alert to its imperatives, to the rapidity of marketplace change today, and that you consciously decide what you can and will do to deliver better value in the days ahead. Towards that end, let's next move to an examination of how firms create value for customers, which inevitably entails a discussion of the "value triangle."

The Value Triangle

As we've seen, every firm, through its offerings, puts forth a Value Proposition. Your Value Proposition may be defined as how you chose to create value for customers. Taken a step further, we can say that your Value Proposition is composed of a triangle composed of quality, service, and price. When that proposition satisfies or exceeds the customer's expectations, the sale goes through. When it doesn't, the sale doesn't.

The Value Veto

When a business loses customers, it's quite often nothing personal. It's just that they have discovered a better Value Proposition elsewhere. In effect, we could say they are "vetoing" that firm's Value Proposition. "It wasn't worth it" is the way consumers usually put it. The pay television subscriber, asked to explain why he dropped the premium movie service, comments that "the prices were too high for the movies they were showing."

The first time customers do business with you, they actively weigh your Value Proposition. Just imagine two springy antennae protruding from their heads, and you'll have the right picture in mind. While talking with your salesperson or receptionist they are listening to every nuance, from how the person represents your firm to how they feel about working there and how badly they want their business. They are also weighing how well your offering seems to meet their need, and numerous other issues. Even if a business really blows it, most customers will put up with the poor treatment or the out-of-whack prices; they just won't come back.

On the other hand there are situations—maybe you've had them your-self—when you did a value veto right in the midst of the transaction. Things were so out of whack that you aborted purchase and exited the scene. This happened to a buddy and me on a scuba diving trip in Maui.

Hungry after a morning dive, we spotted a little restaurant just outside Lahaina with no name, just "Korean Barbeque" neatly printed on a small sign. Inside, the place was hardly spectacular, sort of your basic sandwich shop decor, with maybe seven booths. There was a family at the booth in the back, otherwise we were the only customers. We were greeted by a stone-faced man who merely nodded his head as if to say, "pick a booth, any booth, I couldn't care less." He slapped down menus in front of us and walked off. When we opened the menus, we discovered that the entrees were almost what we had the evening before at one of the finest restau-rants on the island. We kept on with our mile-a-minute conversation, but something began to occur to us: Is it worth it? Is this where we should eat? Or should we leave? Since there had been no welcome, no greeting, no personal attempt at establishing a relationship—in other words, no S Factor whatsoever—we didn't feel obligated to stay. So we just got up and left.

Why Marlboro Faced the Value Veto

The value veto is hardly confined to restaurants. Several years ago, Marlboro found its Value Proposition being vetoed by alarming num-bers of customers. Like other premium brands, Marlboro had passed along steady price increases for almost a decade, and as the price hikes kept coming, customers began switching to discount cigarettes instead.

By 1993, the nearly $1 gap between what Marlboro charged and the price of a typical pack of nonbranded cigarettes was too much for many customers to ignore. Discount smokes were growing at an incredible pace, gaining nearly a share point a month. Marlboro, meanwhile, made by Philip Morris, was losing market share, and company execs were wor-ried that if they didn't do something to slow the boom in discount smokes, smokers who had switched would get used to cheaper brands and be hard to lure back. What to do?

In a desperate move on what came to be known as "Marlboro Friday," Philip Morris cut Marlboro's price by 40 cents a pack, sending shock waves throughout the tobacco industry and Philip Morris's stock plummeting.

Operating income in the year after the move had dropped 46 percent, and Philip Morris was forced to dramatically cut costs.

Marlboro's acknowledgment that even supposedly brand-loyal cigarette smokers could become value vetoers was a wake-up call to all packaged-goods manufacturers. "The price-value relationship got out of line," William I. Campbell, tobacco unit president at Philip Morris, told *Advertising Age*. "Great brands are still great brands, but you have to keep the price value in line with today's discerning consumers."

By continuing to raise prices each year when consumers had new, lower-priced alternatives, Marlboro may have thought itself immune from the Value Revolution. It found out otherwise. What the world's leading cigarette brand discovered was that at some point its customers weren't willing to pay more. The extra price wasn't in line with the perceived extra value.

The good news for Marlboro is that by lowering its price, Philip Morris has been able to recover some of the Grand's lost market share. But industry observers believe Marlboro did irreparable damage. "Sure you can get your [market] share back at a price, but once the consumer learns that private-label brands are good, it becomes a much different game," commented one analyst. "This has radically changed the way people think about brands. It's made brand managers realize they can't keep taking and taking from consumers because consumers have other choices. They can trade down."

And that's the value veto in action. If we think of the Q-S-P as a triangle with the point at the bottom with the Q Factor and the S Factor on the top two corners, it's helpful to think of the value veto as occurring when the triangle is perceived to be turned upside down: The price is perceived to be greater than the quality and service. The would-be customer perceives he is being asked to pay more than what he is getting: a "bad deal."

So far in this chapter, we've spoken about the three factors that make up the value triangle as if they were entirely simple and straightforward issues. In reality, that's seldom the case. Thus it will be beneficial to take a closer look at each of the factors individually, as we explore how customers look at and value different things about them.

Quality: The "Q" of the Value Triangle

Quality is an important first dimension of the value triangle. Customer expectations of what quality is differ greatly, but one thing is clear: Those expectations are constantly on the rise. And as expectations have risen, what is happening is that reputable distributors and dealers simply aren't willing to endure the hassle of endless customer returns of defective or rejected merchandise. Thus, the bar has been raised in increasing numbers of product categories, and is destined to rise further in the future.

Offering higher quality is one of the ways today's innovative firms get noticed. When Lexus, a division of Toyota, entered the U.S. luxury car market in 1989, its strategy was built on offering even higher quality than existing competitors. Its cars were said to contain 300 major and minor innovations. Stories abounded of Lexus engineers pasting on women's fingernails so they could better design door handles that would meet the needs of women customers. Its state-of-the-art engineering revolved around not just satisfying customers but also delighting and surprising them.

"We knew we had to exceed expectations," Lexus manager Richard L. Chitty told a conference on "Designing, Developing, and Delivering Outstanding Service Value" in New Orleans. Lexus then made sure that the quality it designed in was what each customer experienced. It conducts 1,600 quality checks over and above those conducted on Toyotas before the cars leave the factory. There are various quality assurance sign-offs at the port of entry into the U.S., and further signoffs at the dealership taking delivery. Dealers do a 2-hour test before the vehicle is offered up for sale. Each new customer receives an inspection certificate presented at the time of delivery.

Lexus did not stop with the quality of its product. "We knew our dealer network would be our face to the customer," says Chitty. So they next asked: What can we do to reinvent the level of service surrounding the automobile to better please the customer? And they went to work on designing Lexus dealerships from the standpoint of providing a quality dealer experience, from initial sale to after-sale servicings.

In beginning the relationship with the customer, Lexus reinvented the selling transaction. "Sales consultants" regularly attend national and regional training courses to learn about cars, both their own and those made by competitors, and about customers. Lexus does not allow the traditional haggling, instead training its people on a radically different approach: not to hover, not to pry, not to solicit or "close." Consultants are taught to stay totally out of sight until the customer informs the receptionist that he is ready for a consultation. At the point of sale, the consultant ushers the customer into a "product presentation room," an alcove with no doors, no clutter, and a semicircular marble-topped table and three leather chairs that are precisely the same height.

The first two regularly scheduled maintenance appointments of a Lexus are free. Loaner cars are available. When the customer picks up his or her vehicle, it has been washed and vacuumed by a "valet detail specialist" whose compensation, like everyone else's at Lexus, is pegged to customer satisfaction. Mechanics are "diagnostic specialists" at Lexus and wear white shirts, and unlike traditional dealerships, customers are encouraged to speak directly with their specialist to better understand what services have been performed.

Finally, with regard to price, Lexus appears to have asked: How low of a price can we put on the car to truly give the customer better value? By coming into the market with a significantly lower price than other imported luxury cars, Value Innovator Lexus helped fuel a revolution in the upper tier of the car market.

The results of rethinking the Value Proposition was a success uncommon in any industry. It was all the more uncommon in a segment of the market that observers had long assumed was so bound up in heritage and tradition that buyers would never accept a new pedigree that came without a tradition of luxury behind it. But consumers swarmed to Lexus and pushed sales past BMW and Mercedes in just 2 years. And so it went, with Lexus holding the lead for several more years.

Then, by the mid-90s, the tide had turned yet again. Lexus was being beaten in a game it had helped create: introducing value into the luxury tier. Its sales were dropping. When Lexus was first introduced, its price started at a third less than the lowest-priced Mercedes. But Lexus and other Japanese makers were, during this period, facing a rising yen, which necessitated consistent price increases. And Lexus had apparently not retained the strategic insight that its Value Proposition had enabled it to achieve such instant success. The Toyota division had raised sticker prices from $30,000 to more than $50,000 and watched the market respond true to principle.

Indeed, the overall market for luxury cars had shifted, and instead of massive numbers of Boomer consumers trading up as had been predicted, many were opting for luxurious sport-utility vehicles such as Chrysler's Jeep Grand Cherokee or Ford's Explorer. Meanwhile, competitors such as Mercedes, BMW, and Jaguar (now owned by Ford,) made a comeback after learning two important lessons from Lexus: Keep a lid on prices and increase quality. What Lexus failed to remember in the giddy aftermath of its nearly flawless launch was that the customer doesn't care how good you were yesterday—only how good you are and what your price is today relative to your competitors.

Service: The "S" of the Value Triangle

You know about customer service. You know what it means. But you may not realize how powerful it can be to the overall value equation. While service—the S Factor—in the value triangle is a multitude of factors, for the purposes of our discussion, we'll use the S Factor to connote two things: The first is customer service; the second, customer services.

Customer service means the quality of the personal interactions and relationships between your people and your customers. It's intangible, but measurable. This aspect of service is all about perceptions, and perceptions are based on what Jan Carlzon, former chairman of SAS Airlines, terms "moments of truth," those crucial points of customer contact with a firm, its people, products, and services.

Each of these customer service "moments of truth" gets graded consciously or unconsciously by customers on the basis of what they expected would happen compared to what they perceive actually occurred. In other words, what did the customer expect your firm and your people to do for him or her versus their perception of the actual performance? If their expectations aren't met or exceeded, you failed to deliver value. Conversely, if you exceeded their expectation, you delivered more value than they expected, and you delivered better-than-expected S Factor value.

It's important to point out with any discussion of service that the customer doesn't generally see service quality as a distinct entity from your product quality. To most customers, service and quality are inextricably intertwined. A service business has a product, which is "manufactured" in real time, quite often in the presence of the customer, and that is the issue of performance: Did the building get renovated satisfactorily? A separate issue is whether the renovation crew was easy to work with, whether they completed the work when promised, etc. Ditto whether that's a trucking company backing up to your loading dock, or a cruise ship staffer welcoming you aboard for 2 weeks of nonstop service delivery.

While providing exceptional service is the rocket science of the 90s, the payoff for companies that continue to add value to this dimension of the value triangle is plainly evident. Home Depot is a stellar example. Home Depot's success is not due to carrying a markedly different set of products from anyone else. But what Home Depot has done is to serve its customer in a unique way: through empowerment that they can tackle that "do-it-yourself" project, and trust that the company will not sell them anything they don't need. Indeed, Home Depot prides itself on actually not letting the customer buy something he or she doesn't need.

And though it is a national chain, Home Depot partners with the local communities where its stores are located. When Hurricane Andrew hit South Florida, Home Depot cut the price of plywood by 40 percent. In effect, it sold plywood at a loss, but the message was that it cared more for the community's well-being during a time of crisis than it did about making a fast buck off people's misery.

Here's why the personal aspect of service has emerged as crucial to a firm's success:

1. *Today's time-starved buyers mean people value service more than ever.* People—individual consumers and buyers in general—just don't have time for poor service anymore. Because today's buyer is more pressed for time than ever, errors, misinformation, and unreliable support are as unacceptable as poor product quality.

2. *Customer service is the surest way to differentiate a business in a look-alike landscape.* Competing businesses often stock the very same products, completely neutralizing the Q Factor one to another. Other than competing strictly on price, service becomes the only way to add value. How can you stand out if you live in one of these look-alike competitive landscapes? Answer: with the quality of the people who take care of customers. While your value-adding service innovations are important to customers and can give your firm added momentum, they can also be copied by competitors.

3. *Customer service is the surest way to build and sustain competitive advantage.* Studies conducted by Forum, a Boston-based consultancy specializing in customer service, show that keeping a customer costs

one-fifth as much as acquiring a new one. In addition, customers are 4 times more likely to quit buying from a company because of poor service than because they found a cheaper supplier elsewhere. And fielding an effective service team is not something that a competitor can imitate, or assemble overnight. It is built over time by painstaking effort. Yet once you own the customer service niche in the minds of consumers, you have a powerful edge over competitors, although price and quality are still important.

4. *Service is increasingly important, even for discounters.* In the value era, the P Factor of the value triangle has a strong allure. But lower prices alone may not be enough. Lower prices get taken for granted. So major chains such as Circuit City are moving toward improving customer service, while still offering "low price guarantees." Even among discount brokerages, customer service is increasingly important. Waterhouse Securities, based in New York City, delivers share trades for $35 each, well below the discount industry average of $47. But the firm *exceeds* customers' expectations when it comes to excellent customer service. The firm has 41 branches and offers a full selection of financial products, including 700 mutual funds.

CUSTOMER SERVICES: THE OTHER S FACTOR

Just as customers' expectations of service have risen, so too have their expectations regarding *services*, which include the written and unwritten, implicit and explicit things you agree to provide with the sale. Such services might include something as simple as a free car wash with fillup, all the way to the activities inherent in fulfilling the lifetime warranty of a product.

As it becomes harder and harder for products to stand out and have clear differences, differentiation of the product itself becomes more difficult to maintain. In such an environment, companies began to search for what they could do to add value to a product, and providing services is an obvious arena.

Whether service or services, the added value of going "above and beyond" takes on a new dimension of importance in today's impersonal society. Not long ago, Saatchi, the giant advertising firm, dispatched a cultural anthropologist and a psychologist to talk with consumers about the meaning of service and its role in their lives. They heard stories of a man who, after owning a sterling silver Cross pen for 20 years, backed over it with his car and ruined it. Yet he wrote to the company, and they sent him a replacement. When he wrote them a letter to thank them, they said, "No matter what happens to our product, our product is our product for life; we stand by it."

In another instance, a shopper who'd bought a pair of shoes at Bloomingdale's continued her shopping trip, and at Nordstrom found a pair she liked even better. The Nordstrom representative volunteered to take the shoes back for her.

"That was the strongest point to emerge from our research from listening to customers," comments Myra Stark, a research associate at Saatchi. "If the company defines value as merely low price, they are missing a critical dimension of value in our time, and that is the service dimension. This value-added dimension of service centers around understanding what consumer expectations of service are and fulfilling them." Adding value to the service dimension of the value triangle inevitably involves looking at each stage in the transaction and asking, "What might we do to add value at this point in the transaction cycle?" Some of those checkpoints are:

> *Before the sale:* In what ways does your firm deliver an extra dimension of service prior to the sale?

> *During the sale or sales process itself:* On a recent visit to Istanbul, Turkey, my wife and I shopped for rugs in the famous bazaar there. While looking at rugs, we were treated to complimentary cups of Turkish coffee.

> *Servicing the product:* Recall how Lexus distinguishes itself from other car companies by outfitting mechanics in white shirts and encouraging customers to interface directly with them.

> *After-sale service throughout the lifespan of the product:* While you may not be able to offer a lifetime guarantee of your product or service, what special rights and privileges do prior customers enjoy with your firm?

Price: The "P" of the Value Triangle

In my 1991 book, *Managing the Future: 10 Driving Forces of Change*, I predicted that discounting was likely to spread in the 90s. Spread may have been too mild a word. I underestimated the magnitude of this driving force of change. Yet as important as price has become, price alone is rarely the only factor in buying decisions. Instead, the key factor in any buying decision is the *perceived value* to be gained by the buyer. Perceived value is the reason why companies with the highest-priced products and services in many industries often have the lion's share of the market. And it's also why those who become embroiled in price wars so often end up going out of business.

This is not to say that price can be ignored. Far from it. In fact, pricing is of paramount importance in the value era. Given the trend toward buyers having more and more choices in terms of how they'll purchase, and greater ease in obtaining information on products and prices, price equalization will come to many industries, if it hasn't already. The only way to get a higher price will be to add more tangible value via special services, higher measurable quality, or a perception of service excellence.

There are three things you can do with your prices: keep them the same, raise them, or lower them. Before you decide to lower yours, I suggest you think about the longer-term implications of what you're considering, and look for options. Rather than focusing the customer's attention on the attractiveness of your Q Factor or S Factor, a price cut encourages focus on your price tag, and commoditization is likely to be the result (just ask the folks in the airline industry).

If you're hearing from your sales force that "all our customers care about is price," it's a sure sign that you must rethink your Value Proposition—fast. The customer even has *your* people convinced that he's only interested in price, and he has succeeded in narrowing the focus to terms on which you can only lose. You must think long and hard about what uniqueness your firm offers, a subject we'll explore in Chapter 4, before you decide to cut your prices, consider the following eight-point P Factor checkup:

1. CONDUCT A PRICE SURVEY OF YOUR CUSTOMERS

The conventional wisdom about pricing is: *Charge what the traffic will bear.* To be sure, that strategy may point to taking gargantuan profits—for awhile. But such thinking, while understandable, does not factor in the fundamental reality of the era of value, which is that a new competitor can come in overnight and steal those customers away with lower costs.

Thus, to continue to be mindful of your Value Proposition even when

43

you don't have strong price competitors on the scene is prudent today. After all, the strategy of charging what the traffic will bear was what small-town merchants, like so many deer caught in the headlights of category killers (Circuit City, Toys R Us, Office Depot, etc.), got clobbered by.

A simple suggestion is to ask customers how satisfied they are with the price of your offerings at the same time you survey their levels of satisfaction with your quality and service. Using a postage-paid mailer, ask a group of your customers:

- What factors do they think about when they buy your product (how important is price)?
- What factors are key to their decision to buy (i.e., the reputation for quality of the seller, the value-adding services included, the seller with the lowest prices)?
- How satisfied are they with your price based on the factors they list above?

By doing this sort of surveying, you may find that your customers are only dissatisfied with some aspect of your pricing (the extra charge for installation, for instance), and you can then decide how you'll deal with that dissatisfaction based on a clearer understanding of their desires.

Remember the example in Chapter 1 where customers perceived the price difference between AT&T and its rivals to be 20 percent, when in reality it was only 5 percent? That's why your survey should also solicit customer perceptions of your *competitor's prices* as well as your own. The big question here is: How high do they perceive your competitor's prices to be relative to yours, and how accurate are their perceptions? Armed with this information, you can then compare how high your prices, compared to your competitor, are in reality. You may not need to cut prices as much as you need to educate your customers about what they are getting for what they are paying, and why your prices are justified.

2. Rethink How You Arrive at Pricing

Traditionally, most businesses arrive at the price they will charge by adding up their costs, and tacking a profit margin on top. Then, almost from the moment they launch the product, they are forced to start cutting the price. This could mean cheapening the product, redesigning it, or taking a hit on the bottom line, even though it was a perfectly good product. The real reason: *The customer didn't perceive the value was there to justify the price being charged.*

Of course, from the manufacturer's point of view, the price was necessary to cover the costs that went into designing and manufacturing the product. But this is the reason the United States has no consumer-electronics industry today. Value Innovators from Japan didn't come from that paradigm. They knew they had to offer a superior Value Proposition to the consumer to get to first base.

Japanese manufacturers looked at the fax machine in the 80s and did the same thing. A U.S. manufacturer invented the fax and charged the highest price it could obtain. Demand was limited. The Japanese priced their machine 40 percent lower and ran away with the market virtually overnight. Today, only one U.S. fax manufacturer, a niche player, remains.

The new reality of the global Value Revolution is: Customers don't care what your costs are. They don't see it as their job to "cover your costs." They want only the best value (best combination of Q-S-P) that fits their individual needs.

So, instead of setting prices based on cost-driven pricing, the Value Innovator does price-driven costing. This is more than a play on words. It means that much more attention is paid to bringing in the product at a price that is in line with what the customer might be able to afford to pay, rather than tacking on a profit margin at the end of a design and build process that considers the ultimate sale price secondarily or hardly at all. At a minimum, it's the kind of rethinking that will cause you to consider more deeply about the likely behavior of the intended customer.

3. Simplify Pricing

Value pricing has become a popular trend in recent years. Indeed, at General Motors, it has become a source of competitive advantage. Instead of discounting in the form of cash rebates, the GM strategy has included cutting back on the number of models on the market, while limiting option packages to just one or two combinations per vehicle and selling at discounted sticker prices that, in theory, are not negotiable.

Result: GM undercut the competition on similarly equipped cars in the all-important California market. In a recent year, GM's Pontiac Grand Am SE with air bags, stereo, air conditioning, and other options sold for $6,000 less than comparably equipped Toyota Camry DX.

How can you create a selling advantage just by simplifying your pricing schedules? Customers appreciate straightforward, easy-to-understand fee schedules and rate sheets.

4. KEEP PRICES THE SAME, BUT PROVIDE MORE PRODUCT FOR THE SAME PRICE

If you're in a tough competitive industry, lowering your price might seem to be an obvious thing to do. But it's important to remember that there are other options.

Throughout most of the 80s, McDonald's scoffed at lower-priced competitors such as Taco Bell, and got spoiled by its success. Then came the recession of the early 90s. Customer counts and profits declined in its U.S. restaurants. What to do? For awhile it seemed that cutting hamburger prices might be the only solution to get growth back on the front burner.

But instead of simply chopping hamburger prices, the chain linked lower prices with "Extra Value Meals," designed to coax the customer to spend more for a *bigger* meal, a Big Mac, large fries, and medium soda, whereas the customer might have ordered smaller sizes. Coupling this price innovation with a new focus on cost reduction, McDonald's made the numbers work. Result: Per-store sales in the U.S. began to increase, and profit margins at company-owned restaurants rebounded to record levels.

Instead of knee-jerk responses to competitor discounting, remind yourself that there are a host of options to try. What additional services can you throw in? What "extras" that you now charge for might be included as standard? And, taking a page from the McDonald's playbook, how might you provide more product while keeping prices steady?

5. LOWER YOUR COST OF DOING BUSINESS AND PASS SOME OF YOUR SAVINGS ON TO CUSTOMERS

Sometimes, of course, lowering prices does make sense, as Procter & Gamble concluded. Caught in the sway of the Value Revolution, P&G found its premium brands were suddenly out of step with the marketplace. Private-label rivals in categories ranging from diapers to coffee to dishwasher detergent began to emphasize their savings to strapped consumers. And their market share increased dramatically in some categories.

But to its credit, P&G took bold action rather than playing "let's wait and see if this will just blow over." P&G embraced the new imperatives of the Value Revolution, and in a matter of 2 years became a completely different company. Under the leadership of CEO Edwin Artzt, P&G completely rethought its Value Proposition. Artz determined that a two-prong response was necessary: Cut costs and lower prices.

The giant company, long a bastion of lifetime employment, cut 13,000 jobs—12 percent of the company's work force—and streamlined operations by closing 30 of the company's 147 factories. Artzt next moved to simplify P&G's vast array of products, eliminating almost a quarter of the different sizes, flavors, and other varieties of its brands. Unproductive coupon promotions were also slashed. And he poured increasing amounts into advertising to strengthen the brand image of his products.

The biggest and most controversial move involved cutting back on the promotions P&G offered to wholesalers and other channel partners. Such promotions led to "yo-yo" pricing on the shelf, with the same box of Tide costing in one week as much as a dollar less than the previous week. Such pricing not only confused the customer, it also eroded the brands' perceived value. P&G took a huge risk in breaking the gridlock and trying to reduce warehousing and distribution costs and speed up delivery cycles.

Previously, P&G's methods had produced enormous costs while delivering little value to the consumer: Wholesalers pocketed the discounts; there were big swings in production needs as promotions artificially increased demand one week then decreased it the next; and huge overhead costs were incurred to keep track of all the various promotional schemes. At first, the new policies hurt sales; resistance to the new "value pricing" as P&G called it, was rampant. Trade customers and retailers were upset because it hurt their profits. P&G's market share in some categories took a hit.

But the success of the initiatives have allowed the company to reduce the price difference between itself and rivals, including private-label competitors, while giving the customer "more for less" (than other brands). At this writing, the strategy is working well. In the most recent fiscal year, P&G reported the highest profit margins in 21 years, making a tidy $2.2 billion, and competitors who played "let's wait and see what happens" are now struggling to catch up.

Message: When the customer finally shouted that P&G's Value Proposition on many of its famous products had gotten out of whack, its leader had the guts to take decisive action. "We have to become single-minded in our quest to deliver better value," Artzt says. It is a mantra that other leaders might want to heed as well.

6. Offer Lower Prices for Less Service

Huge packaged-goods manufacturers like Philip Morris and Procter & Gamble aren't the only ones who must rethink their Value Propositions in the face of change. Service companies too must ask, "What changes being brought about by the Value Revolution are apt to change our customer's perception of good value?"

Many service companies have raised their prices for years, to the point where their service is no longer affordable to many would-be consumers. Charging "what the traffic will bear" has created not only less traffic but also low-risk opportunity for an emergent Value Innovator to come along and offer less service for a lower price.

This is happening today in the funeral industry. Families suffering the loss of a loved one have traditionally relied on the local undertaker who had served them well in the past. For their customers—families in grief— weighing competing Value Propositions of various funeral services was hardly at the top of their list of priorities—and price was not a major concern. But today, a more mobile population has fewer ties to local funeral operators. Meanwhile, the price of traditional funerals has been rising steadily to the point where they are beyond reach for many. Thus a growing demand is building for inexpensive caskets and no-frills cremations.

Enter Value Innovator Lloyd Mandel Levayah Funerals in Skokie, Illinois. Unlike traditional funeral homes, mourners don't stream in and out of Levayah Funerals for wakes and memorial services. There aren't any. Instead, Mandel arranges simple graveside services, and cuts the price of funerals by $2,000. Mandel also gives the bereaved more choices in how they package the funeral. A fourth-generation funeral director and president of the company, Mandel plans to franchise his operation under the name First American Funeral Store Franchise. The Levayah Funerals division will be aimed at Jewish families, while Infinity Funerals will target nondenominational customers.

7. If You're Competing on Price, Emphasize Savings. If You're Competing on Value, Emphasize Cost

Often, too much talk and concern over pricing adjustments is really a signal that innovativeness in the Q and S Factors has faltered. The customer doesn't perceive any uniqueness between competitors. You haven't done your educational work in defining the difference between the price of your offering (that which you charge) versus the cost (that which the customer must pay), not only in dollars but also in the investment of his or her time, knowledge, risk if buying from someone less reliable, etc.

In your marketing efforts, what you emphasize depends on your strategy. Assuming you are competing on the uniqueness of your Q Factor and/or your S Factor, you must continue to point out the distinction between your offering's "cost" and its price. If the photocopying machines in your office are down for a week because your dealer's service department can't get the needed parts delivered any quicker, what's the "cost" to your company? If you receive inadequate or erroneous information from a low-bidder knowledge supplier to your firm (e.g., key man insurance) what's the cost versus the price?

8. Make Your Customers Passive Beneficiaries of Lowest Price Guarantees

Boise Cascade, sensing that its customers needed more from an office product supplier than just low prices, applied "activity-based costing" methods to help many of its customers lower their costs as well. Boise then went a step further: with a new program that takes the customer's cost savings an important step further.

Called Boise Direct, which its newspaper ads touted as "just another in a long line of value-added services you've come to expect from Boise," the new program puts the onus on Boise, not the customer, to compare its pricing with the advertised sale prices of Office Depot and Staples in Southern California and Las Vegas. If they print a price that's lower than you normally pay at Boise, Boise will lower the price in its computer system immediately, so you automatically get the best price available in the marketplace.

Chapter Summary

So there you have them: the three factors of the value triangle, and the three key elements that make up your firm's Value Proposition. The fact is, most business people don't think about their Value Proposition until trouble hits. A new competitor suddenly appears. Sales taper off. Margins get squeezed. The status quo, which is to say the current Value Proposition, is no longer attracting customers. By then it may be too late.

The best time to think about value is before you have to, before your back is up against the wall, before your feet are to the fire. When a Value Innovator moves to reinvent value in a particular industry, other players in that industry are presented with a critical decision; either they in turn rethink and reinvent their own way of doing business by way of response, or they play an end game of watching customer loyalty erode over time.

By virtue of the fact that you're reading this book, I know that you are a leader who wants to deliver value profitably, rather than a mere follower. That's why, in the next chapter, we'll look at how to become a Value Innovator.

CHAPTER

BECOMING A VALUE INNOVATOR

IMAGINE LANDING AT CHICAGO O'HARE AIRPORT, tired after a long flight. You make your way out to the curb to hail a cab; your expectations of quality are so low that you'll settle for anything that moves. Service? Forget it. If the cabby is willing to get out and open the trunk, it would be a small miracle.

Instead—you must be dreaming—a neatly dressed driver approaches you with, "Sir, while I load your luggage into my trunk, I'd like to give you my mission statement." He hands you a laminated card. "My mission is to provide the fastest, cheapest, safest transportation to your destination in a warm, friendly environment."

Then, as the driver glides away from the airport, he says to you, "Sir, my name is Jake, and I want to tell you about some choices you have." Choices, you wonder incredulously, now he's going to pull nonsense

51

like, "We can take a faster route, but it's gonna cost you a little more money." You brace yourself for the pitch. But instead he says, "Up front here, I've got two thermoses, caffeinated and decaffeinated coffee. I've also got an ice chest full of soft drinks. Oh, and there's also a cellular phone you're welcome to use. If you need to make a call, just insert your credit card. And here, on this card," he says, passing another laminated card back to you, "here I have a listing of all the radio stations in the Chicago area with the station formats: sports, news, weather, rock and roll, just let me know. I've also got copies of today's papers: the *Tribune*, *Journal*, *USA Today*. And, finally, sir, I can give you a fantastic description of the great sites in this city as we pass them, or I could keep my mouth shut. What would you prefer?"

As you arrive at your destination, you realize that not only is this cabby for real but also you've just had a transforming experience. Henceforth, all other cab rides will inevitably be compared to this experience. Talk about exceeding expectations! Look at what this cab driver did. While his prices were the same as every other cab driver's (regulated industry), he provided a noticeably greater overall value in the form of excellent personal service and unique amenities. Some of these value-added services, he charged extra for (cellular service); some were included in the price— not only excellent customer service but a range of amenities that showed his guest that every aspect of the guest's comfort had been thought of.

Or take another example of a service business that adds unique value. This example comes from my friend and fellow professional speaker, Dr. Barry Asmus, the senior economist at the National Center for Policy Analysis. Barry was about to have his shoes shined in the Pittsburgh airport, and he watched the attendant stuff $5 bills in his pocket, one right after the other.

Joe, the shoeshine man, would apply a gooey substance to customers' shoes, light them on fire for a few seconds, and then hit them with a buff rag. Done. Shazam! It all happened in a minute. So Barry had his done. "I suddenly had mirrors for shoes," he told me. "It was the best shoeshine I have ever had in my life."

Asmus gave the man a $5 bill: $3 for the shine and $2 for the tip, and said, "I'm an economist. We often ask personal questions. Sir, how much money do you make shining shoes?"

Joe, the shine man, didn't mind, "This year I'll pull in around $50,000." Shining shoes!

Entrepreneurs like Jake the cabdriver and Joe the shoeshine svengali are Value Innovators. In virtually every industry today, there are Value Innovators, and what they do is redefine the value businesses in that industry can provide. After a trip with Jake, other cabs would be a disappointment. Or with the shoeshine man, Asmus was not the only one who didn't mind adding on a generous tip. Value innovators ask a fundamental question: How can we deliver greater customer value and raise our profitability by so doing?

This chapter is about how to move your own business in the direction of becoming a Value Innovator. To do this, I'm going to walk you through four strategies that make up what I call the value ladder. These are: less-for-less, same-for-less, more-for-less, and more-for-more. No matter where you position yourself on the ladder, the way to win the Value Revolution is to exceed your customers' expectations at the particular level you position yourself at. Let's start with less-for-less.

Less-For-Less: A Popular Strategy with Price-Sensitive Customers

"There's nothing wrong with serving a lousy cup of coffee . . . as long as you always serve lousy coffee," observes Truett Cathy, founder and chairman of Chick-fil-A, a chain of 600 restaurants. Chick-fil-A serves good coffee. But his point is an important one: As long as it's clear to your buyer that you are offering less in the way of product quality and/or service quality, you can still meet or exceed customer expectations, and keep customers coming back for more.

Purchasing coffee from a vending machine is a perfect example of less-for-less in action. You approached the transaction knowing the product quality was going to be low (especially in a period when gourmet coffee has reached an all-time high in popularity). And when the cup appeared and the beverage began to pour, you were satisfied (at least the machine hadn't eaten your coins). Some examples:

- Warehouse clubs, among other new businesses, have proved that there is a huge pent-up demand for lower prices, even if it means less convenience, less selection, and no service. Almost daily, it seems, new airlines are launched with less-for-less as their game plan.

- Wholesaler-distributors are making hay with less-for-less by sell-ing only a limited range of products, rather than by carrying a full inventory of goods.
- Manufacturers are responding to the lure of less-for-less by pro-ducing stripped down, generic, or clone products, rather than by going for ever more bells and whistles that add to the overall price.
- Even insurance companies are climbing aboard the less-for-less bandwagon. San Antonio-based USAA's auto-insurance premi-ums are among the lowest in the industry, yet it still manages to be ranked second highest in the nation against insurers that charge much higher premiums. How? USAA doesn't have the overhead of other insurers, because it deals with its customers entirely by phone and mail, using innovative technology to ensure that mem-bers calling in receive prompt response to questions and requests.

Less-for-less is popular with today's buyer, because, as we saw in Chapter 1, it is driven by declining spending power on the part of many end consumers. Here, the guiding principle is: Find a niche and fill it. Or, said another way, find a market where profit margins are high for the existing players, and attack on price. A plethora of new superstores supplying everything from pet products to educational materials are springing up across the land. In talking with those who launch such new businesses, it's a good bet that we haven't seen the last of them.

CONVERSATION WITH A LESS-FOR-LESS VALUE INNOVATOR

George Orban, a former New York investment banker, has been involved in Egghead Software, Ross Dress for Less, Karen Austin Petites, and Workplace, a pioneer in office superstores that has since been bought out. Before he attacks a new industry with a less-for-less strategy, Orban looks for two things: distribution inefficiencies and changing technology.

In looking at the software business in the early 80s, he observed not only a rapidly growing industry but also one where, on the retail side, nobody was making any money. "Nobody was really performing a service for their customer," he recalled. "Stores were inefficient and unpleasant. The microcomputer software business combined the inefficiency in distribution and great technological evolution. It had both those critical elements." As a result, he was instrumental in growing the Egghead Software chain into a national concern.

Similar conditions made the office products industry ripe for less-for-less. In Miami on a business trip, Orban met an entrepreneur by the name of Harold Jaffe, who ran two office products stores in what had once been grocery stores.

"They were a mess," Orban recalls. "But when I visited those stores, I noticed a couple of things. One, Jaffe was doing a tremendous business in a lousy retail store. And two, as I started poking around, I was astounded by the rate of growth in the office products industry and its consistent performance. The profit margins were high; everybody made money, even in recessionary periods. I made some mental notes about the industry, and then in 1986, a fellow in Boston started Staples, and I said to myself, If I don't get into it now, I never will."

Orban believes other industries are ripe for a less-for-less makeover. "It's now possible," he says, "for a start-up company with relatively limited capital to put in sophisticated computer and communications systems so that they can deliver products to consumers much more efficiently than an existing player in that industry who hasn't kept up."

Making Less-for-Less Pay Off

One key to many less-for-less strategies is to downplay or do away with the customer service side altogether. Since customer service is so difficult to standardize or to ensure, and since people are so expensive, the less-for-less strategy can be easier to execute. Self-service operations of all varieties, superstores, and warehouse clubs are all examples of virtually wiping out customer assistance in exchange for a lower price. Offering less selection, less convenience in terms of location, and less handy sizes in many product areas, warehouse clubs have grown from $1.5 billion in 1985 to $22.6 billion in 1993, sparked by price-driven consumers. In response, supermarkets and countless other retailers have been forced to slash prices on thousands of items to compete against these formidable new competitors.

Increasingly, firms taking a less-for-less approach are connecting with customers hungry for their offerings but unable or unwilling to pay traditional prices. Value Innovators are rethinking industries from travel agencies to legal services, and are coming up with ways to provide less service and a lower price. And the winners here, as elsewhere, figure out ways to exceed the expectations of customers at that price range. Let's take a look at how one airline has almost single-handedly brought the Value Revolution to its industry.

How Southwest Airlines Flies High with Less-for-Less

Dallas-based Southwest Airlines has taken the industry by storm with less-for-less strategy, competing not just with other carriers but with other methods customers might employ to fulfill their need of getting to a destination quickly and cheaply. Southwest fares are so low on many routes, they compete with bus fares and are even cheaper than driving.

The seventh largest U.S. domestic carrier with over 18,000 employees, Southwest has been profitable for 23 years and was the only major airline to realize a profit in a recent year. When it enters a new city, Southwest regularly drops fares 60 percent to 70 percent lower than existing fares of competing airlines.

One way Southwest can afford to do this is that it has 40-percent greater utilization of its aircraft and pilots than competitors. By deplaning and reloading two-thirds of its flights in 15 minutes or less, aircraft availability is increased dramatically. Pilots fly an average of 70 hours per month versus 50 hours at other airlines. The rapid turnaround not only cuts costs, which are handed down in the form of lower fares, but also results in added value by ensuring high frequency, on-time arrival to its many satisfied customers. And flight attendants clean the airplane interiors, not separate crews.

Southwest also keeps costs low by being conservative financially, not over-expanding through airline acquisitions, and staying clear of debt—only 49 percent of equity. Operating costs are kept low by a policy of using only fuel-efficient Boeing 737s, which further translates to lower maintenance costs.

But the most obvious less in the less-for-less formula is the no-frills approach to serving the customer, one that Southwest pioneered in the industry and that many others have since imitated. No meals are served aboard flights, and seating is open. Most flights are short enough so that meals aren't missed, and passengers are quickly and easily seated by agents who issue reusable plastic cards on a first-come, first-board basis. Furthermore, the customer has to call Southwest directly to make a reservation, because the airline does not participate in the computerized booking systems used by travel agents—another way it creates savings to pass on to the customer.

So far, Southwest's Value Proposition seems pretty simple: Cut your costs and services, and dramatically undercut competitors' fares. But numerous other carriers have failed with less-for-less, so we've got to look further and ask what is the perceived value that keeps people coming back to this incredibly popular airline in a tidal wave of customer loyalty? The frequent departures, on-time service, and low rate of baggage loss all add value, but the innovation that makes Southwest a leader is clearly its corporate ethic of treating employees as customers, which is epitomized by the front-line leadership style of CEO Herb Kelleher.

"In a service environment, if your people aren't delivering good service, it doesn't matter how good your niche is," says Dave Ridley, Southwest's vice-president of sales and marketing.

Less-for-Less: How Not to Make It Work

At one time, Sears was *the* Value Innovator, the leader in pushing back the frontier of value for millions of Americans. Through its catalog, Sears provided unprecedented choices to customers in isolated areas who previously had no access to such material goods. Result: Sears prospered as it grew with the nation.

But like many firms that are wildly successful, Sears began to think it had an unbeatable Value Proposition. By the mid-70s, Sears began to lose its cachet as a one-stop, value-leading shopping emporium. In the 80s, its core of middle-class customers eroded, and it faced competition from aggressive specialty stores that were cropping up in malls all over America. Sears watched as a sizable chunk of its appliance business was won over by aggressive new superstore competitors.

It ceded much of its toy sales to Toys R Us and discounters such as K-Mart, Target, and Wal-Mart. By the early 90s, Sears went from being the number 1 retailer in the world to a tired, down-on-its luck purveyor without a clearly defined niche or strategy. Facing tremendous pressure from Wal-Mart, Target, and K-mart, Sears launched, through massive advertising, an "everyday low-price" strategy.

The only problem was, Sears had apparently forgotten a vital component of less-for-less, which is that your costs must also be as low as your prices. Sears began eliminating thousands of in-store employees and back-office expenses. But with a history of doing business in a less-constrained manner, employee acceptance of the change was not automatic, and several tough years ensued before Sears's cost structure was brought in line with its new market positioning.

More recently, Sears has taken some bold and exciting steps toward recovery of its former glory, most noticeably in women's apparel. Indeed, the organization may yet adjust its Value Proposition in the eyes of customers, which is no mean feat. As Sears found out the hard way, shifting from a conventional middle-of-the-road positioning to a less-for-less proposition requires more than a massive communication effort to get the word out to customers. It also requires that a conventional firm redesign the way it does business from top to bottom.

Here are seven questions to ask yourself before you pursue a less-for-less strategy:

1. How can your systems of distribution be rethought to produce quantum cost-stripping improvements?

2. What is the downside in moving to less-for-less for existing customers?

3. How can you partner with your suppliers differently to make less-for-less work?

4. Can customers in your industry really get by with less service, or even no service at all?

5. Can you effectively communicate a change in your strategy such that it will make a difference?

6. Will both your customers and your front-line employees understand the move and support it?

7. What would going to a less-for-less strategy entail and are you up to it?

More-For-More: A Strategy for Customers Who Want Extras and Are Willing to Pay for Them

Despite what we've said so far about the new price-conscious, strapped consumer, there will always be a customer group that wants more and is willing to pay for it. That is to say more quality, more Q Factor, if you will, and more S Factor. In today's world, the level of complexity involved in accomplishing so many necessary tasks is considerable. Therefore, if customers can leverage their time, many will choose to do so. In effect, they are willing to pay for knowledge, expertise, and guidance, insofar as it translates to saving them time.

In an era of the more sophisticated consumer, in an era when we've gone from conspicuous consumption to conspicuous bargain hunting, it might seem that the appeal of more-for-more would be greatly diminished, or even nonexistent. But objective research reveals that nothing fundamentally has changed: If you give customers something they perceive as having extra value, they'll still pay extra money for it.

What is different is that a premium product or service doesn't become premium because its maker puts a fancy label on it or calls it premium. The customer determines the grade. The product must inherently deliver more. Companies can no longer count on positioning a product as "exclusive" or best of class and expect it to be accepted on those merits alone. The restaurant whose service is lackluster, whose food is bland, whose atmosphere is sterile, but whose dining-room attendants saunter around with the attitude that they are the ultimate in cool, may fool people once. But those same people won't come back, if they even stay through one sitting.

Certainly, status is part of the appeal of more-for-more offerings, and whether it's Mt. Blanc pens or Rolex watches or Rolls Royce automobiles, status is a dimension that determines purchase that doesn't fit neatly into the Q-S-P value triangle. But at this writing, Rolls Royce automobiles are not selling well in the wake of quality and service of other luxury cars. And here's what is different in the new era: Whether fine fountain pens or luxury hotels, there are more competitors at this top rung on the value ladder.

There used to be only two categories of hotels: luxury and regular. Today there is luxury (Marriott, Hilton, etc.) and ultra (Ritz Carlton), as well as medium-priced (Holiday Inn), limited service (Hampton Inns), budget, and economy. At the top, what you see is the ratcheting up of expectations, and when you sing from the more-for-more hymnal, you must be prepared for quick page turns.

In the final analysis, value is and will continue to be an important consideration as the buyer weighs and evaluates choices of where to spend more-for-more dollars. So, you can count on one thing with the more-for-more positioning strategy: If you adopt it and run with it, your position is such that you have to keep adding value—continuously.

Let's take a closer look at how two widely divergent firms, one a super-market chain, the other a manufacturer of shaving equipment, have made more-for-more pay off.

How Wegmans Wins with More-for-More

Rochester, New York-based Wegmans Food Markets has bowled over other chains in the grocery business and made its mark as a here-to-stay success. Wegmans is "the best chain in the country, maybe in the world," says consultant Neil Stern of McMillan/Doolittle in Chicago. "They have created something that gets the customer beyond price."

Owned and operated by Chief Executive Robert Wegman and his son Danny Wegman, this privately held business has 50 grocery stores and 15 home and garden centers, capturing as much as 55 percent of the Rochester market. Its revenues are estimated at $2 billion a year, with larger stores producing as much as $1 million per week, 4 times the national average.

Wegmans' approach is to give customers more in all three of the fac-tors of the value triangle. The Q Factor is the most obvious: Compared to the average grocery store, Wegmans offers more quality by offering cus-tomers a produce section 5 times bigger than most. Locally grown produce, much in demand, is featured, with growers' names and regions displayed. Produce supply is meticulously inspected and replenished 12 times a day. Local suppliers deliver directly to the store, thereby avoiding warehouse stays where products might lose freshness. Some apple growers even cre-ate special boxes for Wegmans and use them in place of more conventional deep bins to avoid bruising or crushing of fruit on the bottom.

Wegmans stores have been winning customer loyalty since the 50s by catering to ethnic tastes, albeit at a higher price. Quicker than oth-ers to read the trends, the company saw the rise of working women and the resultant changes in lifestyle, and started early offering high-quality, gourmet-prepared foods ranging from pizza to chicken *cordon bleu*.

More S-factor services are another weapon in the Wegmans' arsenal. Newer stores have up to 35 checkout lines. No one waits in line at Wegmans, a fact Bob Wegman personally sees to when he shows up unannounced and goes through the line himself. Gourmet deli sections, featuring white-capped chefs who toss your pasta or sauté your salmon while you browse, combine elegance with convenience. In-house cafes where you can have Sunday brunch or sip a glass of wine further differentiate Wegmans by providing more services than the average grocery store.

Part of Wegmans' appeal is the added convenience to the customer of having not just foods but also a wide variety of services under its roof: videos for rent, prescription drugs, a card shop, a restaurant, even a patio furniture department. The mix has proved highly profitable.

How does Wegmans manage to appeal to so many grocery shoppers, while price appeals have become so effective in other parts of the country? Why do Wegmans' shoppers spend more on their monthly grocery bill than do shoppers at other chains? The perceived value of the P and S Factors easily overrides the larger grocery bill. Another way that Wegmans keeps costs down is by buying in bulk and bargaining with suppliers on price. Higher profits come from over a thousand private-label food products and nongrocery items. A nonunion work force helps keep labor costs low, and owning 80 percent of the property under their stores certainly helps with leasing costs.

To be sure, competitors such as Tops Markets Inc. in Williamsville, New York, are copying the Wegmans style and nipping at the firm's market share. But for the most part, rival stores have been knocked out by this highly competitive more-for-more maverick. At one time, there were seven grocery companies in Rochester. Today, few remain. "We stood up to A&P and others, but Wegmans blew half our stores off the road," said the owner of a now defunct chain.

A decision to stay small and not grow nationally seems to ensure that the unparalleled quality and service will continue. The close watch maintained over day-to-day operations by the father-son team has been a key ingredient in the more-for-more strategy, something that would be much more difficult in a far-flung operation. Staying local, it seems, has been a wise choice for Wegmans.

How Gillette Strayed from, Then Returned to, More-for-More

Long associated in the consumers' minds with razors and shaving products, Gillette's business churned out steady profits for over a century by not only selling razors but also replacement blades. But in the 70s, Gillette's momentum was zapped by a swarm of Value Innovators at the low end of the shaving market.

Led by Bic, the French pen company, Gillette was upstaged by a less-for-less product that nearly took Gillette down, namely, cheap, disposable razors. In knee-jerk response, Gillette fought back by coming out with its own disposables. Fortunately, the name Gillette on a package of disposables carried some weight with customers, and, for a while, it looked as if shaving had become a disposable activity.

But the disposable dukeout had an unintended impact. The growing popularity of disposable razors threw Gillette's market for replacement blades into decline, and its profit margins plummeted. Sales of shaving systems such as the Atra and the Trac II got cannibalized. Result: The consumer no longer perceived any real difference between disposable maker A and disposable maker B, so why not go for the cheapest one? Commoditization ensued as Gillette stopped innovating and started playing a price game. Takeover battles loomed for the weakened company.

What to do? Not until the late 80s did Gillette's management finally begin to realize the full impact of what had been allowed to happen. They set out to recreate a differentiated solution: a better shave than was obtainable by any other means. Millions of men each morning faced a problem: how to remove whiskers from their faces in the least painful and most effective way possible, so that they could get on with the events of their days. They also faced a choice: pay more to get more, or pay less and get less than the best shave.

Gillette's more-for-more breakthrough was Sensor, an innovation in shaving history, introduced in 1990. In the U.S., Sensor outsells its closest rival 10 to 1. Gillette reestablished its supremacy, but it was a close shave!

What to Ask Yourself Before You Embrace More-for-More

Here are two important issues to consider before you adopt a more-for-more strategy:

1. If you have the highest prices in your industry, consider yourself a target. Somewhere out there, a competitor has his sights on your market share. In many industries, a high price is now a liability. How can you further differentiate your added value?

2. What does "more" mean to your particular customers? The assumption is that if customers see a better-performing product, they'll pay more for it. This may or may not be true with your product or service category, and only you can make that determination.

Same-for-Less: Driving a Wedge in the Marketplace

While less-for-less and more-for-more are at the opposite extremes in the marketplace, they are certainly not the only positioning strategies being used in the battle for consumer dollars. Another strategy is to duplicate all or almost all of the other guy's offering, but come in at a lower cost. Same-for-less is a way for the attacker to gain attention. And that is as true today as it ever was. Just look at the results achieved by a seminar company and a Mexican food purveyor.

Gaining "Share of Stomach" at Taco Bell

Because this unit of PepsiCo had the foresight to move toward a same-for-less strategy, Taco Bell sales doubled in a 5-year period, and operating profits nearly tripled. And that was just for starters. Under CEO John Martin's spirited leadership, Taco Bell was among the first to cut prices on popular menu items by 25 percent, changing the face of fast-food retailing forever. It was able to do so by reengineering the business: preparing foods centrally in off-site kitchens, then delivering to what has become an ever-expanding number of locations. Taco Bell has achieved significant labor and cost savings, and passed those savings on to customers. What Taco Bell has in mind for the future is to take the largest quick-service Mexican restaurant chain in the world and grow it even faster by putting outlets on college campuses, in stadiums, in airports, and on wheeled carts. Or, you might say, Taco Bell has reinvented itself from being a quick-service restaurant to "being number 1 in the share of stomach," as Martin puts it.

How CareerTrack Spawned an Industry Revolution with Same-for-Less

Before this Boulder, Colorado, firm began promoting its courses around the country in the early 80s, three seminar companies dominated the industry and regularly charged $165 and more for a 1-day training course. In 1982, CareerTrack founders Jeff Salzman and Jimmy Calano, both in their mid-20s, had a different idea: Cut the cost of such training, and see what would happen. With $10,000 of their own money invested, they began promoting an "Image and Self-Projection" seminar for women.

"We priced our program $20 less than our lowest competitor just to drive a wedge in the marketplace," says Calano, majority partner and CEO. "We thought we'd get people to try us out to see if in fact we were giving the same for less." Successful in doing just that right from the start, the ambitious duo kept lowering their price to see what would happen. "What we discovered was that if we cut the price in half, the elasticity of demand was such that we didn't just get twice as many people, we got 3 or 4 times as many people!"

What the two had stumbled across was a torrent of pent-up demand for lower-cost training. In studying their marketplace with fresh eyes, Salzman and Calano realized the wave they had caught. A lot of the seats at public seminars in cities like Chicago and San Francisco and Dallas, it turned out, were being filled by managers from companies in smaller cities. This meant they had to fly or drive to the seminar city, incurring travel costs. The seminar fee turned out to be only 20 percent of the cost. By bringing the training closer to where these managers lived, and by cutting the cost of training, "now they could afford to send four people for the price of one."

By helping company training directors get the same instruction for their people at less cost, and by bringing the training closer to the customer in many cases, CareerTrack became a juggernaut of change in the value equation. It greatly expanded, just as Southwest Airlines and many others have done, the market for their product. The competition's reaction?

"They laughed at us," Calano recalls. "They ignored us for the better part of 2 years. They thought it was absurd for us to charge only $45 for a 1-day course." The Big Three did not lower their prices, nor did they follow CareerTrack into the smaller cities.

Result: mayhem in the marketplace. One of the top three players was wiped out, and three of the top regional players quickly went under. Of the two remaining national seminar companies, both tottered on the brink of insolvency. One was sold and sold again; the other reorganized and has made a modest comeback.

By 1990, lower-priced seminars had become the rule rather than the exception. CareerTrack, the erstwhile upstart, was the undisputed leader. Profits continued to roll in. This changed everything. Instead of ignoring the firm, survivors now watched its every move and began to imitate every aspect of what CareerTrack did: its seminar titles and the look and layout of its all-important direct-mail pieces, which necessitated frequent trips to the courthouse to defend its uniqueness.

"These days we have about a 90-day window before [competitors] copy us," says Calano. "And we also have some new competitors, people who've seen our strategy, seen how well we were doing and said, 'let's copy them.'" The intensity of the survival-driven competition combined with rising postal rates continues to gnaw away at profitability. Postal costs were a major reason four seminar companies shifted to a nonprofit organization status. And the relatively low barriers to entry encourage constant new competitors. "The 90s have been very tough," Calano concedes.

Fierce competition has forced CareerTrack to innovate or evaporate, and to rethink every aspect of how customers perceive it. An inability to raise prices necessitates attention to figuring out how to make their strategy work by not only being perceived as the low-price leader but also as a consistent quality and service leader as well. This has produced a constant emphasis on raising their Q Factor and S Factor in areas where customers notice.

"What we try to do is to provide more take-home value training without sacrificing the entertainment aspects of our courses," says Calano. "When we realized that the copycat behavior was never going to end, we began to see that the only way to establish and maintain competitive advantage was by raising our quality."

Realizing that most customers' impression of the firm began and ended with their impression of the 125 trainers who led seminars in hotel rooms across America, the firm began pruning the bottom tier of its trainer corps, upgrading its course content more frequently, tripling its development staff, bringing out more new programs, and looking for additional revenue sources in such areas as back-of-the-room sales. The firm found a new profit center in making all its courses available for sale in audio and video formats, an innovation that now contributes almost half of annual revenues.

Such dramatic market changes, which CareerTrack helped unleash, are part and parcel of the post-Value Revolution playing field. In effect, CareerTrack has had to change its positioning from same-for-less to more-for-less. "Same-for-less doesn't cut it in our industry anymore," Calano observed.

More-for-Less: The Value Proposition Customers Want Most

In the classic text *Competitive Strategy*, Harvard professor Michael Porter asserts that a company can be either a value-adding differentiator or a low-cost leader. But what certain value-innovating organizations are discovering is that they must *figure out ways to do both* in order to win the Value Revolution.

In this section, we'll look at a men's suit retailer, a home improvement superstore, and an electronics giant that offer excellent service. Yet they also offer low prices and, in some cases, a low-price guarantee. What gives with the Porter analysis? The value economy reveals that competition is so fierce that its new imperatives make mincemeat of theories that were solid and reliable only a few years ago. If ever there were a positioning strategy most closely akin to what the customer really wants, it's more-for-less.

Look around the economic landscape today, and where you see the action, you will see more-for-less innovators. They're springing up everywhere and growing at a phenomenal rate.

Breathing Life into the Men's Suit Business

One such more-for-less revolutionist is Fremont, California-based Men's Wearhouse, a men's suit retailer. While many men's suit retailers have shuttered their doors in recent years due to declining sales of business suits and the trend toward more casual dress, Men's Wearhouse has chosen to expand and has, in some cases, taken advantage of huge drops in the cost of retail space. The chain offers low prices on brand-name clothing with such recognizable names as Cardin, Givenchy, Halston, and Yves Saint Laurent. With stores in 21 states, Men's Wearhouse also touts its "more" by including free pressing and follow-up calls to determine the level of satisfaction. Highly visible television advertising raises the company's profile, often using the slogan "I guarantee it."

How One "Discount" Broker Offers More

Charles Schwab pioneered discount stock market investing in 1974, by rethinking the concept of what a stockbroker should be. He looked at the real needs of a segment of the investing public and provided them a different solution. These customers wanted investing to be low pressure, low cost, and fast. They knew where they wanted to invest and didn't need any "advice."

Offering none, Schwab helped investors by doing their bidding, and little else. This is in stark contrast to the usual pressure to buy certain stocks and bonds. Schwab has also been able to personalize the discount brokerage business through the use of his face in the ads. His handsome, trustworthy moniker is found on virtually every piece of advertising the company produces.

"Discount brokerage used to be a sort of faceless, impersonal [business], . . . and Chuck really brings a personality to what we have to sell," observes Jeffrey Lyons, Schwab's senior vice-president of marketing.

Schwab continues to innovate new services at a seemingly unending rate. And it continues to attract new customers. In a recent year, the firm added 800,000 new accounts, up 16 percent over the previous year. Half of those new accounts were new to investing. Better yet, the average age of the customer is 47, a full 10 years younger than the industry average.

In the beginning, the uniqueness of Schwab's approach was enough. However, as more discount brokerages blossomed, Schwab evolved its less-for-less positioning into the more-for-less concept. It has continued a string of value-adding firsts ever since:

- The first to offer 24-hour trading, 7-days-a-week order entry for stock trades.

- The first to introduce automated telephone touchpad order entry available in four languages.

- The first to offer competing mutual funds with a program called OneSource. There are 287 funds from over 27 mutual-fund families that customers buy free of "loads" or transaction fees. This saves the customer the time and trouble of dealing with multiple-fund companies.

- The first to waive annual fees for Individual Retirement Accounts with balances over $10,000. (IRA assets have since doubled.)

- The first to offer trading software packages for customer PCs that allow the customer to buy and sell stocks, bonds, options, and mutual funds; access financial news wires; and research information and forecasts from independent analysts, while saving 10 percent on each trade.

- The first to offer Custom Broker, which uses various news wires and information services to get the data the customer wants, and then gets the data to the customer fast by fax, computer, or pager.

- The first to offer a no-fee dividend reinvestment plan for over 4,000 stocks.

Schwab's rapid growth and success have inevitably attracted competitors who have no recourse but to position themselves in the less-for-less category. So far, however, they have not wrested Schwab's base of cost-conscious stockmarket investors. And Schwab's value-adding innovations, coupled with extensive mass advertising and direct marketing, make it a powerful competitor. Says Lyons, Schwab's marketing vice-president, "We really want to live up to our tagline, which is 'helping our investors help themselves.'"

A Budget Motel Offers More-for-Less

In a segment on the popular television program *60 Minutes*, commentator Andy Rooney focused his attention on the state of the American hotel room. "Why can't somebody come up with a better room at an affordable price?" mused the curmudgeonly commentator.

Hotelier Robert Hazard, CEO of Choice Hotels International, happened to be watching the program that evening, and took the question to heart. The result was Sleep Inns, a budget motel promising more in-room amenities at the same low prices as competitors in that market tier.

"Anybody can build a cheap hotel on a cheap budget," says Hazard, "but getting five-star value at a one-star price is rare. Sleep Inn will thrive now and into the next century because it appeals to a value-conscious market that craves quality."

What's so different about Sleep Inns? Interestingly, its rooms are a third smaller than the average midrange room, but are designed to give the impression of increased spaciousness. It makes up for the lack of size with an addition of amenities not usually found in budget properties. Each room contains a spacious workdesk, oversized walk-in showers, thick 30-ounce carpeting, electronic data ports allowing for hook-ups of computers, fax machines, and other business traveler technology. A state-of-the-art security system allows the guest to use his or her credit card as a room key.

Introduced after extensive research with customers, Sleep Inns have minimal public space, only a small lounge seating area and registration desk, and rooms are accessed via an interior corridor. Further cost cutting is the result of the company's efficient use of employees. The night clerk doubles as the nighttime laundry person, a feat made possible by locating the laundry room directly behind the front desk. Landscaping is composed of low-maintenance shrubs rather than high-maintenance lawns. Maids can clean more rooms per day because night stands are bolted to walls for easier vacuuming and cleaning. The result of these and other cost-cutting innovations are that Sleep Inns are operated with 10 employees but accomplish what competitors do with 120 employees. Concludes Hazard, "Delivering value profitably is an art."

Home Depot: Cleaning Up with More-for-Less

Not long ago I decided that the best way to cut our water bill and to conserve water was to install a drip irrigation system on our property. Never having installed a drip system and being notoriously unhandy, I trudged over to my local home center for materials.

The first clerk I encountered pointed me to the garden center. Neat: They even had a video on how to do it, I discovered. When I finally found the associate in the nearly deserted garden center, he popped in the video. It was helpful, but I still had questions.

"You know," he confessed in a making-friends sort of way, "we don't really sell that much of this drip irrigation stuff. The place you ought to go to is a company that specializes in drip, called____. They're closed today, but they are open during the week. Matter of fact they stole away one of our best guys." "How do their prices compare?" I probed. "Oh, about the same," he replied.

As he was walking me out, we passed by the store's selection of red-wood bark. I asked for his suggestion on a ground cover that would be most appropriate for a sunny backyard. I inquired about prices.

"You're gonna have to pay over $8 a bag if you go that route," he said. "What you ought to do is call one of the tree companies in town. They have all these tree grindings that they'd probably love to get rid of." I thanked him and asked how he liked working at the center. "Oh, it's just temporary," he said, "I'm here through next week and then I'm going back to school."

Sound familiar? That's the level of employee commitment today at many firms. And this one, Builders Emporium, was liquidated in 1994. Now contrast Builders Emporium with Home Depot.

At Home Depot, employees give good advice, walk you through your project, show you how to not overspend. Since company founders Bernard Marcus and Arthur Blank built their first store in 1979, their success has been nothing short of extraordinary. Among the *Fortune Service 500*, Home Depot ranks number 1 in 10-year growth in earnings per share —an average 42.5 percent annually. The company's net income in a recent year rose 45.6 percent. Home Depot is on the march. So what's unique about its positioning strategy?

Is it the prices? True, its prices are low and they often undercut the sleepy and overpriced local home products stores. But try again. It isn't the low prices so much as the way the company adds value by empowering the customer. "Home Depot caters to the do-it-yourselfer," says Bernard Marcus. "But it's the first time he's done it. The fear factor is the biggest thing we have to overcome. That's why our value-added is all the training our people have."

A typical topic might be "How to Install Ceramic Tile." The salesperson shows the customer how to lay patterns of tile and hand-mix batches of grout, while dispensing a steady patter of advice—and a low-key sales approach. "Make sure you have a pair of kneepads to do this," and "You'll want to buy about 10 percent more tile than you need to allow for breakage and replacement—if you buy new tile later even in the same pattern, the colors won't match."

It's interesting how something as obvious as empowering the customer to believe in his or her abilities to do home improvement projects could be at the heart of a firm's winning strategy. And yet, while most competing home improvement centers are hardly as poorly staffed as the one I visited, few have seen fit to copy Home Depot's winning moves.

Circuit City: Blasting Out the Competition with More-for-Less

Richmond, Virginia-based Circuit City has become the nation's largest and most profitable specialty retailer of consumer electronics and major appliances. The company accomplished this remarkable growth and profitability by defying conventional wisdom. It is a value-adding discounter. A contradiction in terms? How can the company provide both?

"What allows us to be both a discounter and a full-service retailer is our market share," Richard Sharp, Circuit City's CEO, told me when I interviewed him. "Our share on the home electronics side is typically 3 to 4 times our nearest competitor's; generally in the 25-percent range or higher. The combination of large market share, efficient operation, and increasing buying clout has allowed us to become the low-cost, full-service producer." What allowed Circuit City to emerge as the low-price leader, Sharp explained, was the fact that when the chain was just starting, most of its competition was from department stores and mom-and-pop retailers. "That gave us an initial foothold. You have to remember that pricing is always relative to the predominant competition."

If the predominant competition used to be department stores, isn't Circuit City vulnerable to the warehouse club discounters? "To a certain extent, maybe," Sharp concedes, "since they have a cost structure that is substantially lower than ours, or any other full- or moderate-service retailer." But Sharp is convinced that most consumers won't seek to buy stereos and televisions and VCRs in what he calls a "zero frills environment," since "buying electronics is a fairly high-anxiety purchase. It's big ticket, high technology, and consumers don't want to make a mistake. They want a broad selection, which the warehouse clubs don't provide. And they want knowledgeable sales counselors, which the clubs don't have. And just as important, they want to know that if they have a problem afterwards, that somebody is there to fix it if it breaks."

In its early days, Circuit City competed almost exclusively on price. Its new slogan is "Circuit City—Where Service Is State of the Art." As Sharp explains, "In the earlier days our focus tended to be more on price. The prevailing attitude was that since we offered low prices, the customer would be willing to tolerate a bit more inconvenience. But as I looked at where the business was going, I felt that with the two-wage-earner families and with the increasing affluence, people would be less willing to be inconvenienced and would demand higher service levels."

The result was a rethinking of every aspect of how the customer experiences value. Out of this process came a more upscale store design as well as an increased focus on the entire customer experience. A typical Circuit City electronics superstore features more than 14,000 square feet of selling space and 2,800 brand-name items. Also contained within each superstore is a credit office, a warehouse, a car stereo installation facility (many discounters don't install), a sales training room, and a service department.

In rethinking its business from the standpoint of its customers, Circuit City came up with value-adding innovations at every turn. Typical example: Product categories are arranged around a central "racetrack," a walkway that guides the customer through the store to individual selling boutiques. Bold, clear signs help customers find their way around. Each boutique displays products by price and features, simplifying the purchase decision while providing the breadth of selection consumers demand.

At least part of Circuit City's brainstorms came from studying the competition. Says Sharp:

> We had studied the catalog retailers like Best Products because they were some of the first discount retailers. They were slow as molasses. You walked in and filled out this paperwork, you stood around for a while, then they called you to the counter and you paid, and then they finally called you to a pickup area and you picked it up, and they sometimes called you to the counter and told you, "Sorry, we don't have this item in stock." It was a frustrating experience. We looked at how much hassle the customer had to put up with and turned our minds inside out looking for better ways of speeding the customer through the purchasing cycle. I made the decision that we needed to commit the extra dollars necessary to have enough sales counselors on the floor.

Even the best customer service in the world is disappointing if the customer can't find what he or she wants, or has to wait while the product is special-ordered. Breakthrough solution: Half of each Circuit City store is devoted to showroom. Result: The customer often gets instant delivery—whether it's a Walkman or a washing machine—even during peak selling seasons.

Finally, Circuit City looked for ways to add value in another arena of constant frustration for customers, in the after-sale servicing of products that don't work. Says Sharp:

> We spent a good bit of time analyzing the best way to provide [after-sale] service. The complexity of the product today, the cost of the parts inventory, the availability of technicians, and the need for adequate supervision make it virtually impossible to have service departments at each store site. Our solution was to set up regional service departments. We have special vans with carpeted shelves that are used for nothing but transporting the merchandise back and forth.

Circuit City has added value to every aspect of the purchasing cycle while still offering customers a low-price guarantee. The combination has proved to be a killer for competitors, and not just the small stores. The firm's ability to raise both quality and service to new levels while offering low prices has made the difference.

Moving Toward More-for-Less

More-for-less is a game plan pregnant with possibilities. Try this strategy in your business by asking yourself right now: How can I give my customers more quality of product, more quality of service, at less cost?

Companies like Charles Schwab, Sleep Inns, Home Depot, and Circuit City did it, and you can do it too, if you model their ideas. None of these businesses is standing still. They're moving forward constantly, looking and searching for new ways to add more and do it for less. Circuit City does it through centralized warehousing. Sleep Inns does it by designing more efficient motel rooms. Schwab does it through technology and creating new techno-edges that save drudgery and man-hours. You can do the same.

Here are some questions to consider as you contemplate moving toward more-for-less:

1. How can you cut back on costs and still deliver products or services that meet customer expectations?

2. What new technologies can you use to lower prices and increase profits?

3. What innovations might you create that will allow you to offer more for less than the competition?

4. How can you combine both low cost and added value at the same time?

Getting Ready to Add New Value

As you read about what various firms are doing to differentiate themselves, you no doubt considered where your company is currently positioned on the value ladder. You may have noticed that this chapter's examination of the "rungs" of the value ladder is incomplete. In reality, there are five other potential game plans (e.g., same-for-more, less-for-more, etc.) that we haven't looked at. That's because these are not positioning strategies that any company should attempt to stand on for too long in the value era, for they are ultimately not viable.

The trend today is inexorable: what customers want, and what they are increasingly able to get, is more-for-less. They'll settle for less-for-less, and they'll gravitate towards same-for-less, but what they really want is more-for-less. So no matter what business you're in, you must provide greater value, and not necessarily charge extra for it, to attract and retain customers.

What else might you do to strengthen your positioning in the eyes of customers? Questioning "the way things are done in our industry" is a good place to start. Following that up with an examination of "the way our business is currently delivering value to customers" will lead you to think outside the bounds of the way things have always been done. It will lead you to try new things, to take risks, to revitalize your business.

But the story doesn't end there. In the next chapter, we'll look at seven powerful ways you can add unique value, no matter where you're positioned.

4

Chapter

SEVEN POWERFUL STRATEGIES FOR ADDING VALUE

IN RESEARCHING THE BOOK *WINNING THE INNOVATION GAME,* I crisscrossed the United States to interview over 50 of America's leading innovators, men and women who were introducing new products, services, and methods that were changing the way business is done.

My mission was to discover what traits, if any, they had in common, that enabled them to succeed in translating their ideas from vision to reality. One of the things I heard many of them talk about was their reliance on intuition. During dinner with Robert Giamo, founder of the American Cafe chain in the Washington, D.C., area, he kept referring to his reliance on his *gut* to guide him in making all kinds of decisions. I wanted to know more about what he meant.

To Giamo, intuition is "accumulated experience in similar situations. It's some kind of internal extrapolation," he explained over delicious plates of pasta. "Gut instinct has an internal logic, but maybe it's not a logic you can document on a piece of paper. It's a lot of internal information and there's something connecting that internal information inside of you that translates into experience. That experience is putting together analysis to a problem."

When it comes to making purchase decisions, today's consumers have a lot of this "accumulated experience" at their disposal. They've made countless decisions about where to spend their money. They've been disappointed, been burned, been ripped off. And too, they've been treated fairly, as agreed, and been satisfied and sometimes even been delighted with the service they've received. Through it all, they've been accumulating knowledge that they bring to their expectations and perceptions of your firm.

Which is why anticipating and meeting the customer's needs in unique ways can be so rewarding.

In this chapter, we'll look at seven strategies for creating customer-pleasing worth that will give buyers additional reasons to do business with you, and give your firm a recognizable degree of difference. The Seven Value Strategies are:

Strategy 1: Make the CUSTOMER'S LIFE EASIER

Strategy 2: Provide GREATER RESPONSIVENESS

Strategy 3: Take on the CUSTOMER'S PROBLEM

Strategy 4: Empower CUSTOMERS through KNOWLEDGE

Strategy 5: Manage the CUSTOMERS COMPLEXITY

Strategy 6: Involve the CUSTOMER in CREATING VALUE

Strategy 7: Provide GREATER CUSTOMIZATION and CHOICE

Now let's look at each of these in greater detail.

VALUE STRATEGY 1: MAKE THE CUSTOMER'S LIFE EASIER

Your business has a "convenience quotient." The customer calculates that quotient by dividing his or her desire for fulfillment by the hassle and annoyance that must be endured to do so. Every time customers consider satisfying a need, they consciously or unconsciously calculate the convenience quotient.

The customer's desire to achieve satisfaction is mitigated by factors such as: "Is the business open when I have time to buy?" or "Will I be able to figure out the directions that come with this product?" or "How much can I accomplish in one stop?" and so on. It's the same with business-to-business buyers. What vendor can supply us with the products we need and can make our lives easier in the process? The result of the convenience quotient calculation is a decision about whether to buy from you or a competitor; whether to buy now or later; whether to use your method of satisfaction or wait a few minutes until something better comes along.

So, here's the message with regard to the power of this strategy: Businesses, products, and services that have a low convenience quotient can count on losing customers to those that respond creatively by asking: How can we make the customer's life easier? And then responding with big and little improvements that do just that.

As you go about rethinking this S Factor dimension of your Value Proposition, take a look at these "convenience checkpoints" that your customer encounters in considering doing business with you. Then ask yourself what new value you can create in each of these areas:

1. *Locational convenience.* Obviously, the nearer the customer when he or she wants to do business, the better. If you can't change your physical location, can you deliver? Can you overnight your product for next morning delivery? Today, businesses from USAA Insurance to sporting goods wholesaler Ellet Brothers to Dell Computer do business entirely by phone, yet still receive high praise for their perceived convenience. Consider new ways to place your offering closer to where the customer is apt to be. *Example:* Taco Bell now serves its Mexican-style fare from kiosks and movable carts in malls, at the corner gasoline station, on supermarket shelves, even in school lunch programs. Taco Bell has quintupled its "points of access" to nearly 25,000 from 4,500, and by the year 2000 aims to have 200,000 outlets, mostly "nontraditional."

2. *Time frame.* How much of the customer's involvement is required to do the research, to sort through various claims and Value Propositions of your offerings and that of other vendors to determine the one that's best? That's what we might call the

purchase *time frame*. What can you do to simplify this search process by giving better and more complete information on your offerings that provides your customer with the knowledge and peace of mind necessary to make an informed decision?

3. *Payment methods.* By offering as many payment methods and terms as possible, your firm can increase its convenience quotient for customers. How can you boost business by making it easier for your customers to pay? What's the most frequent complaint from your customers regarding billing and payment issues? How might you provide incentives to customers to pay you on time with less hassle to both you and them?

4. *Ease of doing business.* In other words, is your business ready to do business when the customer wants to buy? If you have customers on the West Coast and you're on the East Coast, are you open during their business hours and not just your own? If you're a small independent retailer or dealer, do you close up promptly at 5 o'clock, just when your customers are getting off work? The attractiveness of shopping interactively from home holds so much promise precisely because the customer can shop any time of the day or night. In what ways can you make it easier to do business with you?

5. *Ease of correction when things go wrong.* If problems occur, what are you prepared to do about it? How much hassle and inconvenience will the customer have to endure before the problem is fixed? Can the item be returned? Will the customer be allowed to back out of the deal if the initial application doesn't live up to expectations? All of these are issues of convenience, since the customer has, as part of his or her "accumulated experience," memories of transactions when the seller didn't perform as expected. By being up front about these issues, and developing realistic, workable, and fair policies, you'll have fewer misunderstandings and greater trust.

6. *Ease of use.* Everything from the products or services you sell to the way they are packaged and presented can be included in this part of this convenience subset. Is the product easy to get "up and running"? Is it "plug and play" or does the customer have to wade

through hours of complicated and poorly explained instructions?

7. *After-sale service*. Many, if not most, products purchased are not one-time events. Buying an automobile begins what may be a 10- year relationship with the dealership where the car was purchased. This is the case with many products. Purchase of an insurance policy may form a lifetime relationship not only with the selling agent but also with the insurer. So the customer may be as interested in knowing what that relationship will be like before he or she decides to purchase. How convenient is your business after the sale? How easy will it be for customers to receive follow-up service from your firm? Do you have a toll-free number they can call?

All of these areas are vitally important aspects of convenience. Using them as a sort of checklist, you can determine how much you have already done to add value to your firm in this arena, and what you'll want to tackle next to make the customer's life easier.

That's what Value Innovators do. A group of managers at GE's Appliance Division asked the question, "How can we make our customer's life easier (and take some of the burden off our dealers)?" They came up with GE's Answer Center. The Center operates 24 hours a day with repair tips and help for owners of GE appliances who can't get their products to work or who have all sorts of questions.

Asking "How can we make our customer's life easier?" is one that everyone must be encouraged to ask. Yet, because of the crush of daily activity in most businesses, there never seems to be enough time just to get through the "must do's," so issues of the customer's convenience get overlooked and ignored. Few firms ever really think this way. Few get outside their own needs and climb into the heads of their customers long enough to see their convenience quotient as their customers do. Your employees see ways to improve your firm's convenience, because they're with customers every day serving their needs, hearing their complaints and problems. But unless you gather them together from time-to-time to collect their suggestions, unless you have some sort of suggestion system that encourages and gives them incentive to participate, you will probably never hear their good ideas.

Value Strategy 2: Provide Greater Responsiveness

Do you have a perfect driving record? If you're like most of us, you can probably recall how upset you were when you were involved in what people sometimes call a "fender bender." You wanted to get the damage repaired quickly, so that you could forget that unpleasant event.

Plymouth Rock Assurance Company in Boston makes it possible to do just that—quickly. If you have your auto insured with them and you have a mishap, you're instructed just to a give 'em a call. Instead of informing you where to go for a "claims adjustment," they send a white and blue minivan out to greet you. The adjuster videotapes the damages, records the parts, and, with the help of a portable computer, estimates the repair costs and issues you a check right on the spot. Shazam, just like that, in about 20 minutes. And you can take your car to the body shop of your choice, check in hand.

When I share that example with audiences, I sometimes ask how many people would assume that such a responsive service costs Plymouth Rock more to provide. Most people do. Then I share a surprising fact. In a recent year, Plymouth Rock had the lowest cost of doing business per customer of any auto insurer in Massachusetts, and the highest customer satisfaction ratings. The point is this: Value-adding programs providing greater speed don't have to cost; they can pay off on your bottom line.

Speed is not a new imperative, of course. But responsiveness has become an almost universally important component of value with today's time-starved consumer. Saving the customer time, providing the product and service when the customer wants it, has become essential for manufacturers, distributors, service companies, and retailers. Here's why: Customers gravitate to businesses that value their time. Therefore, speed—speed of transaction, speed of repair, speed of error correction, speed of customization—is a factor in the customer's decision of whom to patronize.

Here are some additional suggestions on how to get this powerful source of added value working for you and your firm:

1. *Challenge time-based assumptions.* Most organizations are ingrained in "that which exists"; they don't continue to charge the gates of that which could be." "That which exists might be defined in

your business as "everybody knows it takes 2 weeks to do x." Then along comes someone from outside who challenges this assumption. When that happens, everybody in the industry who hopes to remain viable is forced to adapt to the new speed, which in turn gradually becomes "the way things are."

In the furniture industry, "that which exists" might be how long it takes for the dealer to deliver a sofa after the customer has selected the style and fabric and ordered it. The customer expects that such a customizing procedure will take more time. But if sofa factory A can do the job in 3 weeks, while sofa factory B takes 3 months, sofa factory A has an exploitable competitive advantage.

Service-providing firms, have traditionally considered themselves "above the fray" with regard to speed. In fact, just the opposite rationale for their slowness was sometimes put forth. "We're so good that we can afford to make you wait on us," was the attitude. In some professions, this still works. But as other businesses speed up all around these professionals, that justification for making the customer wait works less well today. Patients have been known to sue their physicians for the waste of their time such that the American Medical Association has put forth guidelines suggesting that 20 minutes is an acceptable wait. Nonmedical practitioners who have the attitude that "we'll get to you when we can" are vulnerable to the Value Innovator who figures out how to seize the speed initiative and then market the heck out of the difference.

2. *Measure your "fulfillment float."* In other words, how much time regularly elapses between when your customer says "I want it" until your customer "has it"? Whether it's a customer's request for product delivery or a journalist's request for information from your public relations department, you're being judged all the time. Measuring the average time elapsed from request to satisfaction will make you and your associates more responsive to the time issue, and will stimulate everyone to look for speed innovations.

3. *Offer more speed to those willing to pay for it.* Even if a new way of adding speed costs more, you'll find some customers willing to pay for it. Just ask Federal Express, which has built a global business on the basis of customers who are willing to pay extra for

speedy shipping. Examine your request-through-fulfillment cycle, and determine if there are bottlenecks that can be eliminated by passing the added cost on to the customer. Then, on a trial basis, check out the demand for such services. Hertz's Number One Club Gold in effect offers the same thing. By becoming a member of this "club," the customer is shaving time off of the car rental process. He or she can step off the plane and go directly to Hertz shuttle buses that deliver them to covered parking areas where a car is waiting with the completed rental agreement hanging from the mirror.

4. *Offer time guarantees.* Can you find ways to increase the overall perceived value of your offerings by guaranteeing action, satisfaction, or completion within a certain time frame? The quick-lube industry virtually stole the oil-change business from traditional auto dealers because it offered not just speed but *guaranteed* speed. Quick-service restaurants promise your meal after a certain number of minutes or the meal is free. Even physicians are getting into the act. Dr. Neil Baum, a New Orleans urologist, guarantees that if the patient is still waiting after 20 minutes of his scheduled visit, Baum waives the charge for the visit.

In every area of your business there is a "fulfillment float" where the customer waits on you, not the other way around. Cut it by 10 percent or more relative to your closest competitor, and you have created a discernible measure of added value.

Value Strategy 3: Take on the Customer's Problem

In the 80s, businesses learned the importance of listening to their customers. "How are we doing?" became the operative question. But in the value era, there is a need to go beyond shoring up poor customer service or quality problems. Quality products and quality service are becoming "table stakes," the minimum price for staying in the game. The value-adding firm goes further in partnering with the customer. It seeks to ensure that its customers receive total value from the products or services it sells. "How are you doing?" becomes the operative paradigm of success.

"How are you doing?" is more than a semantical twist. It's more than *pretending* to care about the customer's well-being. It's figuring out ways to help your customer become more successful, because that will in turn make you more successful. Taking on the customer's problem is an important strategy behind the success of Tyson Foods, America's number-1 chicken processor.

From a one-truck chicken delivery business started in the Depression, the company has grown from its Arkansas roots into a global empire through market innovations that add more for more. It ranks 110th on the *Fortune* list of America's 500 largest companies, with $5.2 billion in sales. Tyson processes 29 million chickens a week, producing twice as much chicken as second-ranked ConAgra. Tyson is now the nation's second largest producer of hogs and is expanding its beef-processing capacity. To complete the menu and dominate what former CEO Donald Tyson calls the "protein center of the plate," the company bought the largest at-sea fishing processing fleet, Seattle-based Arctic Alaska Fisheries, in 1992. In addition to the more than 60 poultry, beef, and pork-processing plants nationwide, Tyson operates 24 feed mills, 35 hatcheries, and 36 fishing and processing ships. Tyson is also one of the nation's largest tortilla makers.

It didn't just happen. Behind the rapid growth lie thousands of production innovations that have increased the firm's efficiency at every turn. But the biggest innovation of all was one of moving from a production orientation to a customer orientation. In short, Don Tyson looks at his business from the standpoint of his down-chain customers, both the consumer and the outfit that sells his products to the end consumer. Tyson takes on the "problem" of both.

Tyson first put its credo of solving the customer's problem to work with consumers. Tyson saw that if you added more convenience by further processing the chicken, consumers would pay extra for it. Processed chicken was Tyson's biggest boom. It debones it, marinates it, cuts it into pieces, presses it into patties, rolls it into nuggets, breads it, batters it, cooks it, and freezes it. In return, processed products command a premium price over fresh chicken. "We're really selling time along with quality and convenience," says Tyson.

Seeing that meat departments needed new products, Tyson "invented" cornish game hens and introduced them with such enthusiasm that few consumers realized that they were really just young female chickens weighing under 2 pounds. Tyson sold them to grocery chains as specialty items for 50 cents each, a higher profit than chickens sold by the pound. The product became a minor sensation, and Tyson realized the power of coming up with new product ideas its customers could sell. Much of what Tyson has done since is a variation on the theme of extracting more value from the basic product.

Tyson chicken shows up in 88 of the top 100 restaurant chains, including mighty McDonald's. In the 70s, as Americans began to turn away from red meat, McDonald's faced a problem: Their main offering, the hamburger, had an out-of-favor main ingredient. But it wasn't until Tyson came calling that McDonald's realized it could diversify its menu away from red meat. McDonald's might have been caught in the mindset that it was a "hamburger" chain, until Tyson helped it develop Chicken McNuggets. It sold McDonald's on how such a product could be integrated into its kitchens. Tyson offered to prepare the chicken, bread it, season it, and deliver it, in short do everything but cook it.

What Tyson did is something every firm must do: take on the customer's problem. Powerful things begin to happen when you go beyond merely trying to sell your products or services and become the customer's consultant, coach, cheerleader, and partner.

Value Strategy 4: Empower Customers Through Knowledge

Home Depot, as we saw in Chapter 3, is a lot like all the other home improvement centers, but for one notable difference: Its associates are highly trained, experienced experts willing to share their knowledge with anybody and everybody. In short, they empower customers by giving them the knowledge they need to solve their own problems.

Empowering through knowledge, in an age of rising complexity, brings incredible benefit to the customer. "Our greatest value to our clients is our tremendous industry knowledge," observes Larry Marsiello, president and CEO of The CIT Group/Commercial Services of New York, the largest factoring firm in the world, and also the most profitable. "Because of our expertise, we have the ability to structure complex transactions with a speedy turnaround time. We have global reach and can help clients import or export from anywhere in the world. Our people are very knowledgeable in their jobs and in our clients' businesses."

Jim Miller, founder of Miller Office Systems in Texas, knows that knowledge adds value, which is why his firm holds frequent seminars for customers that provide important training in how to use its products correctly. Seminars on ergonomics show people how to avoid carpal-tunnel syndrome, a disease that can result if employees don't use computer keyboards and other office equipment properly. After attending a Miller seminar, managers have a much better understanding of how to increase comfort and office productivity while reducing lawsuits and medical costs arising from employee injury.

Customer education, Miller believes, can be the most cost-effective way to spend limited marketing dollars. "Ask yourself what can you teach customers and potential customers that will allow them to understand and appreciate your service or product quality," suggests Miller. "Do your salespeople know how to demonstrate the difference between a leather and synthetic finish? Do the secretaries know your competitors take up to 12 hours to respond to a service call, while you show up in 2 hours? Do your cashiers know why Brand X costs twice as much as Brand Y? If your employees don't know quality differences, how can they explain them to customers?" Miller sees part of the role of the knowledge his seminars imparts as selling the "S Factor" as much as the "Q Factor" in his Value Proposition. And both are vitally important to customer satisfaction and retention. Says Miller: "Customers will remember quality a lot longer than price."

Empowering through knowledge doesn't have to be expensive; it requires no capital spending and no new technology. Often overlooked is the need for creativity rather than for large marketing expenditures in executing this strategy.

Among my own customer groups are the speakers bureaus that serve as brokers for companies and associations that need professional speakers. My associates and I brainstormed this question: What can we do to add value to these bureau partners that is low cost yet has a great perceived benefit?

Before I tell you what we came up with, you should know that speakers bureaus do not have industry analysts to tell them how their industry is doing, what the prospects for the future are, what's happening in the "big picture" out there. They are a cottage industry, literally and figuratively, with many operating out of electronic cottages in the unlikeliest places all over the U.S., Australia, South Africa, Europe, and elsewhere.

Our solution was a survey of the bureaus we work with, soliciting their views on questions having to do with their outlook for the industry, what trends they are seeing, etc., which we then collate and interpret and share in the next regular mailing. The survey has been well received. After all, it doesn't cost them anything, and they can use the survey get a more objective feel for what they're experiencing and how it relates to other speakers bureaus.

The survey is a win for us as well. As we conduct the survey, we invariably learn more about their businesses, which helps us to be better partners with them. And collecting this information forces us to talk about something other than our needs from them, and puts us in the role of listener. Then, when the results go out, we've got something else to talk about with them, since they are curious to find out how their views contrast to those of others. Best of all, the survey positions us the way we want to be positioned—as purveyors of cutting-edge knowledge that isn't available from any other source. The cost, by the way, is so minor we don't even budget extra for it (we would be doing the mailings regardless), yet the value-adding benefits have had a ripple effect in building goodwill.

Knowledge is power, the timeless expression has it. When used to empower the customer to do what he or she wants to do, to solve problems and create opportunities, knowledge becomes something else too — a valuable strategic tool.

Value Strategy 5: Manage the Customer's Complexity

Wal-Mart sells a lot of disposable diapers. Tons of them. Giant stadium-sized warehouses full, in fact. And yet, it wasn't so long ago that Wal-Mart kept running out of Pampers. Wal-Mart found itself miscalculating how many packs of Pampers it would need, when it would need them, and where it would need them. Wal-Mart's miscalculations didn't just inconvenience its customers: they crimped Pampers' sales. So Procter & Gamble came up with a system whereby it, *the supplier*, would manage the customer's task of monitoring the inventory and replenishing when needed.

Wal-Mart and Procter & Gamble developed an innovative way of working together that has become a new industry paradigm. Result: Wal-Mart wins because it's using up less inventory space in warehouses and at its retail centers, while still being appropriately stocked. P&G, which has made projections of inventory need into a science, also wins. Procter and Gamble made it a point to manage its customer's complexity.

This is what F. D. Titus & Sons, a City of Industry, California-based distributor of health care supplies and equipment does for its customers. Like many wholesaler-distributors, Titus is in an industry in which it is difficult to differentiate on the basis of product offerings. Every manufacturer of the products it distributes willingly sells to any and all distributors, offering no exclusivity in the Q Factor. Ditto with regard to differentiating on the basis of pricing.

"You can't use product differentiation, and the manufacturers are selling to everyone at the same price, so you've got to use service differentiation" observes DeWight Titus, president and CEO.

But Titus realized these basic truths about his industry as far back as the late 70s. That is why he began to study up on service differentiation. How could he make his firm stand out from the other players? Out of this searching came a program whereby Titus partners with customers and manufacturers alike to raise overall value, lower costs, and still make a bundle. In every key indicator of success, Titus is right up there at the top: return on assets, gross margins, and operating profit. And in net profit before taxes, the firm outperforms the industry average by double. No wonder the company's value quadrupled in a recent 4-year period.

At Titus & Sons, the game plan has long been to manage the customer's complexity in such a way that you become deeply ingrained in the customer's business. This has bottom-line benefits for everybody. Titus doesn't just sell bandages, throat lozenges, blood pressure gauges, and thousands of other health care products. It *manages the inventory* for customers ranging from health care clinics, surgery centers, extended care facilities, home health care agencies, medical groups, and physicians' offices. In so doing, it promotes savings.

That's not a bad thing to promote, given its market. In Southern California, the Value Revolution struck health care in the early 90s with a vengeance, and cost cutting became the mantra. The traditional customer base didn't fully grasp, nor did it care to, how having 6 months' worth of inventory raised costs. But the rapidly expanding managed care networks understand costs, because they have to.

The first thing Titus does is to get a handle on each new customer's inventory. Says DeWight Titus:

> One of the keys to a value-added program is that unless you have a beginning benchmark on where you are starting from, you can never really demonstrate clearly how much value-added or additional services you've brought to that customer and how much cost you've taken out of your system. We do a large amount of work up front because we've found that most all of our customers do not know what their inventories are. They don't count on how much they have on hand. In most cases, we find that inventories are anywhere from 3 to 6 months in excess of what they need.

> Part of our program is managing the customer's assets that are tied up in inventory and taking these costs out. This means reducing the number of employees, courier services, and all of the other things that get blended into these integrated systems or into these large customers. And our customers, typically, are a health care system where you have a hospital, have individual physician offices. We're seeing whole integrated systems evolving today. Each one of those areas has a different service need. To properly take costs out of the system, you've got to do the study and the benchmark before you start really becoming partners.

> As an example, this week we are going up to one of our large customers in Northern California. They have five major clinics with over 100 physicians in each clinic. We'll do a quarterly review with our key customers to keep them abreast of what's going on, what progress we're making, and, as a partner, what progress we are making to accomplish our objectives. Once you get your partnership together, then mutually you've got to establish what your real goals and objectives are, or the next thing you know your customer is going to be wandering away from you, saying, "You told me you were going to do this, and you didn't do it." It has to be clearly defined and measured as we progress through the partnership.

Because each customer's requirements are so different, each decides to what extent it wants Titus to take over the purchasing function. Customers also decide whether they want to move to an Electronic Data Interchange (EDI) system or stay with their existing system. The old system was one where the distributor *sold* the client and thereby generated an order. With EDI, orders are created from within the customer's system. In some cases, the new system enables a reduction in the number of employees needed by the health care facility.

"The customer has to have some comfort level that they are getting the correct pricing that both parties have agreed upon, and that the inventory levels and purchasing levels are appropriate," cautions Titus. So the firm further manages the customer's complexity by enabling the customer to audit any portion of the system's purchases at any time. In fact, Titus specialists will even train a customer's internal auditor on how to audit the whole process.

Once the customer is up and running, Titus's objective is to make the firm's service invisible. Titus takes product right into the departments within clinics, and, in some cases, puts the product away or on the shelf, and takes the packing material away, so that clinic staffers are not forced to be material handlers. Titus can feed back to the client what its costs are per patient encounter and per department, which aids cost benchmarking and becomes another value-added service provided.

Titus doesn't always provide these value-added services for nothing. If there are unusual services that the customer wants, such as automatic purchasing, Titus charges a fee for that service. "The fee is totally understood, it's clear, the customer knows what he is paying for, and it supports a certain service component," explains Titus.

Titus obviously has a handle on the notion of managing its customer's complexity. It's this firm's way of adding value to customers and effectively shutting out competitors. "No other [health care] distributors are even remotely talking about doing this," says Titus. "It's driven by our information systems, which we've invested a lot of money in, and that's one of the chief barriers to our competition."

How can you manage the customer's assets more efficiently than the customer can? How might you take over a portion of the customer's business that is a hassle to him but is straightforward for you? How can you reduce your customer's aggravation and cut his costs at the same time? Because operating a business today is so complicated, firms welcome those who can manage their complexity in a mutually profitable way. By involving yourself more deeply in your customer's business, you'll also become indispensable.

Value Strategy 6: Involve the Customer in Creating Value

From its roots as a small Swedish mail-order furniture seller, Ikea has become a global retailer with stores in Scandinavia, Europe, and North America. How? By reinventing the value-producing system itself in a way that involves the customer in the process.

Part of Ikea's appeal is the manner in which it has turned a less-for-less strategy to its advantage. Ikea wants customers to buy into the notion that they will derive greater ultimate value by not merely being passive consumers but by pitching in and helping to create the product.

Many items sell for 25 to 50 percent less than competitors' products. In exchange for these lower prices, Ikea sells almost no furniture fully assembled. Its knock-down bookcases, garage storage units, cribs, bunk beds, and 12,000 other items require that the customer figure out how to get home with the item and assemble it.

Through its advertising and image building, Ikea preconditions customers to its Value Proposition in ways that sell the concept: The company subtly sells its philosophy in each of the 45 million catalogs it prints every year in 10 languages. Ikea adds a tone of intelligent thriftiness to its less-for-less positioning with hefty ad spending that helps it compete not only with department stores but also with other national and regional chains, and with independents as well. The ads are hip and informational, and reinforce the Value Proposition in creative ways.

Ikea adds value to its less-for-less proposition by exploiting the perception that it is actually offering *more* for less. In terms of selection, it certainly delivers on the promise of more; its 200,000-square-foot warehouse stores dwarf other full-line retailers. Another part of the "more" image it seeks to create is in the shopping environment itself. The colorful stores have the look outside of some futuristic country's furniture commissary, with distinctive blue and yellow colors and the blazing Ikea logo prominently displayed. Its locations in the United States are accessible from major highways but in out-of-the-way places. Taken together, such features help to position the outlets as more than just a stop-off for consumers doing comparison shopping or making a single purchase.

Instead, Ikea works hard to position itself as a one-stop destination where entire rooms and homes can be furnished in a single trip.

Inside, customers benefit from free strollers, child care centers, even playgrounds, as well as wheelchairs for the disabled, coffee shops, and restaurants that serve Swedish meatballs and other sturdy fare. Customers are supplied with catalogs, tape measures, pens, and note paper to help them make decisions without the assistance of salespersons. That's good, because sales representatives are often in short supply and often lack depth of product knowledge.

Another way Ikea requires the customer to be involved in creating value is in the investment of time in the acquisition process. A customer described for *The Wall Street Journal* having to wait 2 hours in four lines: one line to find out if a bookcase was in stock, another to wait for the bookcase to be wheeled out of the warehouse, another to pay for another bookcase, and yet another line to arrange for delivery. "Great idea, poor execution," concluded the customer, who happened to be a retailing investment banker.

While Ikea's Q Factor and S Factor aren't setting any new standards, what it is doing successfully is bringing the cost of furniture back into the affordability range. With contemporary styles, at significantly lower prices, customers are willing to produce some of the value themselves, obviously because there aren't better alternatives.

Like the warehouse clubs its outlets are sometimes located next to, Ikea offers a positioning choice of less-for-less. How underserved is the low end in your industry? What aspects of your service might customers be willing to do for themselves in exchange for a lower price?

Value Strategy 7: Provide Greater Customization and Choice

It's not just computermakers who are being forced to add value via customizing their products these days. Boeing, the Seattle-based airplane manufacturer, offers its new Boeing 777 in more combinations than a bingo parlor. The $115-million aircraft is designed with customization in mind. That way airlines can reconfigure the cabins to meet shifts in marketplace demand. If the market suddenly dictates increased numbers of first-class seats, or if the airline is to be used for charter and the first class seats are not needed, the plane can be easily and speedily altered. Even the galleys and lavatories are modular and movable. The owner can transform the 777's setup in about 3 days.

What Boeing is doing with its latest airliners, all firms must do to prosper in the post-revolutionary economy. In the case of Boeing, the ability to customize *quickly* adds value to the product. To make this strategy work for you requires anticipating new choice demands from your customer groups, and responding in such a way that you keep customers loyal by virtue of your flexibility.

Choice and customization are the "have it your way" method of offering the customer greater value and thereby achieving a competitive advantage. Until recently, conventional wisdom might have dictated that the more unique choices you offered in terms of colors, styles, features, selection, personalized products and service methods, the more value you added and the stronger your advantage. For awhile, that sort of "more is better" thinking may have been correct. The picture is more complicated than that today, however.

A countervailing force with regard to choice has begun gathering speed. This is the issue of the added complexity that additional choices bring with them. Here again, the best place to observe this countertrend is probably not in business-to-business selling patterns and relationships but in observing consumers.

In simpler times (the 80s, say), the consumer was excited by new choices. New choices added value. Indeed, the consumer who felt affluent and had time on his or her hands valued choices. He or she liked trying new things and believed that such experimentation added to the quality of life.

But the same consumer feels more restrained and cautious when time pressures predominate and discretionary spending is limited. So where the Boomer consumer might formerly have derived added value and satisfaction from abundant choices, choosing itself has become a burden. The sheer number of choices can be overwhelming rather than exhilarating. The consumer is just as likely to feel burned out about having to choose (not wishing to make a mistake) as he or she is liberated about being able to do so. Futurist Alvin Toffler, in his book *Future Shock*, coined the term *overchoice* to describe the kind of anxiety many feel when having to wade through a plethora of colors, styles, textures, patterns, and programs in order to make a decision.

The result of such consumer anxiety about *having* to choose rather than getting to choose has led some firms to cut back sharply the number of choices they provide customers. Nissan, the Japanese auto manufacturer, until recently had over 2,000 model variations and offered 87 different types of steering wheels, 437 varieties of dashboard meters, 300 different kinds of ashtrays, and 1,200 types of floor carpets.

Offering so many choices became too expensive and offered little additional value. Nissan has since cut its offerings by 33 percent. The new thrust is *Sukkiri ga ii*, or "Simple is good." The secret is figuring out which choices add value in the eyes of your customers and which ones add only costs.

If you are responding to increased competition with more options and features in a kind of choice arms race, it's crucial to remember that customers don't really value choices, *and they most certainly don't value having to choose*. They value having their needs met. They value what you're offering, produced the way they want it, solves their problem, and enhances their quality of life. What they expect is what they've been led to believe is possible; that now you can make the impossible happen for them, because of what they've been exposed to from your direct or indirect competitors.

To mitigate this seeming contradiction, some firms are still offering a steady stream of new options and features, but they are figuring out ways not to overload their customers with too much information and too many choices. The goal is to present each customer with only one choice—the right choice. Not, of course, the "one size fits all" choice of the past, but the one choice of product and service that best fits that individual's taste, budget, and other specifications.

In effect, this is the "empowerment through knowledge" that we talked about earlier. And this approach can only be carried off successfully with in-depth knowledge of the customer's requirements, which can only be gained by highly trained sales professionals.

Here's the good news: You can win by providing greater customization and unique choices, but only if you make these features work for you to deliver a perception of added value in the eyes of your customers. This is what Hilton Hotels is doing with its Resort Select program. Included in the special rate for each guest is one premium amenity or service per day , whether golfing, horseback riding, snorkeling, or canoeing. Customers love it, because they are in the driver's seat.

Choice is a moving target to today's customer. It's easy to end up adding so many new choices that you begin drowning in them, much like Nissan did. If that's the case, better management of the choice imperative becomes essential. The question that must be asked and asked again is: What choices make sense for us to offer today? Which ones do we need to add? What can we not afford to subtract?

Keep tweaking the mix in constant communication with your associates, your customers, your suppliers, and the market. An equally aggressive effort must be made to eliminate choice demands that no longer differentiate or add tangible value.

As you've considered these seven strategies, you've gained new insights into where you might strengthen your Value Proposition. In the next chapter, we'll look at how to "think through" new value-adding ideas, with an eye toward separating the winners from the losers, the ones that mean greater profits versus those that merely cause headaches and stress.

5

C H A P T E R

ADDING VALUE
PROFITABLY

"Don't give your customers a free turkey for Christmas this year unless you're planning on giving them one every year."

— Harvey Mackay

VALUE-ADDED SERVICES. THEY'RE EVERYWHERE THESE days. The dealership where you take your car for servicing now offers you a free loaner car. The manufacturer of disposable contact lenses now gets them to you via second-day air. Even the theater company in your community has hopped on the bandwagon with a two-for-one deal.

Chances are you probably have a few of these programs going yourself. So the question is: Are they working in the way you intended them? Are they bringing in new customers? Helping you hold on to existing ones? Are they giving you a leg up over the competition and helping your salespeople demonstrate your added value? Or are they merely a pain in the neck to deliver, meanwhile draining you of profits and causing complaints from customers who see them not as extras but as givens?

"Everything in strategy is simple," observed Von Clausewitz, the great Prussian general. "But that does not mean everything is easy." Clausewitz was talking about making war, of course, but he might just as well have been talking about adding value profitably.

This chapter will guide you through an objective look of your value-adding programs with an eye toward reviewing your objectives in the ones you already have going. Then, I'll also provide you with nine guidelines to use in planning and implementing new ones.

But first, let's start by looking at what's changing with regard to such services in light of the Value Revolution, beginning with a seemingly insignificant matter: hotel bathroom doo-dads.

The Hotel Bathroom Doo-Dad Wars

Assume for a moment that you've just checked into a luxury hotel in Hawaii. This is the hotel you've been anticipating coming to for months: You've heard so much about it. It's definitely in the more-for-more position on the value ladder. So you get up to your room, you unpack, and you go to put your toothbrush in the bathroom. Suddenly you notice that there are no, ah, "doo-dads." You know, the little bottles of shampoo, the hair nets, shoe mitt, shoe polisher, mouthwash, lotion, mineral drops, nail files, cotton swabs, sewing kits, suntan lotion, tissue, and so forth. You feel sure the housekeeping department has made a mistake; you call them only to be told by a pleasant-sounding voice that the hotel doesn't supply "any of that sort of thing," that "they're available at the gift shop downstairs, however."

You can hardly believe it! The audacity! Just who do they think they are? Suddenly this great luxury hotel that you were so looking forward to being a guest at has made a distinctly unfavorable impression. You can't wait to tell your company's meeting planner just how livid you are.

Let's face it: The reason you're shocked is that you have come to expect that particular set of value-adds at that hotel's positioning level. Now here's my point: Unless you're positioning your firm right along the warehouse club, low-fare airline, Hyundai rung on the value ladder, you're inevitably involved in a kind of value-adding arms race to see who can outdo the other players in your industry. This is true today whether you're a manufacturer, wholesaler-distributor, retailer, or professional service firm. To win the Value Revolution, you've got to out-think and out-innovate the competition in the arena of meaningful, impactful, not-easily copycatted value-adding services.

Winning the DooDad Wars in Your Industry

Are you winning the doo-dad wars in your industry? Or are competitors constantly putting you in a reactive, catch-up mode? Here's a quick question to ask yourself: What was the last significant thing you did to add value to the customer experience of your firm? If you're stumped, or if in the case of a large firm, you can't quickly name *numerous items*, this is probably a signal that you've not been leading in this arena.

Of course, if you are one of those rare organizations that hasn't seen any change in either your industry or your market, you may want to skip this chapter. But before you make that determination, stay with this issue for just a minute longer. Some of the signs that your current Value Proposition could benefit from customer-pleasing innovations might include:

1. Your salespeople are suggesting they need something new to talk about other than price.

2. You are hearing about new ideas that others in your trade or professional association are implementing that leave you feeling outgunned and intimidated in their complexity and scope.

3. You're losing business in competitive situations because the other bidders had certain capabilities or threw in certain extras that you simply couldn't match.

4. Your knowledge of emerging technology isn't evolving nearly as rapidly as your competition's.

5. Customers are asking why you charge extra for the same services your competition now provides "free of charge."

6. Competitors are making inroads into accounts you've held exclusively for years.

7. Long-term customers no longer give you all their business; instead they are increasingly sampling other vendors.

8. Competitors begin advertising their extras and pointing out that you don't provide them.

If more than one of these statements apply to you, it could indicate that you're on the verge of losing the doo-dad war in your industry. Look around at some of the no-longer-in-business players in your industry and chances are you'll find that many of them had a common attitude: They believed they didn't have to "play the game" that everyone else was playing in giving their customers more extras. They pooh-poohed such "gimmicks," preferring to do business the old-fashioned way, the way they'd always done it.

If industry evolution were a train, they were the caboose. And—you may have noticed—they don't have cabooses anymore on trains, just a little box full of electronic sensors stuck back there on the final car. In every industry today, cabooses are vulnerable to being run off the track. The reality is that new value-added services are an integral part of success in today's economic environment. Before we look at solutions, it will pay us to take a broader look at not only *why* value-added services have become *de rigueur* but also state-of-the-race in key industries.

Designing and Implementing New Value-Added Services

It used to be a safe assumption that if a nonbasic service added value, customers would expect to pay extra for that service. No longer. The Value Revolution has changed such perceptions. In fact, the greatest concern of wholesaler-distributors is that customers who paid extra in the past for such services will no longer be willing to do so, and yet will expect that they continue to receive them. "In these situations," concludes *Facing the Forces of Change 2000*, a comprehensive survey of trends in wholesale distribution, "services once considered to add value have become commodity services or competitive necessities."

Listen to an association executive in the wholesale drug industry describe the arms race in value-added services for his members, who sell to pharmacists and retailers:

The level of expectation [in that area] is just incredible. The wholesaler not only sends the retailer everything he orders but the order now comes with preprinted price stickers. "That was nice, but what else can you do for me?" the retailer keeps asking.

The wholesaler now has to handle 5,000 customers with 5,000 different prices on every item they buy. The merchandise now comes in so that when he orders goods, they are divided into fine-line classes so that the retailer can order shampoos, foot items, humidifiers, first-aid products, and those things will come in delivered in totes coordinated with the right area [of the store], so when the retailer opens the right box he's got all of the foot stuff in a box. . . but that's not good enough. Now we actually send him pictures and line item descriptions that tell how the stuff should be merchandised on the shelves, so he knows the big bottle of Anacin goes next to the little box of Anacin, which goes next to the bottle of Tylenol, and they get four-color photos of each department in the front end of the store.

And that's not good enough now, so we coordinate the graphs in each of these items that are in the front of the store, and now that's not good enough, so we coordinate it with an ad circular so that he can order all the merchandise for his ad and he has a circular, and that's not good enough any longer, so we do all the paperwork to actually collect the co-op advertising allowance associated for him. And all of that has been going on, and it hasn't slowed down the price competition at all.

The bigger purchasers are demanding lower and lower prices in their bidding process. A hospital group purchasing agency will award that bid every 2 or 3 years on a bid basis. What kind of service levels can you guarantee? What kind of specialized products will you promise to put in inventory?

The big players in prescription drug wholesaling are making it up somehow; more and more product is going through fewer companies and so becoming more efficient. The mindset of the market will be that the low-cost provider wins, but you've got to have excellent service — and services. Otherwise you're out of the game.

NINE STEPS TO CREATING SUCCESSFUL VALUE-ADDED PROGRAMS
The wholesale drug industry is hardly alone in facing rising expectations for added services while keeping prices low. To win the Value Revolution,

you have to become a master at anticipating and leading the value-added services arms race in your field while making your leadership pay off for you on the bottom line.

Let's take a look now at the essential steps toward designing such services.

1. Inventory the Value-Added Services Your Firm Currently Provides

Most companies don't spend enough time evaluating the value-added services they are *already* bringing to their customers. This is a mistake. It is vitally important that you understand what these are and that you continue to monitor their effectiveness in meeting the objectives they were designed for. Otherwise, the benefits quickly become lost not just on your customers, but on your own team as well.

Here's one way to undertake such an inventory: First, on a separate sheet of paper list the special services you offer. Then get your key people together and have them define what *they* think they are. Inevitably, they will ask you to define what you mean by the term *value-added service*. So you'll need to think through a definition before you call the meeting.

Look to identify areas where your programs and policies go "above and beyond" what might normally be expected from a firm in your industry.

The first thing that is necessary is to get clear on who your customer really is. What customer groups are you trying to satisfy? One participant in my seminar on "Winning and Keeping Customers in the Value Era" was the CEO of a manufacturing group of welding torches. The firm sells his products through industrial wholesalers, who sell to distributors, who in turn sell to welding shops. Service and value, he told the group, mean something different to each.

After wrestling with the issue, the CEO and his managers eventually identified distributors as their chief customers. This led to a rethinking of just whom their programs and services should be aimed at. They then scrutinized each of the company's services in an attempt to identify which added value for the customer and which did not. One result: The firm's purchasing department was reduced by two-thirds. The company redeployed its sales force to focus at least half its time on distributors. "Now they are pitching to the people who are actually buying the product," the CEO told me during a follow-up visit.

When the top team at Bryan Equipment Sales, a Loveland, Ohio, distributor of Stihl power equipment, went through this exercise, they came up with the following definition: "Value-added services are those that Bryan Equipment Sales brings to the dealer relationship, which are above and beyond our baseline contractual responsibilities to Stihl, both written or implied." On the list went everything from obvious items such as toll-free phone and fax numbers for customer orders to such things as no-fault problem-solving, free freight policies, and regional and co-op ad programs. Next, the CEO asked departmental leaders to identify costs related to these value-added services.

Conducting such an inventory is an important first step, but that's all it is. While you're at it, make a list of the value-added programs your chief competitor offers. If you're stumped, call up some of your competitors' loyal customers and ask them to help you with this list. Ask your sales team to brainstorm what these might be. Then list them in order of their importance, as you see them, to your competitors' customers.

2. Don't Confuse Your Definition of Value with Your Customers'

Adding the wrong value is easy to do. It happens all the time. A dangerous prescription might be: Just turn inward and become so involved with your internal processes that you forget to ask the customer.

The only thing worse than not doing anything to improve your Value Proposition is to move in a direction that *takes value away*. Instead of adding value, you end up adding something that isn't perceived as such by the customer. Listen to the words of one strategic planner in the transportation business describe his company's early attempts to create new value:

> In retrospect, we were really asset focused on our internal capabilities. We had all this new and expensive equipment and because we had made this investment in the [new] system, we thought we should receive a premium. We were touting it and not getting anywhere.

What the customer really values is whether, when his particular shipment needs to be moved, you have the right equipment in place. Can you move it quickly and on time? It doesn't do you any good to say [to the customer] "I've got 15,000 pieces of equipment dedicated to this marketplace," if not one of those pieces of equipment are in place when needed. So we've had to rethink our asset utilization and logistics flows to be certain we're delivering what the customer really needs. Only in the past 12 months have we begun to be comfortable that we understand our customers' immediate needs. These got studied *ad nauseam* but no lessons were drawn."

What we have here is a failure of leadership. It's the leader's role to pin this issue down by carrying out whatever combination of customer surveys, focus groups, one-on-one interviews and other methods needed to accurately interpret the customer's needs. It is also the leader's responsibility to sort through the complexity of the issues at hand and to peel away the confusion and bias until it becomes crystal clear how the customer defines value, and what services would provide additional value.

While you can, and should, receive suggestions and ideas from your team, it's up to you to "think through" the implications of such new services, especially those that will have a significant cost attached to them, and those that your customer will come to expect in the future. Of all the tasks and responsibilities of the leader, this one most assuredly cannot be delegated.

3. Figure Out What Business You're Really In

Smart companies don't compete; they out-think and out-innovate the competition by adding unique value. The only way to do this is to know what business you're really in. With such a fundamental grounding you can then translate a keener understanding of how customers think and what they want (but don't quite know what to ask for) into new services and ways of doing business.

One company that truly knows what business it's in is McDonald's. When McDonald's growth slowed in the late 80s, some analysts claimed that fast food was on the road to becoming a commodity. And there was excellent evidence to prove them right. Every intersection in America, every freeway off-ramp, and just about every place else seemed to have spawned a fast-food restaurant. And they were beginning to look a lot alike.

Fortunately, McDonald's didn't buy into this way of thinking. It refused to roll over and become a commodity. After rethinking the "highest value" of what McDonald's represented to customers, McDonald's concluded that it was something deeper than buns, burgers, soft drinks, and fries. The other guys had those things. What McDonalds had was a special relationship with kids.

To build upon that relationship, McDonald's began installing playgrounds in more and more outlets: and it began hosting birthday parties for kids. Happy Meals found their place on McDonald's menus. Ronald McDonald, an invention of an earlier era, resurfaced in the marketing of these "we're doing more for kids" campaigns. The result was that McDonald's growth bounced back. What kid could sit silently in the back seat when mom and dad drove past McDonald's?

McDonald's is not in the fast-food business. *McDonald's is in the business of entertaining kids, and giving moms and dads a break.* With this insight, McDonald's had an edge.

Merry Maids: Selling Peace of Mind

Another company that knows what business it's really in is ServiceMaster, based in Downers Grove, Illinois. Executives at ServiceMaster understand the need to think about the highest value of what they do for the various customer groups they serve. At first glance, the company's Merry Maids subsidiary is in the business of dusting, vacuuming, and otherwise cleaning homes, as well as maintaining lawns.

"We used to focus on the process of cleaning, making sure the home was free from dust," says Merry Maids president Mike Isakson.

By thinking about its service through the template of the customer's highest value, it became clear to Merry Maids that the underlying value was not a clean house. Nor was it increased leisure time. It was peace of mind. "Sure, they are paying for the cleaning," says Isakson. "But if a prized possession got broken or damaged or stolen, that negated everything."

Take the time to figure out what business you're really in. It's worth the effort.

4. Rethink Your Customer's "Highest Need"

Before you set off to create a new value-adding service, it's important to keep in mind what might be called the customer's *highest need*. "We've been selling the wrong thing," observes travel consultant Robert Anderson, president of Anderson Associates, Norristown, Pennsylvania. "We've been selling cost savings. It's an important byproduct, but it's not the thing."

What is the right thing for the business travel industry to be selling? Productivity. The days when business meetings offered a leisurely break from the office or a chance to golf with colleagues are long gone for many executives. Nowadays when companies send people out to stay in expensive, doo dad-laden hotels, they expect a return on their investment.

In a survey sponsored by Hyatt Hotels, some 500 middle managers and 100 chief executives were asked for their views on business travel. Key finding: 75 percent of the respondents cited the "potential for increasing business productivity" as an essential factor in picking meeting sites. The study found that business travelers are much more concerned with being productive on a business trip than they were 5 years ago. They're working harder and feeling more pressure to produce.

It's easy to sell the wrong thing. And it's easy to believe that the services you assume are important to customers are in actuality not that important at all. Just ask UPS.

UPS: The Value of Spending Time with Customers

Big Brown, as it is sometimes called, assumed that *on-time delivery* was the paramount concern of its customers. After all, the new kids on the block, overnight delivery services, had stolen an entire market niche right out from under it by providing greater speed. So at UPS, the driving imperative became driving. . .hard. And running fast! Pick up the package or drop it off and be gone. That was the order of the day. Everything else—including spending a moment or two extra with the customer—came second.

The problem was, UPS wasn't asking its customers the right questions. Its surveys barraged clients with queries about whether they were pleased with UPS's delivery time and whether they thought the company could be speedier. Only when UPS began asking broader questions about service improvement did it discover that its customers weren't as obsessed with on-time delivery as previously thought.

The biggest surprise to UPS management was that customers wanted *more interaction with drivers*. If drivers were less harried and more willing to chat, customers could get some practical advice on shipping. "We discovered that the highest-rated element we have is our drivers," says Lawrence E. Farrel, UPS's service-quality manager. "Now, we're viewing drivers as more of an asset than a cost."

As UPS's experience points out, it's easy to misinterpret what customers really value about your service, and your services—even when you may be calling on them every day.

In a sharp departure, the company is encouraging its 62,000 drivers to be a more integral part of the company's value-creating system. One change: Drivers are allowed an additional 30 minutes a day to spend, at their discretion, to strengthen ties with customers. Delivery quotas are still important. But today UPS is willing to add extra drivers so that others are able to spend time with customers. As an added incentive, UPS is paying drivers a small commission for any sales leads they generate. The program costs UPS several million dollars extra each year. But it has generated tens of millions in additional revenue.

5. Develop New Ways to Listen to Your Customers

If you've had one of those "Tell Us How We're Doing" surveys thrust in front of you recently, what you did with it could say a lot about the state of customer feedback methods. Did you excitedly drop everything and fill the survey out? Did you put it aside for later? Or simply drop it in the trash?

The fact is, we've been inundated with these requests on our time in recent years. Do they do any good? Do businesses really listen if we do have a suggestion? What will they really do with this information if we give it to them?

I remember munching on a hot dog in some forlorn eating place in some forlorn airport and looking over and seeing one of those little Plexiglas cases. "Tell us how we're doing," it said. The only problem was that there were no survey forms in the container, and it looked pretty grungy. I didn't rush right up to offer my comments, I just moved on, reminding myself not to eat at such places again if I could help it.

While customers want great service, great products, and great prices, they don't necessarily have any interest in telling you ways to improve your business. They just vote with their feet or their pocketbooks whether to come back and do business with you again. Or go someplace else.

But they will tell you what they think if you show them that you are ready to listen, and ready to act on their suggestions to make improvements. This doesn't take a lot of money. Just your creativity and willingness to try new ways of gaining their interest that gets them off their own issues and needs for a moment, while they spend time on yours. While you don't have to pay them, it is helpful and shows your commitment to offer a token of your appreciation. It doesn't have to be anything big, just something they can walk away with.

You can start doing this surveying right away. More than anything, listening to customers is an attitude. It's how you spend your time. And with whom you spend your time. If you're a small business, don't let the lack of budget for elaborate focus groups slow you down, or become an excuse. Here are some ways of doing this:

1. *Survey your customers (and potential customers) informally.* During the course of your business day, keep a two- or three-question survey by the phone. After you've conducted the business at hand, simply explain to your customers that you really value their feedback, and you'd like their permission to ask them for their ideas.

Robert Hazard, CEO of Choice Hotels International, asks people wherever he goes his favorite question: Do you travel much? This invariably leads to discussions of people's lodging preferences and their levels of satisfaction. Hazard says he actually got the idea to segment Choice Hotels into various tiers—Comfort Inns and Sleep Inns for the economy and budget sectors, and Clarion for the luxury tie—from asking this question to a Phoenix barber.

"In the summer on our 2-week vacation, my wife and I will drive to someplace like Las Vegas or over to San Diego," the barber explained. "When we get to our destination, we'll stay in the finer luxury hotels. But on the open road, since we'll only be there overnight, we'll stay in a budget motel." Hazard realized that his Quality Inns, as his chain was then called, would never get this man's business, since it was neither top end nor budget but in the midprice range.

2. Convene a focus group of your customers from the different niches of your current market. Some marketing experts claim that they've never gotten a good idea from a focus group in their entire lives. What a pity! At the very least, focus groups get you back in touch with ordinary customers articulating as best they can what works and what doesn't about your business. It's like going to church: You may not hear anything dramatically new, but just sitting in that space for an hour can bring you back to the essential questions. If you don't pick up one or two ideas, or reminders, from such sessions, it may be because you're not probing hard enough. One caveat: Focus groups and surveys don't get at what customers deeply value, since these matters require intensive follow-up questioning. They do a great job of gaining insights into the attributes of your operations, what people like and don't like, and what you might do differently in the future.

3. Survey your sales force. Your sales force is an army of trend detectives out there every day getting feedback, taking the pulse, discovering minute-to-minute changes in the customer base. The only problem is, most salespeople never get listened to by management. To mitigate this, one company with which I am familiar has a "question of the week" that its salespeople are asked to report on and investigate during the week. On Fridays, they are asked to call in their comments to a designated person in the home office, who then makes sure they receive a $10 bonus.

4. Listen to your competitors' customers as well as your own. Norm Brinker, chairman of Brinker International, is one of the country's most respected restaurant gurus. In an 8-year period, he expanded Chili's from 20 outlets to 365, generating $1.63 billion in annual sales. The company now operates restaurants in 43 states and 7 foreign countries. Holdings include Chili's, Spageddies Italian Kitchen, On the Border Cafe, and American Grille, among others. Shortly after purchasing Chili's in the 80s, Brinker began to recognize that consumers were growing more health conscious. He responded by adding salads and other health-conscious items to broaden his menus.

More recently, he noticed that Boomer consumers were shifting away from cheaper fast food toward higher-quality restaurants with more atmosphere. So he purchased Romano's Macaroni Grill, a San Antonio, Texas, restaurant that he has since taken nationwide.

How does Brinker observe the changes in what customers value? One favorite way: He likes to pose as a confused tourist outside his own restaurants. He asks departing patrons if they were happy about their experience. (In a nutshell, "How'd you folks find the value equation here?"— although he doesn't word it that way.) He also visits competitors' restaurants, walking around as if he owns the place, stopping at tables to inquire about the food and the service. "You have to listen to customers on an ongoing basis," says Brinker.

5. *Keep a record on why you lost each large sale.* Review for trends quarterly.

6. *Become the customer.* Think like the customer. Call your 800 number and place an order. Play the role of a befuddled customer who doesn't quite "get it." Call your office and ask for information about the company, and see how you're treated. Immerse yourself in the process of understanding what benefits your customer values most and what aspects of the transaction detract from the customer's quality and service experience.

7. *Do "follow them home" research.* When it comes to innovating new ways and learning from customers, Intuit Corporation, makers of the best-selling personal finance software Quicken, have a unique method. Intuit gets permission from retailers to have its market researchers position themselves near the registers where they wait for customers to come to the counter with purchases of Quicken software. The researcher then gets permission to go home with the new customer to watch how she or he actually unpacks and installs it, what hitches if any are encountered, and how much time it takes for the customer to get "up and running." In addition, there are continual customer surveys and focus groups and a well-staffed telephone service operation to provide free support—and gain yet more information on what customers actually want the product to do for them.

Company founder Scott Cook is fanatical about research, and about refining the listening process. Good data is the cornerstone of Cook's management philosophy, which stresses the need to make decisions based on information, not rank. He sketches an organizational structure in which the senior executives are not at the top of a pyramid but rather at the center of a circle.

"In most businesses, decisions are based on judgments," Cook says. "And when decisions are based on judgments, the highest-paid judgment wins. But in a truly consumer-driven company, decisions are based on data, so the person with the *best data wins*."

With such attention to detail, Intuit was able to introduce Quickbooks, an accounting program for small businesses, that seized 60 percent of that market in its first 2 years, all in the face of repeated frontal assaults from Microsoft.

8. *Host an off-site meeting for key customers*. As someone who makes his living speaking at these meetings, I may be a little biased here. But it has been my experience that such meetings can have dramatic results in smoking out what's really on customers' minds. The environment has a lot to do with it. You want to hold one of these meetings as far away from the normal rush-around world as possible. You'll want to throw in some recreational activities, not so much competitive activities, but activities that cause people to cooperate, communicate, and, maybe even have a little fun. Keep any sales pitches to an absolute minimum; the less you talk the better. And sure, bring in an outside speaker or two to get the juices flowing, to give people some value in the form of ideas they can take back and apply to their businesses.

And food. Don't forget to have plenty of it. But then the gleaning starts. You'll say something like: Thanks so much for coming to our customer meeting, we really value your comments, ideas, and feedback on how we're doing.

At first they'll think you don't mean a word of it. So they'll just be polite. You'll want to continue to probe, and when one of them says something, repeat back what he or she just said. The last thing in the world you want to do is have somebody make a comment and you then call on the next person. Instead, engage each person a bit. Ask a follow-up question or two, and don't fall into the trap of explaining why you did what you did, why you have certain policies that you have, as it will only destroy the rapport. The minute you start explaining your customers will shut down, and shut up. This will be a signal that you are trying to convince them about why you do things the way you do. It will signal them that you aren't really there to listen but to sell, to do "public relations."

If it's a good meeting, it won't be an easy meeting. You won't like everything you hear. The discussion may get heated at times. Certain people may even start "getting on your nerves" because they're getting into what might be starting to sound like criticism. If this happens, don't become defensive. It could be the best thing towards getting the other participants to open up and share with you their less-guarded thoughts, suggestions, and ideas. Hang in there.

This list, of course, only scratches the surface of possible ways to gain valuable, up-to-the-minute feedback from customers. Oftentimes I'll ask executives how they listen to customers, and they'll refer to their formalized systems for doing this, as if to say, "That's a marketing function; it isn't something I care to be involved in." This is a mistake of the highest order. Every innovative, cutting-edge, successful company I've ever known or worked with has a well-thought-out system for information gathering and involving key senior executives who maintain a keen interest in leading these dialogues. And in an era when customer value, and customer values, change as rapidly as they do today, the wise exec will continue to try new methods, new ways of gaining this type of information.

6. Brainstorm for Unusual Ways to Add Value

Ask DeWight Titus, the health industries distributor whom we first met in Chapter 4, for his thoughts on developing new value-adding programs, and his suggestion is: "Get out of the box." What's the box? The imprisonment of the everyday crush of meetings, deadlines, emergencies that can easily leave us feeling that we've worked as hard as we possibly could. Titus explains:

> Our business is so transaction oriented. It's so easy to get caught up in that [activity]. Here's a customer complaint, let me go handle it. Or there's a delivery out back, somebody's got to sign for it. The computers are down, let's work on that. These are things that people love to do, because it keeps them busy. But if you're caught up in the transaction part of the business, you can get totally buffaloed into that. So, you've got to want to come up with value.

Titus also believes it is necessary to spend time, especially if your industry is changing rapidly, in the field.

I spend a large part of my time trying to learn strategically where we are going, what we are doing, what is happening to our customer, what is happening to our competition. I dwell a lot on the outside forces of the company, because I have really good, exceptional people running the company inside. If you do this, it becomes clear what you need to do as a company to combat or to go forward and be innovative. We're all talking about what is the next thing we are going to do right now to differentiate ourselves. Everybody is thinking the same way and we cross-fertilize."

Before you change or add a new service to the ones you already provide, it is important to try to anticipate which ones will provide a new advantage, and how long you can count on having that advantage before competitors are able to neutralize your service by coming out with one of their own. New services can be expensive initially, and, quite often, customers are slow to glom on to them and see their value immediately.

What is true of all successful value-adding services is this: Creating and implementing them will involve all of your skills as a leader—your intuition, your sense of where your industry is going, your instincts, your organizational abilities, and your ability to "sell" your vision of the new program to your people so that they can in turn "sell" its value to customers. It's where you really earn your keep, so to say. Others can do the work of following through on the plan; others can implement and execute. But it's here that your leadership skills are urgently needed and will be tested.

7. Figure Out the Lifespan of Your Proposed Value-Added Service

Harvey Mackay's funny saying about not giving your customers a free turkey for Christmas if you don't intend to do it every year has a serious point. Once you add a service, it's an expected part of what you provide. You can cancel a value-added service, but not without repercussions. So it's better to concern yourself with the lifespan of a proposed new service before implementation. Is the new service only supposed to be temporary or for a limited time? Is it an experiment? Then you'd better communicate these things to customers up front. Another question is: If competitors immediately copy our new idea, what will be the net result? Is being first still worth it?

But not all value-added services are easily copied. Titus Medical doesn't worry too much about competitors copying its most important value-adding service: inventory management for health care alliances and other customers. In fact, company executives go to their trade association meetings and openly share what they are doing with their competition sitting right out there in the audience. Pretty brassy, huh? But their competition doesn't much try to duplicate what they are doing because, apparently, they don't believe they can. At least not on the scale that Titus does. So the company has enjoyed a good run on its value-adding services.

Products have always had life cycles. They've always been replaced by newer, better products promising greater benefits, more features, more choices, more options. The new reality is that services also have life cycles. A new service added to your repertoire gives you a unique competitive advantage. It is a major point of differentiation. Your salespeople use it effectively to close new business—until, that is, your competition wakes up and matches your new wrinkle.

8. Look for Ideas You Can Borrow from Other Industries

Mention the name Bryan Equipment Sales among power equipment distributors most anywhere in the United States and you'll get a nod of recognition. They know the name. Based in Loveland, Ohio, Bryan is a top distributor of German-made Stihl chain saws, lawn and garden equipment, portable power tools, and cleaning systems. The distributor serves a thousand independent dealers in Indiana, Kentucky, Michigan, Tennessee, and West Virginia. So what are they doing at Bryan? Where's the cutting edge?

I put that question to Tom Jones, the president of Bryan, and he described for me a powerful, profit-producing new service that has helped his firm tremendously. He freely admits he borrowed the idea from a completely different industry, department stores.

The idea took root when he attended a competitor's breakfast. He listened as the speaker talked about the power of value, and it set him to thinking. "What are we doing to add value to our dealers?" he began to ask himself. And he didn't stop there.

Jones was well aware of the struggle independent dealers were having with surviving mega-stores such as Home Depot and Wal-Mart. These chains were undercutting the prices of independent dealers largely with two brands: Homelite and McCulloch. The shakeout started in the early 80s and continues unabated. Moreover, his was a mature industry. It was a truism to say that you couldn't compete on price with the discounters: that you had to compete by adding more value. But what additional value could Bryan bring to dealers?

The light bulb went on one day when Jones was in a department store. In the menswear department he noticed the way Timberland had its own "boutique." Why not something like this for his dealers? "I don't want to give you the idea that this was 100 percent my idea," says Jones. "It was an amalgamation of little things that I saw; but nobody really ever pulled it together and put a bow around it. That's really what we did."

To perfect his basic idea, Jones brought in a merchandising display consultant who showed him "what works and what doesn't." Jones realized that he needed to help his dealers in merchandising techniques and upgrading their selling professionalism.

Bryan eventually came up with three prototype displays that could be expanded or modified to meet each dealer's needs. The next thing Jones did was to test-market the idea. Did they really have something that would have an impact on sales, or was it just a "neat" thing? As Jones describes it:

> Understand that we are in a mature industry where sales increases of 8 to 10 percent are extremely exciting. So, we saw that after the first year the dealerships in which we had put a Stihl Concept Store were up 41 percent over the previous year. [Why not roll the concept out instantly for faster results?] Because it's a complex idea and it really takes manpower to convey to the dealership so he understands what is going on. We've got a waiting list of dealers who want these stores installed. People have tried to copy what we are doing, and they don't realize that it's the details that make it work.

> In our line of business our dealers only price big things and the little things our dealers will leave unpriced. So when you get a Stihl concept store installed in your place of business, we give you a price

gun and we teach you about the fact that customers won't buy things that aren't priced. Another thing that is common along the price line is that in dealerships, it's real common to hang a handwritten price tag on a product. Research shows that a handwritten price tag is considered an invitation to negotiate. A preprinted price tag carries more authority. The larger the price—meaning the larger the physical dimension of the numbers —the higher the perceived value.

Equally important to the success of the new system is the training the dealers receive from Bryan on how to make the physical display pay off.

We go into a dealership and explain how it's got to work. If they don't buy into the process, we walk. I'm saying that boldly, but we do it more politely than that. Either they come on board the system or we'll go somewhere else, because we have a waiting list of dealers who want to do it.

A lot of the value-added is in Bryan Equipment's teaching and sharing of experience. "What happens," says Jones, "is once you get the vision on a day-to-day basis, keeping the store maintained and keeping sharp on the little details is nothing. But it takes a while to catch a vision of the details and why the details work. Once you catch it, you say, 'This is so easy. And yet it works—right on the bottom line.' "

And to think, the idea all started when Jones was walking through the men's department of a department store.

9. Consider the Long-Term Implications of Any New Value-Adding Service

In the rush to implement innovations that add value, the biggest mistake is not thinking through them enough. Key questions aren't answered, and the kinks aren't worked out before the actual launch. It can have negative impact, if, say, you're going to offer a giveaway/incentive program, only you haven't got enough of the giveaways when your customer/winner comes a-callin'. It can happen to the big guys, and sometimes does.

Take the frequent flier programs, first instituted by American Airlines in 1982, and quickly copied by other airlines. Sure, you rack up all those miles, maybe dream about that big vacation trip you want to take to someplace exotic—only to discover that your airline doesn't have an "allotment" that allows you to use your miles to get there. Maybe they tell you that you'll have to wait a year or so until there's an opening to use your free miles on that route.

That's what happened to one frequent traveler, and it's why he took Northwest Airlines to court. The flier was attracted by Northwest's advertising campaign that touted the ease with which miles could be exchanged. The rates were more complicated than that.

This customer wasn't the only one. A small but vocal minority of frequent fliers became increasingly outspoken about being shortchanged on their frequent flier programs so much so that the International Airline Passengers Association (IAPA) began looking into the situation. So what began as an added-value feature to create brand loyalty has turned out to be a public relations snafu.

A Message for the Value-Adding Leader

What's the message for the value-adding leader? You've got to think through the implications—for good or ill—before you put it out there for the public. What is it going to cost us? How will our customers receive—and perceive— it? Can we really carry it off? And is it really going to add value? How long before our competitors copy our innovation and neutralize it? These questions, and others like them, are essential to adding value profitably.

So there you have some of the guidelines for developing your next value-adding service innovation. One final word: As powerful as such programs can be in luring new customers, the fact is that almost any program you come out with can and will be copied eventually. To create lasting customer loyalty, you need to focus on the intangibles, too. Which is why, in the next chapter, we'll take a closer look at the subject of gaining customer loyalty in the age of the disloyal customer.

Is it possible? Turn the page to find out.

C H A P T E R

CUSTOMER LOYALTY AND VALUE

"We don't sell products. We capture customers."
—Alfred Zeien, CEO Gillette

RESEARCH BY BAIN & COMPANY SHOWS THAT ON average, 65 percent to 85 percent of customers who chose not to maintain a relationship with a business report that they were "satisfied" or "very satisfied" with their former supplier. What gives? If they were satisfied, why'd they leave? Simple explanation: *They discovered better value elsewhere.*

Companies as large as AT&T and as small as the corner grocer are discovering a painful truth: Today's customers do not feel loyal to brand or company, do not feel loyal to a particular way of purchasing a product or service, and do not feel loyal even to the way they satisfy a need.

The situation is hardly hopeless, however. This chapter will guide you toward a completely different way of viewing customer retention and will arm you with loyalty-producing strategies that are both low-cost and proven in effectiveness.

To get started, let's look at just how important customer retention is, and why it's so difficult to achieve. Let's take a quick look at how the Value Revolution is affecting an industry—credit cards—that, until a few years ago, could pretty much count on keeping customers for life.

How the Value Revolution Affected Customer Loyalty in the Credit Card Industry

Earlier, we saw how American Express got hit by changing values on the part of charge card holders. But American Express is not the only card company to face the Value Revolution. Before we look at what has happened, a few facts are in order: The typical American has an outstanding credit card balance of $1,700, and two of every three credit card users carry balances from month to month, so they have to pay interest. Moreover, card usage in the United States continues to rise. So, in this industry, it's not a matter of a shrinking pie, but a matter of who gets the pie. And in this regard, revolution is almost too mild a word to describe what is happening. Consider:

- Until 1992, most cards had annual fees. Today, feeless cards are commonplace, and issuers can't rely on customer loyalty.

- Until 1993, interest rates uniformly hovered close to 20 percent. Two years later, some cards had dropped their rates to 6.9 percent.

- Industrywide profits, according to research by Merrill Lynch, fell from an average of 40 percent to less than 25 percent between 1990 and 1994, and are continuing to decline.

What happened? In simple terms, the Value Revolution caused the collision of two giant forces. Number 1: The growing sophistication of users facing tougher economic times resulted in their demanding value from the firms they chose to do business with.

Number 2: An explosion of new credit card issuers, and greater competition among existing players, all combined to bring the card industry's run of lush profits to an end. Value Innovators took a look at the industry and knew they could give more value to their customers yet still get more back in the way of profits and other benefits.

When the history of the "credit card revolution" gets written, it may well turn out that Sears, a retailer not known in recent years for starting much of anything, set things off when it introduced the Discover Card in 1986, basing its appeal on a "cash-back rebate" of purchases. What a concept! A credit card that actually gave the customer something back, paying users on a graduated scale, from one-quarter of 1 percent for the first $1,000 in purchases, up to 1 percent for purchases exceeding $3,000. Not a lot, certainly, but the first crack in the dam. Of course, the regular players in the industry were unfazed by Discover Card and largely chose to ignore it, hoping it would simply go away. It didn't.

But then the dam began to show major fissures. Giant AT&T, looking for new profit centers and a way to increase the loyalty of its long-distance customers, launched its Universal Card (Visa or Mastercard). Knowing it had to come to the consumer with a dramatically better Value Proposition, Universal Card offered credit cards, for a "limited time only" without annual fees for life, plus 10 percent discounts on long-distance calls. To further sweeten the pot, it charged a variable interest rate on unpaid balances tied to the prime rate, that during the first several years of the new card's launch kept going down. Other major bank-issued cards, with much higher fixed rates, kept them there.

AT&T did not stop there. It rethought every aspect of the Value Proposition that all competitors were then offering. The customers' chief service need turned out to be fast, responsive phone assistance when they had problems. So Universal Card reinvented customer service from the ground up. It designed everything from application forms to lost or stolen card policies with an eye toward exceeding the customers' expectations. It allowed customers to consolidate many outstanding card amounts onto one card at a lower rate, and provided incentives for doing so. Bingo: Today over 20 million customers perceive better value and have obtained one of the new cards.

It's interesting to look at the response of players who once had the market all to themselves. Traditional issuers, most notably large money-center banks and regional and national issuers, began to raise eyebrows as customer erosion became a flood.

But according to Universal Card's first president, it took competitors a full 2 years before they began to realize that ignoring AT&T was probably not the best policy. As a result, the battlefront became who could offer the best rewards: from airline frequent flier miles and discounts to retirement annuities and finance charge refunds. Discover Card raised the ante with "something extra," a range of merchandise and travel discounts based on monthly outstanding balances.

On another front, Visa and Mastercard began aggressively pursuing American Express customers, which its surveys showed could be increasingly lured away on better value appeals. Visa targeted trendy restaurants and upscale merchants—typical American Express customers—in a bid not just for prestige but for a greater stake in additional corporate charge business. American Express's worldwide charge volume shrank during one period of the first half of the 90s from 18.8 to 15.9 percent, with the number of green, gold, and platinum consumer cards in use declining steadily since 1991. Its Optima card, overreaching for new business, encountered steady defaults and lost money for the company.

To combat the free fall, American Express hopped back on the value-added services bandwagon. While not the innovator in granting frequent flier miles for card purchases, it finally matched Value Innovator Citibank. AmEx also introduced Optima True Grace, a new value-adding twist on its much maligned revolving credit card that, unlike AmEx's other cards, allowed the customer to maintain a balance.

As its name implies, True Grace added an entirely new value: It lets customers avoid paying interest on new purchases for 25 days, even if there's a balance on the account. Other major card issuers, as True Grace's advertising was quick to point out, allow a grace period only when accounts have no outstanding balance.

"Grace periods have been a sacred area," observed one analyst who follows the industry. AmEx promptly pointed out that Visa cardholders in the U.S. would save $2 billion a year if Visa issuers were to match Optima's grace period.

At mid-decade, the credit card revolution is still evolving as a host of new players enters the industry and continues to sweeten the pot with value-adding inducements and features. The result: "The industry has evolved [to] where added value as part of the product is expected," says Mava Heffler, vice-president of promotions at Mastercard. "It's no longer a bonus."

The tough head-to-head competition of the credit card industry is a kind of metaphor for what may well be in store for other industries in the future. And this is why retaining customers becomes more important with each passing day.

Why Customers Are Less Loyal Today

At various points in this book we've looked at the big reasons customers desert: We've seen how a stagnant standard of living for many consumers combined with the explosion of companies all vying for the consumer's business have combined to create a customer who demands high quality, great service, and a competitive price. Now let's dig deeper to discover the real reason that customers don't come back: A *poor experience with their existing provider gave them no reason to be loyal.*

Consider these statistics on why customers leave:

- 68 percent quit because of poor service.
- 14 percent are dissatisfied with the product.
- 9 percent leave for competitive reasons.
- 6 percent develop other relationships.
- 3 percent move away, discontinue business, etc.

While all businesses want loyalty from customers, the actions of firms speak louder than their words. Retailers, for example, have recently jumped aboard the customer retention bandwagon. Yet while many talk about the importance of customer service, many retailers do a terrible job delivering it. A recent Mastercard survey showed that 62 percent of customers left a store without buying an item because a sales clerk wasn't available. About 60 percent of those surveyed said they asked a question that the sales clerk couldn't answer.

Retailers are hardly alone. One oft-cited survey shows that customers are *5 times more likely to leave for poor service than for other reasons*.

Manufacturers want loyalty, brand and otherwise. Yet with rebate programs having turned into rebate wars, customers vote for the biggest and the best at the time of purchase. And, as we've seen, wildly fluctuating prices at the shelf denigrate the perception of value in consumers' minds. If Tide sells for $3 one week and $4 the next, what's the real worth of Tide?

The house brand sitting on the shelf beside Tide, with a more constant, lower price, might just deserve a trial.

Finally, research shows that a loss of 10 to 20 percent of customers every year is not unusual for many companies, yet most of these losses are avoidable. The problem: Companies are often so concerned about attracting new customers that they denigrate their unique Value Proposition to loyal customers. They focus instead on chasing down the next sale, competing on price, and compensating employees more for winning new accounts than for keeping existing customers happy and loyal.

The upshot of all these statistics: Customer loyalty is not just an important issue; it is a critical issue in business today. Customer retention is a set of specialized activities that must take place alongside efforts to enhance the overall Value Proposition. Indeed, as we'll see in this chapter, a customer retention program is the best measure that your partnership with customers is delivering and continues to deliver best value.

Loyalty: The Bottom-Line Benefits

Why emphasize loyalty? Because when customer loyalty goes up, profits follow. Boosting a company's customer retention rate a mere 2 percent has the same effect on profits as cutting costs by 10 percent, according to studies by Bain & Co. And if that's the result during one 12-month period, consider the positive effects of creating a loyal customer over a lifetime.

Consider these statistics, compiled by the Technical Assistance Research Programs Institute (TARP), a firm specializing in customer service systems:

- The lifetime value of a customer to the local pizzeria is $8,000.
- Cadillac estimates that its customers are worth $332,000.
- Corporate purchasers of commercial aircraft could be worth literally billions of dollars.
- A typical supermarket shopper, when all his or her weekly purchases are added up, is worth over $380,000.

- Dallas automobile dealer Carl Sewell estimates that each person who ventures into one of his showrooms represents a potential lifetime value of over $300,000. He arrives at this figure simply by calculating the number of automobiles each new customer is likely to buy during the course of a lifetime and by estimating their average price, along with the service his own dealership can expect to deliver and charge for.

- A General Motors vice-president for consumer development, after accounting not just for cars purchased and after-sale service rendered but also income from auto loan financing, figures that a loyal customer is actually worth as much as $400,000 over a lifetime.

What about your customers? How much are they worth to your firm if they were to continue to do business with you over a lifetime?

Of course, thinking about "lifetime loyalty" in this day and age of change may seem to be an unrealistic objective. Perhaps it is. But when you begin to consider even the lifetime value of a relationship with just one of your customers, it may cause you to think about that customer in entirely different ways. For example, you might be more inclined to give a refund to the customer who's just brought back a half-eaten bag of potato chips and demands a refund because they are "stale."

Becoming a Loyalty-Engendering Firm

Customer loyalty must be earned by consistently delivering superior overall value. And a commitment to retaining customers can't be a "flavor of the month" program looking for a quick boost. Most companies look at the companies that are successful and adopt one or two of their practices, then wonder why they fail to get the same results. Instead, it must be an integral part of your firm's overall business strategy.

Researchers who have delved deeply into the area of customer retention, such as Harvard University's Frederick F. Reichheld, find a common pattern: Few companies have been able to implement what turns out to be meaningful and measurable improvements in customer loyalty. Those companies that have are worth studying. One of them is USAA, the financial services giant based in San Antonio, Texas, that is often cited as a model for the way it creates lifetime customer loyalty.

How USAA Earns Extraordinary Loyalty

USAA is an example of a Value Innovator that identified the unique needs of its customers and provided them services they could not get elsewhere. The firm was founded in 1922 by 25 army officers who recognized they had an unmet need and decided to meet it for themselves and for others like them.

Since they and other army personnel moved around so frequently, car insurance was difficult to obtain. Having to find new insurance in each area was time-consuming and frustrating. So the officers established a firm to serve the unique needs of members of the military and their families. The firm turned the locational impermanence of this group into a basis for loyalty.

USAA has no agents in the field; thus, individuals can change addresses without having to change agents. No big advertising campaigns are necessary since most customers come by word of mouth. It markets only its own customer base with new products. And new products are a frequent occurrence at USAA in response to customer needs. From its base as an auto insurer, USAA has branched out over the years to now offer a wide range of services, from life insurance to mutual funds and annuities. It's from these data that it has branched out from auto insurance to mutual funds, banking, credit cards, life insurance, health plans, and annuity products and has become a financial services company with more than $30 billion in assets. It is of course a no-load company, charging no sales commissions on insurance policies or mutual funds, nor does it charge credit card fees. All employees are salaried.

Having grown to 2.7 million members and the fifth largest auto insurer, USAA has also developed a reputation for superior service. "In today's business battles, customer service is the secret weapon," says USAA's CEO emeritus Robert McDermott. "We cultivate 'customer intimacy,' a thorough knowledge of our market coupled with the ability to tailor products to the specific needs of that market." To stay on top of the loyalty issue, USAA does both mail and phone surveys extensively and uses the information to develop future products.

So how does USAA inspire and motivate its employees to give this sterling level of customer service? It has applied the above principle of knowing the customers' needs to knowing their employees' needs as well. It goes to great lengths to keep its employees happy. And its turnover rate of 9 percent is well below the national average and an indicator that their principle of "happy employees make happy customers" works.

"If you aren't at USAA, you want to be," says one sales rep. That's because USAA is one of the top-rated workplaces in America. Contained on the 286 acres of USAA headquarters are four cafeterias, two fitness centers, two general stores, six tennis courts, and two softball fields, all for employee use. "If they'd open a dry cleaner and a pharmacy, I'd never have to go home," comments another employee.

The second way USAA motivates employees is through training programs. With a company policy that ties bonuses to increased training and learning new job skills, the organization has 30 percent of its employees enrolled in education and development programs at any one time, spending more than $19 million a year, roughly twice the industry average. Says McDermott, "The goal of all our training is to have employees gain the greatest possible benefit from their talents and create a companywide *esprit de corps* to improve service and ensure customer loyalty."

Employees wouldn't be able to do the job they do, however, if McDermott hadn't believed in operational excellence and invested $130 million in computer systems. When other firms were first hearing about such systems, USAA made a risky move to install a state-of-the-art image-processing system that allowed all correspondence to be digitized and accessible on any one of the 17,000 computer terminals. This system is USAA's techno-edge, working invisibly behind the scenes to allow faster service (the customer's account pops up on the rep's computer screen within 2 seconds), but also to process and pay 85 percent of the claims within 1 day of receipt.

And this is only for starters. USAA is in the process of testing multimedia information systems that will allow filing of recordings, photos, and video documents electronically for immediate access at workstations. Says former CEO McDermott, "Think of that for a minute. You could call 5 times and talk to five different USAA employees. But they all will have the same file right in front of them, the same audio recording, the same photos or video."

How can your firm create a higher rate of customer loyalty? Let's turn our attention now to the key strategies that could turn your company into the USAA of your industry.

1. Gather Strategic Information on Your Customers

It's sometimes said that technology has made our world impersonal. But today, technology is increasingly being used by value-adding firms to do just the opposite: to reestablish, or in some cases to build, a bond between customers and company. Let's look at how several firms in a variety of industries are getting to know their customers on a whole new level.

How Sauder Woodworking Compiled a Powerful Database

Take Sauder Woodworking, as an example. Based in Archbold, Ohio, Sauder used to confine its marketing effort to the retailers who sell its products to end customers. The manufacturer of ready-to-assemble microwave tables and other furniture, Sauder doesn't view the retailer as its *only customer*, despite the fact that it has earned coveted shelf space with outlets such as K-Mart, Sears, and Caldor.

The key to Sauder's redefinition is warranty cards. By using them creatively, the company was able to change completely its approach and its dependency on mega-retailers. By building up a database of roughly 1 million customers, "We found out a lot of interesting things," said Keven Sauder, vice-president of sales and marketing.

First off, warranty-card analysis showed Sauder just how wrong it'd been regarding a critical piece of information: who exactly their customers were. It turned out that it wasn't just students and low-income people who were buying their product, as they'd long assumed, but lots of other interesting subsets as well.

Armed with such strategic insights, Sauder was able to add value to its relationships with its retail "partners" as well. Being able to tell retailers, by region, which of its products were most popular with which customers, for example, enabled more targeted displaying and advertising of Sauder furniture. Product design also benefited from a direct relationship with customers, since likes and dislikes could now be fed back into new product design and design improvements.

Because of the advantages Sauder has achieved by simply taking advantage of warranty cards and turning them into strategic insights into its customers, the company now has much more ambitious plans for the future. "We were a $350 million company that no one had ever heard of," Sauder says. "We wanted to change that." And he believes the relationship his company has with consumers will continue to pay big dividends in the years ahead.

NBO Stores: Getting Paid for Being Nosy

Manufacturers like Sauder aren't the only ones busy gathering strategic information on customers these days. Some forward-thinking retailers are too. At NBO Stores, a discount menswear retailer, sales staffers are paid to be nosy. NBO gathers information from credit card transactions, alteration tickets, and address cards that customers are asked to complete. NBO uses this information to compile a customer database that is then used for a variety of purposes. One example: to track individual responses to its sales promotions. Each customer file has 28 categories that note, for instance, what items shoppers buy, what they paid, where they live, and which NBO stores they frequent.

"We don't know their [political] opinions, we don't know their religions," says Jim Frain, NBO's director of marketing. "But we do know what they like and don't like in men's clothes to a very specific degree."

2. Discover and Meet the Unique Needs of Your Customers

Whether yours is a business-to-business relationship or a business-to-end-consumer relationship, your customer is less likely to switch when his or her needs are being met in some unique way. What's unique about the way you meet your customer's needs? What can they get from you and no one else?

It is in defining and redefining your uniqueness that builds loyalty. Reminding customers of the ways you are addressing their unique needs reestablishes the bond that continues to provide the basis for customers' loyalty over time.

If you'll think about your own life for just a moment, you'll realize how inconvenient it is even when you're dissatisfied with a supplier to make a shift or make a change to a new one. Suppose, for example, you were to become dissatisfied with your bank. Consider how difficult it would be to close your checking account, shop around to find a new bank, and establish an account there. Time-consuming and not much fun, to say the least. It's the same with many of the purchases you make as a consumer. And the same in the business world. Every customer group has unique needs. The successful companies survey often to find:

1. What are the unique needs of our customers?

2. Who are the "right" customers for us to target?
   a. Ones likely to do business over time.
   b. Customers to whom we can deliver superior value.

Blacks-Industrial: Giving Customers the Key to the Store

Blacks-Industrial, Inc., a wholesaler of heating and air-conditioning equipment based in Spokane, Washington, identified its customers as contractors and heating and air-conditioning repair persons. What Blacks did next was to open warehouses in smaller towns in Idaho and western Washington. Then, rather than staffing the warehouses with people, it puts contractors on the honor system, gives them a key to the unstaffed warehouse, and allows them to shop at any hour of the day or night, 7 days a week. The contractor fills out the sales invoice for the items he's purchased and puts the invoice in a lock box, then he's off to do his job for his customer.

At first it might seem that giving your customers a key to your store would be an invitation to theft. Yet Rolly Johnson, vice-president at the firm, reports that there is actually less shrinkage at the unmanned stores than at its manned branches. Reason: Customers value the access and the convenience so highly that they make sure to adhere to the rules.

"We find that they do come in at all hours of the day and night to pick up items they need," Johnson told me during an interview for this book. The additional advantage to Blacks is that the company is able to expand into towns where having a full-time staff person would not be economically feasible. The innovative approach has paid off on the bottom line and has allowed it to become established in areas that later could support manned stores.

Is there any question that this company has raised and met the unique needs of its customers to a new state-of-the-art?

How Tierney Metals Engenders Loyalty

Tierney Metals is the world's largest distributor of aluminum-extruded metals to the aerospace industry. If you can spot an airplane out your window as you read this, there's a good chance it contains aluminum parts that were sold to the aircraft's manufacturer by Tierney.

Just across the street in Los Angeles from Tierney's headquarters are several prominent superstores, selling everything from office supplies to auto parts, testimony to the rapidly changing retail landscape. To Tierney CEO Robert Stoltz, who must drive past these superstores each day to and from work, they may be tangible reminders of how rapidly customer values can change, and of the punishment received by players who no longer exist because they did not see how the value equation was changing and did not adapt and respond quickly enough.

So although Tierney has an excellent reputation for quality, selection, and service, and enjoyed record revenues and profits in recent years, Stoltz freely admitted that he doesn't believe these differentiators will be enough to survive the future.

"We are trying to think faster and more diligently than any of our competitors about an industry that is rapidly changing," observes the studious-looking Stoltz, whom close friends call by the more formal "Robert" rather than "Bob." Stoltz believes that value-added services are its only hope for survival.

Tierney Metals is a middleman in an era when the customer wants to reduce costs. Tierney, like most other distributors, doesn't carry unique or exclusive products. The six mills that mine aluminum ore and mill it into tens of thousands of parts for aircraft and aerospace do not grant distributors exclusivity, so in this sense Tierney is selling a commodity. The company buys from the mills (such as Alcoa) that make the aluminum and sells its portion of products direct to the customer, who, in this case, is usually an aircraft manufacturer like Lockheed or Boeing. But because the mills sell the heaviest materials, aluminum floor beams or wing spars—very heavy stuff—directly to Boeing and Northrop, they have a relationship. "Tierney is sort of a preferred provider, although Tierney has had a reputation over the years of being a little more expensive than the other ones, but providing better service, better quality." This relationship, in and of itself, gives Stoltz little reason to feel secure.

In fact, what he is concerned about as he looks to the future, and what is driving him and his top team at this closely held company to create and bring additional value to Tierney's relationship with customers, is the possibility that the distributor could be eased out of a job if it doesn't add value that creates loyalty. In simple terms, the very mills that supply parts to Tierney and other distributors have started to explore selling direct to certain classes of customers.

One of the issues that I face and have been facing is how I can either serve the marketplace or alter the way the marketplace wishes to be served, to have that result enhance my survival and prosperity at Tierney. In other words, it's as if a mill said to the customer, we can do everything you need. You don't need the distributors. And we can do it for less because there's no need for a middleman. If that really sells as a philosophy, I'm in trouble long-term. Our customer base is trying to decide which way it wants to go. I'm trying to get them to do things that not only favor me over my traditional competition, but that will also give me a continuing *raison d'être* over a mill. So if I can install a very exotic computer system with EDI and bar codes, and I'm keeping inventory and replenishing every day, a mill's going to have a very hard time—even a big one like Alcoa—duplicating that service.

Customers can choose to bypass the distributor and buy direct from the mill, and they can get a much lower price. The product becomes a commodity; delivery times are diminished to once a quarter—drop the stuff off in a box car at a railroad siding—and the customer is responsible for taking care of it from there: warehousing it, getting it onto the factory floor on a daily basis. There's no value-added, and the product in effect becomes a commodity.

I'm in effect saying to the mills, look, you do what you're good at, which is making the stuff in the best possible way, and let me be the marketing agent to the customer and the servicing entity with the computers, the bar coding, the customer contact, the worrying about all the customer's new nuances and needs. If I can sell this idea strongly enough, the mill's going to stick to its knitting.

It's going to see that going direct is not the way to go. It's going to see that what the customer demands from the guy that sells it to him are things I can't supply.

3. CREATE A LOYALTY PROGRAM

What are they getting that's special, that will keep them coming back? A program a car wash might institute is: Buy 10 car washes and get 1 free. A theater might offer this program: Attend five movies and get the sixth one free. What are you doing? What is going to work for you?

Because loyalty has become such an important arena in the midst of the Value Revolution, and because new information technology enables firms big and small to keep better tabs on who their customers are, loyalty programs have increased in popularity.

Consider the spread of loyalty programs:

- Waldenbooks' Preferred Customer program offers discounts and rebates, but also segments its database to measure who buys what types of books, so a reader gets targeted announcements.

- Club Arby's electronically tracks purchases and offers food prizes to repeat customers.

- Grocers are faced with intense competition from membership warehouse clubs, discount stores, specialty shops, and consumers who now spend over half their food budgets eating outside the home. As a result, they are embracing reward programs to win loyalty from price-sensitive shoppers. Supermarket consultant Carlene Thissen, president of Chicago-based Retail Consulting Systems, predicts that by the year 2000, 80 percent of the nation's supermarkets will offer frequent-shopper programs that give loyal shoppers better deals.

- Automobile manufacturers, seeking to win dealer profits and customers' long-term loyalty to their brands, are stepping up their efforts to convince owners they should bring their cars and trucks back to a dealership for both routine maintenance and more complex repairs. New surveys say that if a customer is satisfied with his or her dealer in maintenance and repairs, that dealer is more likely to get the next vehicle sale.

Not all loyalty programs work or prove effective in keeping customers. The customer's question in weighing such programs is the same as it is in weighing any Value Proposition: What's in it for me? Who really gets the value-added?

Shopping malls, and retailers in general, will have to fight harder to retain customers, in light of the rise of "nonstore shopping." Noticing the statistic that 80 percent of a shopping mall's business is done by only 20 percent of its customers, The Plaza, a regional mall in West Covina, California, instituted frequent-buyer programs. The programs add value to customers who are loyal in bringing their business to The Plaza, and the mall in return gains valuable strategic information on who these customers are and how to keep them loyal. The Plaza then markets this to its lessees to improve and attract better businesses.

4. Create a Guaranteed Service Program

Some companies are taking a bigger risk than the loyalty programs we discussed above and are guaranteeing service satisfaction, or they are offering various forms of freebies.

At Delta Dental of Massachusetts, if you get transferred from phone to phone, you will be mailed a $50 check. Better yet, you can receive a 1-month free premium if the transition wasn't smooth when you transferred from another dental plan.

Hampton Inn will refund your money if you are unhappy with your hotel room. It advertises 100-percent satisfaction guaranteed. Hampton Inn initiated this program in 1989. Its figures show it is keeping repeat customers it would have lost, and receives $8 in revenue for every $1 paid out to dissatisfied customers. Over 300 guests invoked the guarantee in the first 6 months, and 100 of them said they already had stayed at Hampton Inn again. A recent survey indicated that 2 percent of the guests chose the Inn because of its guarantee.

The Marriott hotel in Minneapolis used a service guarantee to solve an internal quality problem: Housekeepers complained about not being able to get supplies they needed. Manager Kevin J. Beauvals instituted a guarantee that any housekeeper who couldn't get supplies on any given day would get $5 from the supply department. He made sure everyone knew about it. The result: a more efficient system of ordering supplies and lowered housekeeper turnover, and all for a minimal cost.

Who can make the best use of a service guarantee? Christopher Hart, president of Total Quality Management Inc., a Cambridge, Massachusetts, consulting firm, says it's any company standing above the competition in an industry known for poor service: "An island of excellence in a sea of mediocrity—that's the ideal situation to hammer the competition with a guarantee."

What constitutes a workable guarantee?

- It's easy to measure and understand.
- It's quick to use.
- It's painless to invoke.

Some pitfalls to watch out for:

Abuse. Studies show that actual abuse is limited to 3 percent, so don't spend a lot of time trying to plug every loophole.

Watering it down. It will lose its effectiveness. Stay away from too many conditions or restrictions, especially if they are in the fine print.

Lack of communication. If only some employees know, it will cause more confusion. Make sure all employees know and all locations participate. Nothing is more annoying than arriving and finding that the guarantee you thought you were getting is not being honored or participated in by that particular location.

Launching too fast. Make sure your company people can meet the guarantee. GMC, which originally launched a fast-oil change to compete with the fast-lube specialists, changed its program from "a 15-minute guarantee and full money-back" offer to "29 minutes or the next one's free" after testing showed that the 15-minute guarantee would prove too much for some of its dealers.

Make it easy to use. If you create a guarantee that's too hard to use, you'll not receive the value you're looking for. Example: Texaco, seeking complaints about its Star-Mart convenience stores, offers a $5 in-store certificate, but first you must mail in a form that requests the name and physical description of the employee who caused the dissatisfaction. Only one customer bothered to do so in the first year. Texaco has since switched to an 800 number to make it easier for the customer.

5. Look for Patterns of Discontent Among Defectors

Defectors are, in effect, vetoing your Value Proposition. It's important to know why your customers become ex-customers, and to pin down the reasons. Was it your prices? Your service or services? Or was it your quality? Did they leave because they thought they could get better value elsewhere?

By conducting interviews with former customers, you'll not only develop new insights into how you must shore up your Value Proposition, you might even win back some deserters. For example, at one credit card service organization, a phone call to question cardholders who had stopped using its cards led to the immediate reinstatement of one-third of this group.

A Final Word About Loyalty

Gathering strategic information on your customers, discovering their unique needs, creating loyalty and guaranteed service programs, and looking for patterns among former customers are all helpful methods of raising your loyalty rates among customers. And in the value era, when customers are less loyal than ever, retaining customers is putting money in the bank.

But in the final analysis, programs and policies can only go so far. Loyalty comes from what you do, and whether you're prepared as a company to go that extra mile for your customers.

As a child growing up poor in New York's Lower East Side, the late entertainer Eddie Cantor used to earn money delivering groceries to the housewives in the neighborhood. His customers always insisted that he go to a certain grocer whose store was several blocks farther away, even though there were grocers closer by. Whenever he went to a local grocer, thinking it wouldn't make any difference, the women always noticed, and chastised him. Eddie couldn't understand how they could tell: After all, a quart of milk was a quart of milk, right?

One day while using the preferred grocer, Eddie noticed that the man filled the milk bottle above the line that indicated a full quart. And then, when the order called for six bananas, the grocer put in seven. Eddie called the error to the man's attention, but the grocer replied, "Eddie, that's no error. Remember, whatever you do in life, always give a little more than you are asked, and it will make a big difference." Eddie Cantor never forgot that man's words, and he attributed his success as an entertainer to living that credo in all his performances.

How about it? Are you giving your customers just what they expect, or more than they expect? Putting the "extra mile" philosophy into practice could be your best loyalty program of all.

Now that we've examined what leading edge firms are doing to earn customer loyalty, let's turn our attention to how the arena of marketing has been changed by the Value Revolution. In the next chapter we'll cover marketing and communicating your value to customers.

7

C H A P T E R

MARKETING AND COMMUNICATING VALUE

"The company is the product now."

—Hans Decker, vice-chairman,
Siemens Corporation

AS PART OF A CONSULTING PROJECT, I WAS DOING some mystery shopping at a large, international waste removal firm, seeking to find out how responsive the organization was.

"Can you get a dumpster over here this morning?" I asked the person who answered the phone.

"Certainly," she said. "What's your address?"

"Can you get a dumpster over here in an hour," I followed.

"No problem," she replied. "Where would you like it delivered?"

"Can you get a dumpster over here in half an hour," I pressed.

"I'm working on it, sir," she said. "What is the location?"

Whether she realized it or not, that dispatcher was marketing and communicating value. She instinctively realized she had a time-conscious customer on the line, and she did not mince words. She did not talk about what she *couldn't* do; she did not make me feel that my request was unusual or that I was being a burden.

In that brief telephone interchange, she *heard* me, and each time I upped the ante, she accommodated. I was the customer making demands; she clearly saw her role as trying to meet those requirements.

If you asked this woman what her job title was, she would have probably said something like "receptionist" or "dispatcher." But her value is really in marketing. From the receptionist to the sales team to the CEO, marketing in the value era is everyone's job. Of course, if your Value Proposition doesn't meet customers' needs and doesn't render good value in their eyes, no amount of marketing will ever make it a winner. But assuming that it does, customers still need to understand your firm's unique value, how your company gains customers in situations like the one above by communicating in ways that respond to each customer's needs. And that's why marketing is so important.

Businesses that will win the Value Revolution are those in which every associate, regardless of job description, understands that he or she is in marketing as well. In the value era, marketing becomes more than an activity or a series of events or product introductions or "created news." It must go beyond manipulation, beyond image, beyond hype, giveaways, gimmicks, public relations, and advertising. It goes to what you really are and how well you are able to communicate that to consumers in an overcommunicated world.

Even employees who don't ever get near your customers are part of your marketing team. If nothing else, they interact socially with acquaintances who form impressions of your company based on their responses to such questions. Your employees, suppliers, stockholders, and members of the community in which your facilities are located all have impressions of your firm and its products. Only businesses that are able to articulate their value and to speak the language of customer value have a hope of survival.

What is the role of marketing in the value era? In this chapter we'll look at how certain leading-edge firms are answering that question. We'll examine strategies they are using for reinventing the marketing and communications function of your organization to meet the demands of today's sophisticated consumer.

1. Marketing's Role Is to Build Trust

Ask the average person what the role of marketing in a company is and she or he will likely say, "to hype the company and its products and manipulate people to buy." The role of marketing at firms that are winning the Value Revolution is different: It's to form a relationship with the customer, one that is built on trust.

Throughout this book, we've seen how the Value Revolution is being driven by consumers who have more information than before at their disposal, who are more experienced at making choices than ever before, and who have more options available to them than ever before. Yet despite these dramatic changes, many businesses haven't caught up with the attitudinal shifts taking place in consumers' minds. Many of these businesses today actually still believe they can hoodwink consumers and get away with it. The evidence of such beliefs is as close as today's newspaper.

As I write this, I am looking at a page from the *Los Angeles Times*. It's a page of the business section. There are three articles on this page: "Auto Repair Complaint Settled," "Hospital Rating Panel Makes Reports Public," and, the third, "Consumer Group Picks Year's 'Most Misleading, Unfair and Irresponsible' Ad Campaigns."

Each of these articles, taken alone, might be considered an isolated issue. Taken together, they point to a disturbing tendency. Taken together, they tell us a lot about why consumers don't trust, why independent ratings of products and companies are growing, and about how difficult it is for any business today to win trust.

Take the article on misleading ads, which reported on a Washington-based consumer organization (The Center for Science in the Public Interest) that bestows "awards" to draw attention to what it considers to be unethical advertising. Here are a few named:

- Prudential Securities, for ads promising "straight talk." The company had recently paid a $600-million penalty for misrepresenting risky limited partnership stakes as safe investments.
- GMC Trucks, for claiming its Safari minivan was "safe enough for your precious cargo," even though the van ranked near the bottom in government crash tests.

137

- Van Den Bergh Foods, for Promise Margarine ads advising consumers to get "heart smart." The margarine is high in total fat, which is a factor in obesity and heart disease.

These firms are hardly alone in having their hands slapped. In recent years, major financial, accounting, and insurance companies, as well as manufacturers, retailers, and service firms, have been attacked by the media or hauled into court. Even Littlehampton, England-based The Body Shop, whose founders Anita and Gordon Roddick claimed was the "most honest cosmetic company in the world," was pilloried for overstating its boast of being a socially responsible and environmentally friendly firm.

Attacked by *Business Ethics* magazine for having betrayed its customers, the exposé noted that "The Body Shop uses many outdated, off-the-shelf product formulas filled with nonrenewable petrochemicals . . . has increased its use of ingredients that at some point have been tested on animals despite [founder Anita Roddick's] high profile opposition to animal testing . . . and, although it is a centerpiece of the company's image, The Body Shop sources a tiny amount of ingredients from rain forest Indians and other tribal people through its Trade Not Aid program"—among other charges. In response, the firm obtained the subscriber list of *Business Ethics* and mailed a 10-page rebuttal.

The Body Shop brouhaha is significant in that even companies that profess to do good deeds are not above scrutiny. Given the pressures to perform, to build the bottom line, there is and will continue to be pressure on company leaders to manipulate the truth, hide the bad news, inflate claims, knock the competition, and otherwise create situations where distrust reigns.

The truth is that sometimes, perhaps even oftentimes, you might just get away with it. Sales go up. Only a few complaints get voiced. The issue might seem to have gone away. But then it comes back in some form or fashion to bite you. And the goodwill you've worked so hard to build with your customers suddenly crumbles in the face of a headline, a microphone stuck in your face as you leave your building, a shareholder lawsuit, a consumer boycott.

Who needs it?

In contrast to the headlines like those cited earlier, consider Johnson & Johnson's handling of the "Tylenol Case." In 1983 in Chicago, a saboteur put cyanide into Tylenol bottles. Seven people died.

J&J decided to meet the threat head-on. They recalled *all* Tylenol packages from around the country, mounted their own investigation, and developed tamper-proof packaging. The move cost Johnson & Johnson millions of dollars, but today, Tylenol is selling better than ever, and J&J is considered one of the most trustworthy names in corporate America.

The recent history of marketing has been a series of flavors of the month: Relationship marketing. Cause marketing. Database marketing. Environmental or "green" marketing. More recently it's been loyalty and retention marketing. I propose a new gimmick: trust marketing. Here are some elements of what it's about:

- Give the customer the facts and only the facts.
- Use advertising and public relations to build your credibility, not bring it into question.
- Provide detailed information on your products and services.
- Invite independent evaluation of your claims (environmental, social, etc.) and live with the results.
- Use advertising to communicate as much as to persuade.
- Resist the temptation to knock the other guy's offerings; instead, tell the customer what's unique about yours.
- Be prepared to substantiate any claims you make in your advertising and promotions.
- Run your company in such a way that the best marketing you do is free, because it's performed by satisfied, delighted customers—yours! That's called "word of mouth" marketing.

2. The Role of Marketing Is to Build the Market

So often in industry publications these days we read statements like this: "More competitors are fighting over a pie that is not growing as rapidly as it once did." When Value Innovators hear these words, they know it's time to *build a bigger pie*.

Lorna Riley, president of American Training Association, is an expert on time management and sales, and a professional speaker based in Thousand Oaks, California. Riley occasionally runs across prospects who've never used the services of a professional speaker before to sharpen the skills of their people. When she comes across such an organization, Riley always suggests that "maybe it's time you did!"

How Reynolds Aluminum Won the Soft-Drink Can Market

What Riley is doing with that seemingly simple suggestion is building the market for herself and for professional speaking as an industry. Other clients have found tremendous bottom-line value in her services, she suggests, and maybe it's time you took a look at the possibility that these benefits could accrue to your company.

To succeed in today's increasingly competitive business climate, companies must stop viewing their existing markets as their only markets. Instead of focusing on slugging it out with competitors, innovative companies go about searching for new arenas where they can flex their muscles without having to take on all comers. That's what value-innovating companies like Reynolds Metals Co. are doing, with tremendous results.

Reynolds, of course, makes aluminum. As you might expect, aluminum's biggest competitor has always been steel, and therefore steel producers. Until hard times hit the steel industry in the 80s, steelmakers enjoyed years where demand far outstripped supply. Most didn't even have marketing departments.

Not Reynolds. Reynolds has never been content to simply serve existing customers. Instead, it scanned the horizon for markets where it might replace steel. The four sons of the founder implemented daily brainstorming sessions to come up with new ways aluminum can replace existing metals, and everything else. Over the years these sessions produced some pretty wacky ideas, from aluminum coffins to aluminum cocktail dresses.

"People thought we were far-out nuts," one retired Reynolds brainstormer told *The Wall Street Journal*. The coffins were a flop; mourners felt they were too light to be dignified. And the aluminum dresses didn't exactly take the rag trade by storm either. Another loser: Reynolds "tapper" beer kegs, which fit in home refrigerators, and lost fizz when they weren't returned. Even a once-successful product—aluminum siding— eventually lost out to vinyl.

Undaunted, Reynolds kept it up, even convincing General Motors to build engine blocks out of aluminum. A major setback occurred when the Chevrolet Vega and Camaro overheated, and consumers turned on the product.

Along the way, Reynolds and other aluminum companies have had some hits too. Remember when soda cans were made of steel? The conversion to aluminum didn't just happen. It was all part of a concerted effort on the part of aluminum makers like Reynolds to market the value benefits of their product. With just such an attitude of building a bigger pie, it's interesting to see the long-term results when compared with a firm that simply takes orders.

Steelmakers once owned the beverage can market. Their "tin" cans were far cheaper than those of rival materials, and canmakers had big investments in the machinery that soldered the three-piece steel cans together. Rebuffed by canmakers, Reynolds came up with a new canmaking technique that stretched molten aluminum to form an inexpensive two-piece can. The process is about 5 times faster than the three-piece process, and Reynolds, by using stronger, thinner alloys, uses 40 percent less metal per can.

To sell its new cans, Reynolds bypassed the intransigent canmakers and called on its customers, the beverage companies. When steel companies heard of Reynolds's efforts, they dismissed the competition. "We kind of laughed at it and said, 'This is going to go away,' " a former steel company executive commented.

But Reynolds kept knocking on doors, hoping for converts. To provide the very best value equation to potential customers who were willing to give the new packaging a try, Reynolds matched the price of steel cans, even though doing so meant it was selling below its own costs until volume grew. But getting customers to switch required inventive Q-Factor benefits beyond equal price, so Reynolds stressed such qualities as aluminum's lighter weight and resistance to rust. Later, as the environmental issue became more of a concern, aluminum makers could boast that their product was completely recyclable as well. Finally, a regional brewer signed on for a trial, and then Coca-Cola switched to aluminum, and with that the selling process grew considerably easier. Steelmakers laughed no more.

Today, aluminum beverage cans have captured 96 percent of the market, and Reynolds is busy targeting other markets long held by steel. Among them: autos. They're betting that the movement to lighter, fuel-efficient cars will allow aluminum increasingly to replace steel.

And what's next after that? Aluminum bridges, that's what, according to David Reynolds, the retired chairman. "I'll grant that steel makes a good railroad rail, but anything else, we've got a shot at."

How Cintas Goes After New Markets

Reynolds Aluminum is hardly alone in constantly searching for new users outside its industry's existing identified customer base. Look at the leaders in any industry and you'll find this attitude of "building the pie" permeates marketing thinking.

Cintas—based in Cincinnati, Ohio—the fastest-growing and largest publicly held industrial laundry and uniform company, attributes its success to an innovative program of identifying and going after new markets. When management at Cintas realized that increased overall quality in their industry was making it very difficult to increase further their share of the $3.5-billion market, they reframed the question of who their customer was. Company CEO Richard Farmer estimates the potential market for his firm's services is at least 3 times the market currently being served. This potential $10-to-$12-billion market has become the focal point of Cintas's attention, and its efforts are paying off. In recent years, two-thirds of Cintas's internal growth has come from clients who have never before had uniformed employees.

How did Cintas begin the process of converting new customers? According to Farmer, the first step was to identify occupations that lent themselves to a uniform program but weren't currently using them.

"Our challenge is to understand what our nonusers would value," Farmer shared in a recent speech before fellow members of the Uniform & Textile Service Association. "We've got to understand their needs. We've got to know their businesses." In order to do that, Farmer focuses on one or two new segments at a time, because the company couldn't be experts on all the businesses that are involved in the unserved market."

Company staffers read their trade journals, visit their trade association meetings, and attend trade shows, often spending months visiting with the key players in the industry and learning their business.

"We became recognized experts and, most important, we begin to talk their language," says Farmer. Only then does Cintas put together a service that could help it improve its business in a meaningful way. By learning everything possible about a prospective customer, Cintas has been able to pinpoint needs that its service can fulfill.

Only then does the work of marketing and communicating value begin. Then Cintas representatives sell the value of uniforms as a way to improve their company image, professionalism, and morale, and thereby to increase business. Proving to potential customers that they even have a need requires thinking outside the box.

Cintas president Robert Kohlhepp recalled targeting a national company that offered delivery of its product but whose drivers didn't wear uniforms. Initial efforts to even obtain a meeting with the client were met with indifference. He was finally able to arrange an interview, but before going to the meeting, he had photos taken of the firm's delivery people in various locations around the country. Kohlhepp explained:

This company's offices were absolutely beautiful, so I asked the president how much the building had cost.

"Millions," he replied. I then commented on the size of the firm's advertising budget and fleet of corporate vehicles and inquired about how much they had cost.

He again replied, "millions." I then asked him what he thought his company's most important asset was, and this time he answered, "the people." When I got him to focus on the fact that people *were* his most valuable asset and that public image was important to the success of his company, I showed him the pictures we'd taken of his drivers. Guys wearing Grateful Dead T-shirts and jeans with holes in both knees. These drivers were also salespeople for his company! Then I showed him a picture of a driver wearing a clean, crisp, professional-looking uniform, and I asked him who he thought customers would rather do business with. We got the account on the spot.

Result: Three years after starting the new market-building program, two out of every three new customers were first-time users, representing over $1 million in weekly volume added to the industrial laundry industry in 1 year. One of the benefits the firm has gotten out of the build-the-market program is the realization that we've got to move our quality standards much higher than we had them, and that will benefit not only our new customers but our existing customers as well.

> We're learning that these nonusers frequently require special garments, and that's a big no-no in our industry. The only way to approach new markets is to take the fence down and say that we're going to discover a need, and if garments have to be dry-cleaned, for example, we'll dry-clean them. And if they have to be processed in smaller machines, we've got to get smaller machines. It's just that simple. Are we going to go out and sell what we've got, or what the customer needs?

If it's a product you're selling, don't be content to think of your market as the known users of that product, be it plywood or plumbing supplies or chickens. If you're a service business, rethink who could possibly need your services and go after them. Take a leaf out of the Reynolds Aluminum success manual and brainstorm new uses, new markets, new customers. Competition getting too stiff in the existing market? Rethink your offerings, looking for unserved markets and underserved markets. If the suburbs are overserved by your product or service, try the inner cities.

The effect of such initiatives will be to energize your entire company with new hope, new future focus. Instead of lapsing into a mindset of looking backward at the "good old days" when competition was less fierce and making money seemed easier, you'll engender a future-focused attitude that says, "the best is yet to be."

In good times or bad, there are those who seem to defy industry trends and keep moving forward. One way is by doing what Cintas and Reynolds and American Training Association are doing, which is building and expanding the market for their services, rather than fighting over the same pie.

3. The Role of Marketing Is to Educate the Customer

Several years ago I was invited to be the keynote speaker before the American Optometric Association's annual meeting in Las Vegas. At about the same time, as these things go, I began to realize that my eyesight was deteriorating. I was beginning to have to read with the printed page placed at arms length, but now my arms were getting too short, as the expression has it, meaning that I could no longer read newsprint without having to hold it away from my eyes to bring the words into focus.

I decided to take notes as I went through the experience of informing myself about solving a consumer problem I'd never had before: corrective lenses. The first choice I had to make was between optometrists and opthamalogists, who are MDs specializing in eye care. I chose optometry, feeling that my problem was a simple one rather than one needing the treatment of a physician. I pulled out the yellow pages and began phoning around, getting a feel for how a call from a prospective customer (*patient* is the word these professionals strongly prefer) might be fielded. I quickly discovered that most of the people assigned to answer the phones in optometrists' offices had not the slightest clue that they were in fact in a marketing role.

While these conversations ranged from pleasant to brusque, from inviting questions to being downright suspicious that someone wanted to learn about optometric services, there was no understanding of just how ignorant I was about this new service. Any questions that I asked in an attempt to differentiate the various optometrist's services were treated as if I were prying, overly cautious, and . . . they were busy. I ended up visiting three optometrists and reported my findings to the 800 delegates in Las Vegas. I described:

Dr. 1957. I gave him this name because of his office decor. When I asked how long he'd been in his present quarters, he said he'd been there since 1957. In his early 60s, my first optometrist was able to see me right away, which was a real value to me since I'd been putting off getting glasses for far too long and wanted to get this necessary but time-consuming transaction out of the way with as little delay as possible. I noticed that his rather large waiting room was deserted and that he was the only one in the office. I wondered what that said about his practice. He ushered me back and started in with the eye exam, looking into my eyes and adjusting various pieces of equipment, all of which, at age 40, was new and strange to me. The thing that struck me was how ancient both his office (green linoleum floors, ancient pictures of himself beside trophy fish) and his equipment seemed, but at this point, I had no frame of reference through which to compare. Perhaps this was the latest technology; what did I know?

Dr. Medical Model. This optometrist, based in Los Angeles, was booked up several weeks in advance. My host at the optometric association had referred me to Dr. Medical Model after I'd shared my impressions of my visit with Dr. 1957. As he was a former president of the association, I had high expectations of Dr. Medical Model's quality and patient service. His fee, higher than others I'd called, also reflected a more-for-more positioning. If the process of creating a committed patient begins with the first contact, this one failed the test. I arrived several minutes early for my 3 p.m. appointment and was put to work, without any sort of greeting, filling out an insurance form. The office was in the sterile style of a typical doctor's, the only exception being a few toys for kids in the waiting room. I wasn't called back for 25 minutes, at which time I was directed through a series of initial tests by the "office manager." Again, no greeting, no warmth, and little-to-no communication about the purpose of the tests I was being put through, and poker faces as far as the results I was producing.

Finally, Dr. Medical Model appeared and took over the testing. But 2 or 3 times during the process, he would suddenly dart out of the semi-darkened room I was put in without so much as a word of explanation. I'd brought along my pocket tape recorder, and I used it to describe how I was feeling: "Kind of depressing, sitting here, turning 40 next month. I'm balding and now I'm losing my eyesight, and I've been abandoned here in this semi-darkened room." I was even less pleased when the doctor returned and, with only a perfunctory, you-have-no-choice attitude, put eyedrops in my eyes that dilated my pupils wide open for the next several hours. Leaving the office, I drove up a winding mountain road intending to go to a library but soon realized I wouldn't be able to do any reading, and my anger continued to build as I squinted in the afternoon sun, trying mightily to read the color of traffic lights, and cursing this optometrist under my breath.

Dr. High Tech/High Touch. So named because this optometrist had the most up-to-the-minute technology and exceptionally good communication skills. He was the nearly perfect combination of having modernistic, seemingly cutting-edge, high-tech equipment, combined with a warm, caring, and attentive manner. Shortly after I'd arrived and was greeted warmly by a friendly receptionist, this eye doctor came out to the waiting room to meet me personally. He shook my hand, looked me in the eye, and appeared genuinely interested in me as a person. We spoke for a minute or two before he ushered me back to get down to business. And he conducted the complete exam himself, almost all from a comfortable chair that resembled a dentist's chair, using modernistic equipment that enabled him to bring it to me, rather than have me tromp from room to room to get to it. Not having to rove from room to room added to my enjoyment of the exam, and Dr. High Tech/High Touch projected his eye chart on the screen. A slide or two from his recent vacation in New Zealand added to the tone that this meeting was not drudgery but an enjoyable interlude in an otherwise hectic day.

All three exams produced a similar result: a small piece of paper with a few numbers scribbled on it that I could then take to an optician to have a pair of eyeglasses made. But two of the experiences left me unsatisfied and did nothing to induce loyalty on my part. And if we look at these three visits from the standpoint of marketing, they were anything but equal to me as a customer.

Optometrists, like many other professional service providers, face increased competition in many areas. Until recently, they have been reluctant to embrace customer satisfaction, much less value, even while the rest of society is affected by the customer-driven Value Revolution. By hanging onto the word *patient* many, but certainly not all, optometrists also hang onto an era when designing their practices around their customers' needs, rather than their own, was hardly the operative paradigm. But the Value Revolution came to optometry during the past decade in the form of national optical chains that often operate in conjunction with an adjacent optometric office. Optometrists also face competition from ophthalmologists, who can increasingly use surgery to correct numerous eye maladies.

What Dr. High Tech/High Touch did—and what I later shared with delegates to the American Optometric Association—was to understand marketing's role in differentiating one nearly identical practice from another. He understood that marketing was not hoopla or hype, but rather the rethinking of service. In this case, service meant educating a customer new to the industry, and making a customer for life.

4. Marketing's Role Is to Tangibalize Your Value-Added

Webster's New World Dictionary defines *tangible* as "that which can be touched or felt, having actual form and substance." When you "tangibalize" your value added, you bring your value to life in the eyes of customers. To tangibalize your value, it is necessary to dream up and innovate new ways to make value tangible. And it certainly doesn't have to be just big things. The challenge is to look for opportunities to bring what you are doing for the customer to his attention, and to show him how this benefits him. Where might you put information about your value-added service into your brochure, your display ads, your television commercials, your annual report, even on your price tags?

If your associates have been with your firm for a longer period of time than the competition's, and this gives them advantages in terms of depth of product and trouble shooting and expertise that benefits the customer, the role of marketing is to brainstorm new ways to excite you, your associates, and your customers about these differentiators.

The result of such effort and emphasis on the part of the leader is that everyone in the firm begins to understand and use the language of value. People in your company who serve internal customers only will begin to smile when they talk about how what they are doing "adds value." It gets to be a game, but one that serves a bottom-line purpose. Everyone on the team begins to think harder about the value they are producing for the end customer, or, if they only serve internal customers, they begin to realize possibly for the first time just what these buzzwords are all about. When you prepare the annual report, the issue of what would add more value for our customers and shareholders comes into play.

Tangibalizing your firm's value-added services and methods is quite possibly the lowest-cost, but highest-impact, activity you can do to market your company. How so? Because chances are there are efforts you are *already* making for your customer that you're not taking advantage of from the standpoint of differentiating your firm from the other guys. What are they? Chances are, if you make a tangible list, you'll find, as my executive seminar participants do regularly, that your list is longer than you thought.

Provide a Checklist of Your Value-Added Services

But how to do this without being obnoxious? One winning technique is to simply provide a checklist of the extras you offer. Little things. Big things. And those in between. If you don't know many specifics in terms of what your competition does and doesn't provide, make it a priority to find out. One office products dealer uses a laminated checklist to tangibalize the many features and benefits it offers its customers: customized computer reports, guaranteed accuracy on order fills, free advice on getting the most use out of the products it sells. The bottom line is this: Your customers or prospective customers don't know what you do unless you tell them. And your current customers will soon forget unless you remind them. And your prospective customers don't know or may not know unless you educate them about what good value is in your industry. If you move mentally from around your side of the selling counter and stand with the customers on their side, you'll suddenly realize incredible new ways to tangibalize your uniqueness, strengths, services, and people who work on the customers' behalf.

How Miller Office Systems Keeps on Selling Its Value

One Value Innovator is James Miller, founder of Miller Office Systems in Fort Worth, Texas, and author of *The Corporate Coach*. Says Miller:

> Our buyers and decision-makers aren't in the stands for every game we play, so we send them descriptions of what we are doing for them. We send report cards on our past performance—report cards that are based only on the work we've done for them. Those report cards don't include companywide averages, only how we have performed for them. Customers deserve to know how we have performed for them. Customers deserve to know how many of their orders were filled accurately, what percentage of their orders were filled completely within 24 hours, and so forth.

Miller doesn't miss a trick. And to top it all off, it affixes a sticker to orders that read: "Back orders cost you time and money. Miller Office Systems saved you both with this 100% Filled Order! Thank you for your business."

5. The Role of Marketing Is to Challenge Commodity Thinking

Before Frank Perdue came along, chicken was a commodity product. It was found in the frozen-food section, pale-white, hard as a rock, with no brand name. Then Perdue developed a new breed of big-breasted chicken that he fed a diet of corn and marigold petals to bring out a healthy yellow color.

Then he redesigned the distribution system. Instead of delivering freezer-burned birds to distribution centers for later shipment to stores, he bought a fleet of trucks to take his chickens directly to supermarkets. That way his product could be kept fresher than commodity poultry. Next he put a brand name on his packaging, and he advertised.

What was the consumers' response? It turned out that if the customer was given a choice between a rock-hard, pale-white commodity and a plump, yellow Perdue chicken, many would choose Perdue. Perdue's premium poultry is typically priced a third higher than the commodity price, yet he has become one of the biggest producers in the nation.

How Arbor Mortgage Challenges Commodity Thinking

And what Perdue did to chicken, Arbor National Mortgage did to mortgages. Conventional wisdom might hold that differentiation in mortgages is a fallacy. The only thing the customer cares about is, "What's your rate?" But Arbor National doesn't do business that way. A midsize company based in Uniondale, New York, the lender has a slogan: "We never sell products based on price." Arbor focuses on niche products, repackaging plain-vanilla mortgages, and providing funding to customers other lenders reject.

Yet instead of charging customers with poor credit ratings at rates that assume high default rates, Arbor does extensive appraisal work on potential customers' finances, and, as a result, suffers fewer losses. Another value-adding innovation: the Arbor Home Bridal Registry. Couples register with Arbor instead of with a department store, so friends can contribute to the newlyweds' first home. Arbor's bottom-line results are testimony to the company's challenging the commodity assumption and adding unique value that customers appreciate.

6. The Role of Marketing Is to Ensure That Your Distribution Method Is the Best for the Customer

Manufacturers and wholesaler-distributors alike know that it is all too easy to forget or ignore the final user's needs. It's easy to get caught up in serving the next link in the value chain and often get blindsided by end-use market developments right along with others in their distribution channel.

In the personal computer marketplace in the late 80s, as computer users became more knowledgeable, more sophisticated, and more price sensitive, superstores and mail-order operations started popping up all over. At first they were ignored by the Businesslands and Computerlands of the world, but pretty soon these alternative channels of distribution were eating their lunch. Meanwhile, at least one major computer company was loyally propping up its traditional dealer channel, and responding painfully slowly to consumer preferences for different ways of buying computers. The mistake cost them big. The company, of course, was IBM.

By contrast, Dell Computer and other clonemakers began selling product to customers direct by phone, cutting out the costs associated with middlemen in the distribution channel. IBM was mired in a distribution system that assumed that people would not buy without seeing it firsthand and trying it out with the help of a salesperson, and it has been forced to cede a significant share of the market that it had once created.

What responsibility to down-chain intermediaries does a producer have if it is not serving the customer in a way that the customer wants to be served? This is a question that many manufacturers face, and one for which there are often no easy answers. Yet with some creative, "out-of-the-box" thinking, the situation doesn't have to be either/or, all or nothing. Let's look at two such examples.

Why Goodyear Changed Its Distribution Channel

When Stanley C. Gault took over the helm at an ailing Goodyear Tire and Rubber Co., the company had watched its share of the U.S. replacement car tire market fall from roughly 15 percent to 12 percent. A big reason for the drop was Goodyear's distribution system. It simply wasn't putting Goodyear tires where shoppers wanted to buy them. And where they wanted to buy was at multibrand discount outlets as well as warehouse clubs. But Goodyear continued to sell its brand exclusively through its own stores and through a network of independent Goodyear dealers. The problem, as Gualt soon realized, was one of consumer perception of Goodyear's Value Proposition: Dealer stores had a pricey image, while the product's Q Factor or the Goodyear dealer's S Factor weren't perceived as justifying the price.

Gault immediately began to rethink Goodyear. First, he stepped up new product development, coming out with the Aquatred, which was designed to provide superior performance over rain-slick roads. Next he boosted ad spending by a third, and then he dropped a bomb. He jolted Goodyear's dealer network by announcing that Goodyear would sell seven Goodyear-brand tire lines through Sears, Roebuck & Co. It began selling its Kelly-Springfield tires to Wal-Mart and other discounters.

Gault insisted that the whole Goodyear family would prosper from the new marketing approach. At first, dealers were upset. Yet 2 years after the move, Gault proved once again that boldness in the face of a changing market was the only way to go. Today, profits are up at most Goodyear dealer stores, and they are selling more competing brands as well as their own. In addition, mass retailers are moving the firm's other products, and Goodyear is back in control of its destiny.

How Pella Rethought Distribution and Won

Like Goodyear, Pella, the window manufacturer, distributed its meticulously crafted windows exclusively through some 369 Pella Window Stores in the United States. The positioning was definitely more-for-more. "Our philosophy was, if you built a better product, then somebody would come buy it," says senior vice-president Hillary Keeney.

But Pella's revenues, which had risen at an average annual rate of 9 percent for almost 40 years, began to fall flat. The tough years of the early 90s hurt upscale door and window sales. A slow-growth economy and the trend toward inconspicuous consumption combined seemed to have slammed shut the window of growth opportunity.

What to do? Pella commissioned an in-depth study by a consulting firm that helped it understand that it had to change structurally if it was to again thrive. One conclusion the study pointed to: Pella had blindly followed Value Strategy 6: Offer Greater Choices. But now offering an ever-expanding number of choices was leading to an almost unmanageable situation.

Put simply, Pella was producing too many products for too few buyers. Customers could order windows and doors in literally dozens of combinations, and the company was about to drown in complexity. Pella's management team went to work. After completely rethinking the firm's Value Proposition based on the "new consumer," it began making changes. The company now offers windows and doors in fewer variations and has grouped them into the contemporary Designer Series or the more traditionally styled Architect Series. Next it took a hard look at how its products came to market.

It was obvious that more and more consumers were shopping at home supply stores, yet Pella's top team didn't want to betray its distributors, which previously had been the only place to buy Pella residential products. Solution: It launched a more moderately priced series of windows and doors called ProLine, which it offered to home centers.

Unlike former offerings, the ProLine comes in far fewer sizes and shapes than the designer models. Still, the windows have the high-quality, solid-wood frames that sandwich energy-saving panes, yet sell for 12 percent to 20 percent less than the up-market models.

Pella distributors quite naturally were worried. As one distributor said, "We're concerned about ProLine being sold in national chains with hundreds of other products by people who are more interested in volume than quality and service, and who foresaw a drop in the customer's perception of Pella's quality and service." In other words, part of the reputation for quality was contained not only in the product itself but also in the service surrounding the sale offered by businesses that sold only one brand. The fear was rightfully placed. But Pella addressed such concerns by transforming distributors into the quality cops for all ProLine products sold in their territories! Distributors now train local retailers and help their customers with installation and service. Most important of all: Pella distributors were granted a commission on every ProLine window the chain outlets sell.

Back at the factory, Pella also stopped doing business as usual. In order to meet the demands of the very demanding home-center retailers, Pella set up Japanese worker-management teams to search for ways to continuously improve work flow and aid productivity. Members of a 12-person crew descended on the sliding-door operation for 4 days, moving machines, eliminating inventory, consolidating tasks, and reassigning people. As a result, productivity increased 25 percent. Improvements such as these have helped Pella reduce order fulfillment cycles from 5 weeks to a mere 10 days.

"We've virtually redefined who we are and what we are about," says Pella Chief Executive J. Wayne Bevis. The makeover is working in the marketplace, with the distribution channel, and on the bottom line. Pella's revenues topped $400 million in a recent year, and earnings, which the privately held company doesn't disclose, are moving up again.

What Dell, Goodyear, and Pella represent are firms that realized they had to change distribution channels in response to customers who had themselves changed. As painful as it can sometimes be, the message of the Value Revolution is clear: Serve the needs of the end customer first and foremost. And if this means that your distribution methods must also change, so be it. Not to change with change is a surefire prescription for every channel partner to go out of business.

Six Questions to Ask Yourself in Rethinking Marketing

Here are some questions to ask yourself as you go about rethinking the role marketing plays inside your firm.

1. How do your marketing programs, methods, and strategies add value to your firm's offerings?

2. In what ways do you regularly seek to build relationships with customers?

3. How honest and straightforward is your marketing communications?

4. How well does your marketing effort differentiate you? Help to define your uniqueness?

5. How well does your marketing help to remind your customer of your value-added services and service levels?

6. How well do your marketing program and people demonstrate your value?

A Final Word

Now that we've looked at some of the tough issues that marketing in the value era present, you've gotten, we hope, an idea or two about how to adapt your own efforts in this regard. Next, get ready to do the same thing to your products themselves as we look at how the Value Revolution is won with regard to the products you sell.

CHAPTER 8

ADDING VALUE TO PRODUCTS

"Consumers today are taking the time to decide what a product is really worth."

—Grey Matter, a special report of Grey Advertising

IF YOU'VE READ THIS FAR, YOU KNOW THERE'S A WAR on, and you've got to use everything in your arsenal to win it. Adding value to your products isn't an elective these days, it's a *requirement*. If you're inclined to skip this chapter because you're a service company, hold on just a minute: These days, service companies have just as many *products* as manufacturers, and smart manufacturers are creating an array of new *services*.

In this chapter, you'll gain new insights into what gives your "product" added value for today's consumer, and you'll master five factors that are critical for adding value to your offerings. They are:

1. *Innovation*: the need to "think outside the box" and come up with whole new products, as well as to improve continually your existing offering in ways that enhance your customer's perception of quality, service, and price.

2. *Affordability*: designing or redesigning your offerings so that your price matches your customer's needs.

3. *Customer feedback*: the need to involve customers in your offering and to analyze the customer's way of using and devising value from your product.

4. *Simplicity*: what we might call the "keep it simple" factor.

5. *Serviceability*: the before-and-after sale factor of keeping the customer satisfied long after purchase.

By applying these five factors to your offerings, you'll discover new ways to out-think and out-innovate the competition, regardless of what type of business you're in. So let's dive in.

CRITICAL FACTOR 1: INNOVATION

You wouldn't be reading this book if you weren't on the hunt, searching for competitive advantages in an ever-more competitive landscape. Innovation, as I wrote about in a previous book, *Winning the Innovation Game*, is the process of coming up with ideas and bringing them to life. These can be breakthrough ideas, or they can be ones that continuously improve your existing offerings.

To win the Value Revolution, you need both. But since you can't count on breakthroughs—try as we might, they don't come along every day—you must focus on tweaking your offerings in ways that keep them on the cutting edge in the eyes of your users, that differentiate them from commodity lookalikes, and allow you to charge a premium because your perception of value is so much greater. Take carrots, for example.

How "Baby" Carrots Became a Hot Product

Not too long ago, the carrot just sort of sat there in the produce section, and as far as the consumer was concerned, producers were interchangeable. A carrot was a carrot was a commodity. Sales were flat. Margins were thin. All in all it was a pretty humdrum game. What could a carrot grower do to change things? Not much, it seemed.

Enter Mike Yurosek, founder of Mike Yurosek & Sons, a Bakersfield, California, carrot grower who didn't buy into the commodity mentality. He was intrigued when, in the late 80s, he saw a New Jersey firm begin marketing 3-ounce bags of celery and carrot sticks as snacks for the health-conscious—and time-conscious—consumers.

And then one day he heard his wife complaining about the time it took to peel all those carrots for a meal she was preparing. "Can't you do something about this?" she demanded, and Yurosek got to thinking. Yurosek thought ready-snack carrots might be a use for his "culls"—the split or broken carrots that normally ended up as livestock feed. Out of these observations, Yurosek developed a method of creating "baby carrots," the now popular miniature carrot that requires no peeling or cleaning.

Baby carrots are actually made by cutting fully grown carrots into sections of 2 or 3 inches. The sections are tapered and peeled in a revolving drum with a sandpaperlike action, resulting in a product that looks like little carrots, and is perceived as such by most consumers. But actual baby carrots are inedible, since the sugars don't start to develop until the later growth stages.

The product has given new health to the industry, ratcheting up carrot demand by 40 percent in a few years. Soon, the little chubs began accounting for 20 percent of carrot sales, and over 40 percent of carrot revenue. Perceiving a higher value in the product, consumers are willing to pay much more for them. A 1-pound bag of fresh "babies" commands triple the retail price of a bag of regular carrots. To top it off, no pun intended, the demand for baby carrots has not come at the expense of regular, full-sized carrots, according to the California Carrot Advisory Board. Now, how's that for innovation?

Before long, Yurosek had competition, of course. But not all producers could afford the big investment in new equipment, leaving Yurosek with a big lead over rivals. And like the Florida citrus growers and the California raisin producers before them, Yurosek and other producers are just beginning to exploit the market potential of their new product. They are racing to market the convenience and healthfulness of stashing 3-ounce bags of babies into school lunches and office snacks. They're also going after new distribution channels, making inroads with stadium concessionaires and airlines, as well as fast-food restaurants. What it all adds up to is the power of innovating an existing product to give it an additional perception of value for today's time-short consumer.

Bombay Co.: Using Innovation to Produce "Class" for Less

Sometimes innovation is merely taking a product and rethinking it—figuring out a way to sell it for less, as Japanese firms have been so masterful at. Or taking a product that people might want, antiques, say, and mass producing lookalike products.

That's what Bombay Co. did. What began as a small, mail-order business in New Orleans has exploded in the past 10 years through the retail-creating husband-and-wife team of Robert and Aagje Nourse.

The Nourses first saw the 18th- and 19th-century English-style furniture catalog in 1979 and sensed something important: The inexpensive reproductions had the attraction of a "class" product, but were available at very reasonable prices. The couple correctly intuited that making these fine furniture reproductions available through mall retail outlets would catch on with the average consumer: class for the masses.

The Nourses bought Canadian rights to the name and products, and opened their first retail store in Toronto in 1980. Three years later, they had 13 flourishing outlets, and sold to Radio Shack's Texas parent, Tandy Brands. Through a combination of savvy manufacturing in countries such as Korea, India, and Malaysia, the Bombay Co. has been able to supply newly manufactured "olde" English furniture to its 500 retail outlets every 7 weeks.

How Not to Innovate: Why Cadillac's Cimarron Failed

Today's buyer is indeed taking the time to decide what a product is really worth. GM's Cadillac division might have seen that its strategy with Cimarron was fatally flawed from the start. The car was intended to be Cadillac's answer to the foreign invasion of BMWs, Mercedes, and Audis, and it was the company's hope that the new model would win back the young, affluent professionals who'd been deserting U.S. car manufacturers in record numbers. Smaller and sportier than its older brothers Eldorado and Seville, Cimarron featured leather seats, a luggage rack, and lots of chrome. They stamped the Cadillac logo on it and stood back, anticipating Cadillac style sales.

But buyers stayed away in droves. The problem: Cimarron was merely a dolled-up version of Chevy's Cavalier and Olds's Firenza. Cadillac tried to pass itself off as a more-for-more product, when in fact it wasn't. After 3 years of making no headway, Cadillac made another effort to reinvent the Cimarron and came out with a bigger engine and a few other bells and whistles. But that wasn't enough. Competing with imports that were identifiable as status symbols, the Cimarron tried to command a heftier price than its value commanded. Soon the Cimarron was history.

Has GM learned its lesson? One would think so, but recent reports from Detroit suggest that it may repeat the same mistake. Seeing the tremendous popularity of sports utility vehicles, GM is reportedly considering borrowing a chassis from Oldsmobile or GMC and creating an upscale version. If it does, one can only wish it good luck.

Here's the point all of us can take away from the Cimarron disaster: You can't enter the more-for-more race with a product that lacks more-for-more quality, features, and after-sale services. The days are long gone when Cadillac—or anyone else, for that matter—can sell its product on logo appeal alone.

Finding Your Unique Product Benefit

Service companies such as Charles Schwab, CareerTrack, and USAA Insurance, among others, have grabbed the lead in their markets by innovating new product offerings that meet customers' needs. Take a look at these winning new products:

Kitty Litter. By adding absorbent materials that solidify around liquid, this product provided an ease-of-use advantage to its customers, making it easier to clean the kitty box. Value was added through packaging when leading kitty litter manufacturers switched to more convenient plastic jugs. Result: The new product grabbed a third of the market, resulting in a 12-percent increase in sales for the category.

Personal Computers. Engaged in an all-out war for market share, PC makers in recent years have created differentiation in bonus packages that add value to their products. Some are throwing in everything but the kitchen sink—an escalating variety of software products, improved screens, video and audio chips, and extended service contracts.

Condoms. To protect its 60-percent market share, Carter-Wallace recently rolled out value-priced Class Act, a signal that even the condom industry is subject to pricing pressures from consumers. "In the mid-80s, when the AIDS crisis hit, people did not worry about price because they were concerned first of all with their safety. They knew they were putting their lives on the line," said a Carter-Wallace competitor. "There was an impression that the more expensive, the better the condom." But a variety of cheaper foreign brands, particularly from Japan, were beginning to signal a possible "Marlboro defection."

Deodorant. Helene Curtis Industries created an innovation success for itself with the introduction of its Degree antiperspirant line. Chemists at Helene Curtis came up with a "heat-activated" formula for Degree and advertised it as an innovative feature that the competition didn't have. That unique product claim, combined with Helene Curtis's cut-rate pricing, helped the product catapult from its 28th rank in deodorant sales to number 5 in a recent year.

Whatever the product, using innovation to add value to your product challenges you to come up with a way to provide a margin of benefit for everyone: the end consumer, your dealers or wholesalers and distributors, and yourself. Innovation can often be a new spin on an old standby, a new method to provide your customers with a greater perception of value than they'd previously experienced. Innovation requires that you assess your output from a different angle than the one you've been using normally. Here are some questions for you to consider:

1. What was the last truly innovative new product your firm introduced, and how well has it done?

2. What is the unique claim of your key products?

3. Given the changes in your market, what types of products will you need to introduce over the next 5 years?

4. If your products are largely considered to be commodities, what might you do to differentiate yours?

5. List three different approaches you might take to produce more and better innovations in your firm

6. How innovative is your firm at present (on a scale of 1 to 10), and how innovative does it need to be to meet the challenges of change?

Take the time to brainstorm with your team on the subject of your overall innovativeness, and get feedback from your distributors and your customers for future directions. Where is there the greatest need for innovation? Is it in the manufacturing of the product? In its distribution? In your affordability?

Critical Factor 2. Affordability

What the customer finds affordable one minute is changed the next. Take the $42-billion medical technology industry, producers of life-saving devices ranging from magnetic resonance imaging machines to defibrillators to kidney dialysis machines.

Several years ago, if you'd asked most executives of a medical technology company what customers valued, they might have laughed. The answer would have seemed that obvious. "Customers want more bells and whistles and better products," they'd have answered. For years, equipment sales were driven almost entirely by technological advances. The operative question was: Is it better? Is it of higher quality? Does it do more for me, give me more benefits, have more features than the gizmo I've got?

In effect, to relate how the customer looked at and sized up the value equation, think of a huge Q. That's because Q in the value equation far outweighed S and P, primarily because neither suppliers nor buyers worried about costs. And who was the customer? Individual doctors and hospitals, who passed those costs on to insurers and government payers. "We were rewarded for introducing whiz-bang technology at a rapid pace," one imaging systems sales manager commented.

But what the customer valued evolved with surprising speed. As everyone knows, in the early 90s, talk turned to health care reform. Alliances began forming all over the place, and lowering prices became the operative paradigm. Every expenditure got looked at, and looked at again. Do we really need this new machine? Why exactly do we need this new machine? What's the cost of this machine? Can't we do without it? What's so great about it that our existing equipment doesn't provide?

Increasingly, the primary buyers of medical equipment are not just physicians. Now the customers are the penny-pinching, bean-counting groups that buy gear or dictate decisions for hundred of doctors, and dozens of health care facilities. And they were simply responding to what their customers, the senior management team, were yelling at them.

In a very short while, things changed dramatically. The customer's needs changed. The customer's value equation changed. Buyers of medical equipment are now focusing on affordability—with a vengeance! The new credo is: We still like medical technology innovations, but they also better be cost effective.

Med-tech makers that fail to adapt to the change in what customers value do so at their peril. Companies that were wedded to the old paradigm were sluggish about adapting to the new reality. U.S. Surgical, a $1-billion maker of surgical instruments, watched sales tumble 25 percent in the second quarter of 1993, and 32 percent in the third quarter, as the new customers with green eyeshades began demanding comparison bidding. The company had to furlough 20 percent of its employees and cut $150 million, or 20 percent, from capital expenditures.

The fast-responding firms got the message. They saw the handwriting on the wall. They glommed onto the new paradigm. They got out of denial and into gear. Some firms now routinely consult with insurers and corporate health care buyers on what they're willing to pay for improvements—before they crank up the assembly lines. They're asking: What is this worth to you? They now view the payers as their customers too. GE's medical products unit responded with lower-cost products with fewer features, and began hawking their products abroad with a vengeance.

Not just in medical technology but in all industries, affordability is subject to change. Things may not change quite so rapidly as they did in med-tech, but they will surely change. What will your customer value tomorrow? What will the customer be able to afford tomorrow?

How the Recreational Vehicle Industry Faced Up to Affordability

In the late 80s and early 90s, when high interest rates and lack of disposable income threw the economy into a downhill slide, it put many in the recreational vehicle industry in the ditch. The problem was that

Winnebagos, Airstreams, and other vehicles had engaged in an arms race of features that put the typical coach out of reach, price-wise. "It was like a contest to see how many gadgets you could get into a vehicle," Recreational Vehicle Industry Association President David Humphreys commented, referring to the chandeliers, dishwashers, and built-in bathroom scales that were crammed into motor homes.

No wonder that Boomer consumers, the 35- to 55-year-olds who might have been expected to be prime RV buyers, were bringing with them a much more circumspective approach to making large purchases. They shopped around, and shopped around some more, sometimes spending 2 or 3 years in the "looking and comparing" stage before finally making a purchase.

But the RV industry bounced back, by rethinking its product and matching its affordability to the customer's ability to buy. Value Innovators in the industry realized that the younger, RV-buying family was more concerned with affordability than with excessive comforts. And they worked hard to engineer the costs out of their products.

The popularity of low-cost trailers produced by Thor Industries of Jackson Center, Ohio, forced the nation's 100 or so RV makers to follow suit. Fleetwood Enterprises, America's largest RV manufacturer, created a pop-up trailer that sleeps up to eight people and includes a stove, refrigerator, and sink but sells for the price of an economy car rather than a home. By scaling down lower-end vehicles and matching the consumer's affordability factor, models like Fleetwood's Mallard are selling briskly and increasing the company's bottom line. In the case of the Mallard, the company is going for a less-for-less strategy, and the increased sales show that it's paying off.

The Manufactured Housing Industry Gets Affordable

At a time when fewer and fewer working people can afford to purchase their own homes, the market for manufactured homes is escalating. After working hard to overcome the public's perception that pre-fab homes are little more than over-embellished trailers, this industry is finding more than a foothold. For roughly half the cost, the buyer of a manufactured home can purchase a four-bedroom/three-bath home, permanently attached to a foundation. Manufactured home builders, as a result, are working overtime to keep up with the growing demand.

Perrigo: On the March with Same-for-Less

Matching price to customer's needs has rocketed private-brand labels in the over-the-counter drug marketplace as never before. With a focus on today's value consumer who's always on the lookout for a same-for-less deal in essential but nonprestige purchases, Perrigo Company, a virtually unknown Midwest private-label supplier, offers retailers over 800 "knock-offs" of products like Pepto Bismol, Oil of Olay, and Efferdent.

Producers of these products—giants like Procter & Gamble, Warner-Lambert, and American Home Products—are angry about it, but have little recourse. In a recent year, Perrigo Co. did over $500 million in sales, demonstrating that the impetus for today's value consumer is the drive for perceived equal value at less cost, and this trend shows no signs that it will abate anytime soon.

The Message About Affordability

Producers, whether of goods or services, have to be in tune with their audience's affordability. If the product is over-engineered, and consequently must be priced to match, it can have devastating consequences, as happened to the over-engineered Mercedes-Benz. Conversely, a product may have high affordability but lack the quality to sustain its reputation, as happened with Hyundai's problem-plagued Excel. And Marlboro cigarettes, as we saw in Chapter 2, also took a major hit when forced to fight back against cigarette discount brands. Drastically cutting its retail price, Marlboro was able to corral back some of the customers it had lost, but at a cost in perception of what its product was truly worth.

Take a moment here to think about the affordability of your products as you consider these questions:

1. Is there a way to add still more value to your product by matching your end user's affordability factor?

2. When did you last measure your price to the end user's affordability factor, and what were the results?

3. What system or method could you put in place to ensure that your price continues to match the customer's affordability factor?

4. When did you last compare your P Factor with those of your nearest competitors? What were the results?

CRITICAL FACTOR 3: CUSTOMER INVOLVEMENT

We saw in an earlier chapter how the creators of the Quicken software program, developed a "follow-the-customer-home" research system that gave it up-to-the-minute feedback on how its product is being received by customers. It's all part of a movement to get closer to customers, to suss out their values, wants, needs, and hidden desires. While customers can't tell you what they would want before they see it, it's no excuse for ignoring them as useless. Smart companies get some of their best ideas from customers.

The converse is the "over-the-wall" approach. You've heard of the over-the -wall approach to product development. It works like this: The marketing team comes up with a concept and throws it over the wall to the research and development team, who work on it. Then they throw it over the wall to the manufacturing team, which sets about creating the product. When they've accomplished the manufacturing, that team throws it over the wall to the sales group, who is responsible for selling it. This approach worked well for many companies for many years. But it doesn't work so well in the value era.

"Today's products are far too complex to follow this traditional path," says Hewlett-Packard's Manuel F. Diaz, general manager, Worldwide Sales & Marketing. Diaz advocates instead a "customer-centric" approach, replacing the company's earlier "technology-centric" focus. A new customer feedback process has been developed to replace "over the wall." It involves surveys, focus groups, and feedback systems to "capture what customers think about H-P products."

As the company has gone about changing its development process, each division now assumes responsibility for ensuring that "products and services deliver value to customers." In remarks at a symposium on value marketing sponsored by the Conference Board in New York, Diaz suggested that "there are too many opportunities for miscommunication, and H-P is too large an organization to rely on this [over-the-wall] approach."

By establishing a multidisciplinary team approach, the firm transcended the over-the-wall approach, with all its various teams contributing and communicating back and forth with each other through a central umbrella team. The result of careful analysis of their systems and operations, and the ability to implement new ideas rapidly, has enabled Hewlett-Packard to remain in the forefront of numerous volatile and highly competitive industries, from medical technology to printers.

How Hewlett-Packard Outgunned the Laser Printer Manufacturers

In 1985, the Japanese made four out of five personal computer printers bought in America. They completely dominated the market with their speed-to-market and economies of scale.

Today, however, it's a different story. H-P's printer division decided to rethink all assumptions about how to win that market. Its operative mantra: Learn from the enemy. Adopt his tactics. In the mid-80s, getting into computer printers meant going head-to-head with Epson and Okidata, but H-P's people had to come up with a better offering. And they did: Inkjet. The concept itself took some getting used to: shooting ink onto paper. But it had a key ingredient: It had mass-market advantages over costlier laser printers, because when it hit the stores, the Inkjet came in at a cheaper price, while providing quality printing for its customers.

Who wouldn't want laserlike quality for a PC if it were affordable? H-P grabbed the market's attention with its Inkjet innovation and maintained an aggressive price-cutting posture in a competitive market. When Canon was about to introduce a color Inkjet of its own in 1993, H-P quickly cut the price of its own version before the rival product even reached the market. Result: H-P dominated 55 percent of the world market for Inkjet printers in a short period of time.

How Thermos Reinvented the Backyard Barbecue

Barbecue grills are a $1-billion annual business, with a phalanx of inexpensive competitors vying for their share of the overall sales. Analyzing both the market and its operations, Thermos company was able to successfully rebuild a better mousetrap—in this case, a new, electric barbecue grill designed to provide that outdoor barbecue flavor without the fuss and muss of the standard-brand, charcoal-fired grill of yesterday. Thermos, which was already competing in the field with its own gas and electric barbecue grills, determined that it had to come up with something new that would give it an edge in the already challenging market.

Thermos's CEO, Monte Peterson, had a clear understanding of today's value consumer: Clever promotion and expensive advertising won't cut it in today's market, which demands value at reasonable prices. But what Peterson did that was novel to Thermos's operations was to use savvy consumer analysis in his preproduction stages and combine it with innovation in product design.

Peterson's team knew that the old standard image of dad out by the smoky barbecue grill wasn't the whole picture anymore. Millions of single moms also liked to barbecue and cook out with the kids, and this share of the market hadn't been targeted. The result? A barbecue grill that is extremely easy to use, clean, electrically driven, and a runaway seller in a highly competitive market.

Tallon: Terminating Termites Without Toxins

Market trends also play an important part in customer involvement. As today's consumer becomes more and more interested in toxic-free environments, certain traditional industries may have to rethink their products, or at least offer alternatives. Take pest control, for example.

For decades, pest control involved the use of chemical pesticides, the tenting of your home or office building, and inconvenienced consumers by making them stay off the premises, in some cases, for as long 3 or 4 days. But in the mid-80s, Tallon Termite & Pest Control, a Long Beach, California, company, came out with a new way to get rid of the little buggers: As their ads said, "We Freeze Their Little Buns Off!"

Tallon, a family-owned and family-operated business, had analyzed the market and was struck primarily by the consumer's growing interest in and awareness of the dangers of environmental and chemical pollutants. In a patented process developed by Joe Tallon, Jr., the son of founder Joe Tallon, Sr., the company is able to use liquid nitrogen on the insides of buildings and bring down the temperature to minus 20 degrees Fahrenheit. At that temperature, termites and other unwanted guests literally freeze their buns off. While expanding throughout California, its home turf, Tallon is now looking to additional markets in Florida.

Analyzing the Flops for Clues About What Customers Want

Today the economic landscape is littered with new product failures, dead-on-arrival entries that went nowhere because not enough time went into the analysis before the launch. Consider a few personal favorites:

- Premier, R. J. Reynolds's "smokeless" cigarette, was designed to counter the growing argument against second-hand smoke. The problem was that the cigarette tasted lousy to the smoker. The product was launched only on a limited basis, and customer reception was, well, hardly incendiary.

- NeXt, the computer, was unveiled to great fanfare and media blitz. NeXt failed to get off the ground because its technological "improvements," the high-tech optical drive, was not something the average customer wanted or needed. The optical drive made life "more difficult" for the multitude of home computer users, one of the main markets. On top of that, the PC carried a $10,000 price tag.

- Newton, the MessagePad, is a hand-held notebook. Apple thought it was on to something—and I'm sure they're right—when its designers came up with this hand-held, all-around computing machine. Unfortunately, it was brought to market before all the kinks were ironed out, and the kinks made more news than the machine's good features. That error in judgment was topped by a retail price, over $750, which strained most buyer's affordability.

Analyzing What Customers Tell You

Successful analysis requires more than time; it calls on you, the leader, to examine great failures, as well as winners, when you're doing your own, personal research. You've got to take a look at the combined factors— innovation, affordability, simplicity, service—during your analysis, in order to come up with the most impactful results, for yourself and for your offerings.

Analyzing must include three basic aspects of operations: your company and its offerings, your customers' wants and needs in light of the Value Revolution, and what your competition is doing. Start with a serious look at your company and its output or product/service:

1. Ask yourself, where, and what, can you innovate to add value to your product/service?

2. Analyze your customers' wants and needs and how they may be changing.

3. Take another look at the competition's product. What are they doing that you're not? What are you doing that they're not even onto yet? Are they making some errors of judgment that you're, thankfully, not making? If so, make a note of it, so that you don't lapse into imitating their offerings and dissipate the perceived value your customers find in your offerings.

Critical Factor 4. Simplicity

Many innovators get caught up in the miracle of their ideas, and lose sight of one of the bedrock ingredients for adding value to your offering: *simplicity*. Your customers, or end users, don't just want value for their money. They want to be able to use your product quickly and efficiently, no fuss, no muss. In an age when we have so much new technology to master, the time it takes to conquer the complexities can detract from the experience of using the product.

Who of us hasn't come home from our local electronics outlet with some wonderful new item, hot to fire it up, only to be stymied by the complexity of the instructions booklet? Or in too many cases, the instruction booklet is really a *manual*, too often a complicated and many-paged piece of work that would require someone with an engineering degree, at least, to figure out. In some cases, the consumer has to go back to the place she or he bought it and ask for assistance before using the product itself. Is this adding value to your product? Hardly.

If you took a quick survey, you'd discover that the most common problem with manuals is that they're often too technical, their language written for engineering students, not the general public. And this applies to many products, not just computers and electronic gear. It can also be applied to other aspects of the business world, including your own field of endeavor.

Earlier, we saw Circuit City's innovations on the sales floor—among them, the "racetrack" setup of the store's design, so that the customer smoothly moves through the whole store, passing through one sales "boutique" after another, then ends up at a central purchasing point to pay for his selections. That one bit of simplicity gives Circuit City an edge it might not have had in the highly competitive field of electronics retailing.

Adding value through simplicity is one method available to all of us who are in the business of marketing our products or services. The trick is knowing where to look and where to find areas you can simplify to greater advantage, for both yourself and your customer.

If you're a retailer, start by taking a look at your surroundings, at your "playing field," let's call it. Are there any areas of operation you can streamline which will result in greater ease and/or convenience for your customer? How about the positioning of your products, in relation to one another, on the shelf and/or on the floor? Is there a way to redesign your floor to increase your customers' access to what they're looking for?

If you're a service provider or wholesaler, take another look at what F. D. Titus & Sons did, as we discussed in Chapter 4 of this book. By forming an innovative partnership with its customers, health care clinics, surgery centers, extended-care facilities, and physicians' offices, Titus not only simplified its customers' inventory systems and accessibility to new products, it also brought overall prices down for customers. In an industry where there isn't any differentiation of product, Titus came up with a new spin on the S Factor. The firm developed a method of entering into a partnership with its customers and aggressively pursued the new setup so that by simplifying its clients' merchandise flow, Titus now outperforms the industry average by double!

Consider your own operations: What can you do to add value by simplifying, either under your own roof or in your customers' perception, or both?

CRITICAL FACTOR 5. SERVICE

Cecil B. DeMille, that movie-making mogul, coined the phrase "location, location, location." If DeMille were in business today, I'd like to think he'd agree that the best way to add value to your company's offerings would be "service, service, service." The fact is, there's a kind of doo-dad war going on with regard to out-servicing the competition.

First, Mercedes introduced roadside service. Then Cadillac glommed onto the idea, and Volvo and others began to follow. Then Ford Motor Co. introduced free emergency roadside service to all buyers of its 1994 models, including trucks. The free roadside service covers flat tires, failed batteries, engine failures, and the like. Now that Ford has introduced this attractive, free service, rivals had to follow in order to stay competitive. They did. By 1995, roadside assistance was available even on the GM Metro, which sold for under $10,000.

Roadside service, and services you offer to customers that support your products, have a similar trajectory toward more. There are lots of ways you can increase your S Factor for your company. Some might be costly at first but profitable in the long run, like an 800 number. And some might be as simple as adding another service-oriented feature. A small independent garage in our town advertised free "loaners" while your car was in its shop. Business shot up by 25 percent.

Again, service is everybody's business, in one way or another, from the highest ranks to the lowest. How you and your staff handle the S Factor in your operations can add value to your product, or detract from it.

Which takes us back to the oldest adage in the book: *The customer is always right*. A recent case of forgetting this adage developed in the troubles Intel Corporation had when problems arose with its Pentium chip. The powerful and speedy Pentium microprocessor, installed in many new computers—including IBM, Compaq, Dell, AST, and Gateway 2000—was discovered to make mathematical errors in highly technical computations.

A brouhaha erupted when Intel acknowledged that it had known about the possibility of errors but had not discussed it with its customers. Then thousands of computerphiles on the Internet and America OnLine started angrily demanding that Intel replace the chip, at its cost, in fairness to the consumers.

Finally, Intel acknowledged its errors and agreed with its consumers that it was responsible for replacing the problem chip, at the company's expense, but its response came some 4 or 5 weeks after the problem had first surfaced, and Intel suffered a public relations crisis as a result.

The Pentium chip problem, more perceived than actual for most of its users, had another implication. Whether he or she is buying a computer or a washer/dryer, today's consumer has come to expect a kind of perfection. "The tolerance for something not working immediately and working all the time is zero now," advertising executive Mark Kvamme notes.

Often you might already be providing excellent customer service but not advertising it to your potential clients. In today's world, the value consumer is looking for the edge, something that differentiates you and your product from the next guy's, and great service can give you that edge. Indeed, most of the value that financial markets assign leading-edge companies is due to their ongoing services competencies, not the hard assets that the buyer acquires. This is true regardless of whether the company is in services or in manufacturing.

Customizing or tailoring your service to individual customer's needs, as we discussed earlier in this book, is another way of adding value to your product. Take the Perrigo Co., the pharmaceutical "knockoff" manufacturing firm we discussed earlier in this chapter. Not only does Perrigo provide excellent and low-priced "equals" to name-brand drugstore products, it also customizes such items as pain relievers, stomach-upset products, and cough syrup. If a retail chain wants it packaged or labeled in a specific way, Perrigo obliges.

When you're striving to add value through the S Factor, just remember: *Service comes in all forms, at every level, on every business day.* It's hitting a thousand singles everyday, rather than batting a home run once a month. Every time one of your people interacts with a client or potential client, it's like a time up at bat: Are they going to "connect," to continue the baseball metaphor, or will they strike out?

Remember the story about the Chicago taxi driver in Chapter 2, with the cellular phone, thermoses of coffee, fresh fruit, and newspapers, all ready for his clients? Imagine if all your people were as focused on service as that fellow. What would happen to the perception of your product's support?

A Final Word About Value and Products

Before you leave this chapter, take a minute to review the five critical factors of adding value to products: innovation, affordability, customer involvement, simplicity, and service. Review the notes you've taken, or, if you haven't, take a moment now to make some notes for yourself, jotting down the ideas that are in the forefront of your mind. See if you don't already possess some clues specific to you and your operations that you hadn't previously spent time with, clues that will help you increase the value of your products.

That done, let's now turn our attention to how to sell those products in the value era.

C h a p t e r

VALUE-ADDED
SELLING

THROUGHOUT THIS BOOK WE'VE SEEN HOW THE
economic landscape has changed, and is changing, because of the Value
Revolution. Nowhere is this more evident than in the arena of selling.

In this chapter, we'll look at how to remake your sales operation into
a unit of added value, and we'll look at what certain firms are doing to
sell effectively in today's fast-changing economy. As you'll see, we'll
return to the seven strategies for adding value that were first outlined
in Chapter 4, only this time from the salesperson's perspective. Before
we dive into the solutions, however, let's look at the changes taking
place in the arena of professional selling.

The New Selling Environment

Here are a few of the fundamental forces that are creating a vastly different sales environment than the one that existed even 5 years ago:

- With high staff turnover, long-established sales relationships go by the wayside.

- More people are involved in the decision-making process leading up to a sale, and often the salesperson never gets to meet key decision-makers.

- The sales cycle is now longer from start to finish.

- Partnering between companies is altering or virtually eliminating the traditional selling relationship.

- Customers are more dependent on information from salespeople since downsizing has resulted in a thinning of the ranks of management and operations.

Until recently, salespeople too often sold without seriously considering the customer's needs. The strategy employed involved trite phrases, memorized sales presentations, manipulative techniques, and hard-sell closing strategies. These methods no longer work, and relying on them is a sure recipe for sales force disaster.

In the value economy, the sales process becomes even more important to delivering the value that today's demanding customers are seeking. Relationships between customer and supplier are even more critical, with customer-vendor "partnerships" becoming increasingly common. Even the words, *salesman*, *saleswoman*, and *salesperson* are increasingly anachronistic. They've been replaced with titles such as *sales consultant*, *adviser*, or *sales engineer*. The names have changed because the nature of the position has changed.

With the fierce competition for today's dollar, the new selling environment requires that your sales team excel with customers in a number of new ways. Communication must be on more than just price alone. Your team must articulate and deliver the Q Factor and S Factor of your Value Proposition, and make each tangible to your customers.

By moving from the traditional methods of selling based solely on reputation of product, old-time contacts, or regional attitudes, the new requirement is a sales team that focuses on meeting the unique needs of each customer. Studies have repeatedly shown that while sales staff represent a significant cost in the overall operations, customers credit the salesperson with about one-third of the total value created during a sale. You create value for your customers when you educate them and keep them up-to-date, in addition to all the other services you provide in the area of sales.

In response to the changing selling environment, large and small firms alike are redesigning their sales operations, downsizing sales staffs, and demanding more productivity and professionalism and profit from those who remain, in exchange for greater opportunities and higher commissions. And none too soon. As with other professions, salespeople must add value . . . or get run out of town.

The Value Revolution Hits Pharmaceutical Sales

This is happening in certain industries, such as health care. Previously, pharmaceutical sales were handled by drug company "detailers," who used to be a welcomed source of information, free samples, and goodies such as prescription pads, pens, and tickets to sports or entertainment events.

But more and more, the pharmaceutical manufacturers fall under the watchful purview of managed-care organizations whose goal is to hold down costs. Translated, this means they still expect a high Q Factor but now demand a low P Factor, and thus are willing to do away with the perks of the S Factor. These health organizations generally have a pharmacy committee that makes decisions about preferred drugs and provides physicians with information that was once provided by the sales reps.

The pharmaceuticals have responded to changes in their marketplace by reducing sales personnel, providing drastic price discounts, and assigning sales teams to work with managed-care organizations. But the relationship is not the same. Kaiser, the USA's largest managed-care organization, is especially harsh in its new mood toward detailers. "With very few exceptions, there is no legitimacy to drug detailing . . . it's selling," Francis J. Crosson, Jr., Kaiser's associate medical director for Northern California told *The Wall Street Journal*. "The costs are just being passed on to little old ladies who need their hypertension medicine. The whole process is offensive, and we have no interest in promoting it."

Wal-Mart's Message to Sales Brokers

Health care is not alone in rethinking the costs associated with full-service sales. The megalithic Wal-Mart chain in recent years has moved to eliminate completely the third-party sales broker or independent manufacturer's representatives from the company's product buying systems, preferring to deal only with manufacturers' suppliers. Wal-Mart's chairman and chief executive officer, David D. Glass, made the move in an effort to further utilize electronic data interchange (EDI) with direct links to its suppliers, a system that provides a way for each supplier to know just how much product is on the shelves and in warehouses so the manufacturer can upgrade or alter production schedules in response. In one fell swoop, Wal-Mart sliced away a whole layer of salespeople and sales brokers, in effect saying, "You're only adding costs, not value, to our supply chain."

In a similar move, Sears Roebuck & Co. has also moved to eliminate independent salespeople and brokers, in an effort to consolidate purchasing practices and keep retail prices down. All across the economic landscape, major corporations are seeking to reduce the number of suppliers they work with, and midlevel and smaller corporations are moving in this direction as well. In the past, the idea was that multiple and competing suppliers would keep prices low. Now, however, in a less-is-more philosophy, companies are paring down the number of suppliers who sell to them, making the selling environment all that more difficult in both manufacturing and services.

Against this backdrop of rampant changes, one thing is increasingly clear. Willy Loman, the hapless, sample-case carrying character in the play *Death of a Salesman*, who got by "on a smile and a shoeshine," is history. Selling today is a complex, demanding, yet rewarding profession for those who understand the new imperative: Figure out how to create greater value in the act of selling itself.

CREATING GREATER VALUE IN THE SALES PROCESS

Value, as we've seen, is created by adding something that the customer wants, such as information or the meeting of special requirements. Conversely, it can be created by taking something *away* the customer doesn't want.

The value-adding sales professional knows that each customer has wants and needs that are as individualized as fingerprints. Understanding and translating that understanding of those needs and wants are where the rubber meets the road in the new selling environment. Indeed, the same downsizing and reengineering that has created such a challenge for sales organizations has also created an opportunity. For as organizations flattened out their hierarchies, legions of middle managers have been squeezed out, taking their knowledge and expertise with them. The remaining managers are often desperate for information, ideas, and creative solutions to their problems, a gap that can be filled by the salesperson and sales force with training in problem solving and creative expertise.

In the past, sales training was *based on the salesperson*, on perfecting his or her ability to pitch the product and inflate the customer with self-serving slogans and complimentary phrases, all intended to appeal to the customer's ego. Focusing on the customer's problems and issues was secondary at best. That method of selling is now history. It's either add value at the point of sale or lower your price in an ever-descending spiral.

Here are some specific ways sales professionals can add value:

- By providing information about product, features, industry trends, and competing products, the salesperson becomes a valuable part of the decision-making process, a consultant, in effect.

- The salesperson can extend the customer's network and often provides key contacts to other suppliers or industry experts.

- Salespeople can become quality-control ensurors of their own firms. By facilitating critical delivery schedules, tailoring inventory flow, and meeting other unique customer requirements, they become indispensable.

- By training your people to see themselves as industry experts, your sales team is able to help build the customer's bottom line, reduce costs, find key personnel, streamline business operations, and often locate sources of capital or financing, and otherwise bring more to the relationship.

With these methods of rethinking the role a salesperson plays, let's revisit the seven value strategies we first discussed in Chapter 4, this time from the sales perspective

Value-Added Sales Strategy 1:
Make the Customer's Life Easier

Making the customer's life easier isn't a single thing a sales professional does; rather it's a matter of the entire approach to selling. "We make the customer's life easier in the application of knowledge and contract responsibility, and we customize solutions to individual client problems," says Bill Whitcroft, president of Babush Corp., a Menomenee, Wisconsin, distributor of conveyor systems. "Ours is not an inventory-on-the-shelf kind of business. We don't know how to build a building, and we don't know how to do sewers, and we don't know tank removal, but we sure as hell know how to move packages."

Babush's sales engineers sell solutions. Their "hard" product is package conveyor systems, but what they're really selling is peace of mind to industrial customers throughout the state of Wisconsin. As a team, they work together to make the customer's life easier in countless ways.

> Our customer is confident that we know what we're doing, that we are people of our word, and that we will give him more than the minimum standard, so he doesn't have sweat in the palms of his hands anymore. We earn his business and his trust.

Whitcroft's company, with $6-million annual revenues, sees its mission as a "wholesaler of engineering solutions" involved strictly in the conveyor field. According to the terms of his company's agreement with its principal equipment manufacturer/supplier, Hytrol, Inc., of Jonesboro, Arkansas, the company operates only in Wisconsin. Babush Corp., which Bill Whitcroft bought in 1969, specializes in conveyors that move packages, anywhere from a 2-pound box to a 6,000-pound pallet.

Whitcroft and his 11-person sales engineering team, in addition to 4 independent dealers/sellers, provide customized services to a variety of industries in need of package conveyor systems. Their typical projects often have a 26- to 30-week life span, as he and his sales engineers design, manufacture, install, and start up the operations of their conveyor systems.

Whitcroft's sales engineers make life easier for customers by listening to customers and learning what their wants and needs are, and then by tailoring the project to solve their problems. "If they want one purchasing order or 19 of them, that's what we give them," Whitcroft says.

"If they want to be their own general manager, it's their choice. I haven't hidden the talent under a green eye shade in the office," Whitcroft says, referring to his sales engineers.

> They're out there talking to the customer face to face, because I don't think a customer ought to waste his time with clerks. That's helped us a lot, because it's given us terrific repeat business. I put a lot of authority in those sales engineers. They're the ones who determine the final selling price. They are the ones that commit on the delivery schedule; they manage the cash flow of the product. They have a lot of authority and the customer knows that. So, in effect, when customers are dealing with my sales engineer, they're really dealing with the "owner" as far as they're concerned.

At Babush, the downsizing that has so decimated midlevel management ranks is turned into an opportunity. "With all the changes in middle management, particularly in the manufacturing area, engineering departments have gotten thinner and thinner, or in some cases, evaporated," Whitcroft explains. "Now they have to spend capital money and they haven't got the brainpower to help them buy [complex] capital equipment. So they are leaning more and more on specialty houses like ours."

Whitcroft also sells *trust*, for it is trust that makes his customers' lives infinitely easier. His customers have to know that Babush cannot only make the bid but also provide the knowledge and expertise necessary to make the system he sells and installs make money for them. He keeps his customers' "palms from sweating," and that certainly makes their lives easier.

Making your customers' lives easier starts with knowing your customers' business and how you can creatively solve their problems and address their concerns. When was the last time your sales team did in-depth profiles of your customers' operations and their concerns? What are the extras that your salespeople can perform to let your customers know that you are out to make their lives easier?

Value-Added Selling Strategy 2: Provide Greater Responsiveness

As the leader, you're also the top sales consultant, and responsiveness to the customer begins at the top and works its way very quickly to your salespeople. What this means is that your salespeople can only be as responsive as you encourage and enable them to be.

Dell Computers founder and CEO Michael Dell knows the power of responsiveness to customers. Every Friday morning, the company holds a "customer advocate meeting" with reps who handle both incoming and outgoing calls, review the week's customer complaints, and come up with solutions for the problems discussed. Dell associates know the computer marketing company's credo: The customer must be "pleased, not just satisfied." That sense of responsiveness has worked; in less than a decade, the firm has risen to the top in computer sales and customer satisfaction.

Ron L. Yates, vice-president for sales and marketing for Jefferson Smurfit Corp., the nation's second-largest manufacturer of corrugated packaging, also lives by responsiveness. Smurfit, based in St. Louis, had been producing corrugated packaging for General Electric refrigerators when GE suddenly found itself in need of increased packaging for its new plant in Decatur, Georgia. Yates responded to the customer's challenge by coordinating inventory from three different plants, balancing shipments from other designated schedules, and keeping GE's rapidly changing needs satisfied.

Sometimes greater responsiveness comes about when staffers who support salespersons discover ways to enable it. When Robinson Brick, a Denver-based, family-owned brickmaker, wanted to increase its sales, the firm initiated a plan in which salespeople would take one employee into the field with them at least once a month. New ideas and information flowed back into the plant, and the company developed new ways of delivering product and customer service. Result: The firm expanded its distribution base from 15 brick distributors in 1987 to 115 by 1992.

Another word for greater responsiveness is *speed*. Speed of satisfaction of the customer's request, need, problem. Bill Whitcroft of Babush recalled a request for a proposal that needed to be on the customer's desk within a day and a half. Here is the way Whitcroft described what happened next:

> Normally, it was the kind of thing that would take 10 days to 2 weeks, because of other workload that was ahead of it, plus a couple of days on the drawing board, a couple of days of pricing, but

this client needed the proposal to show to his decision-making team within a day and a half. It was either go for it, and give it to him in a day and a half, or forget about it. My people just rolled up their sleeves and did it. It totaled $300,000 and required a lay-out system that we did on our CAD equipment. We met his deadline and got a $300,000 competitive proposal, well-engineered, within a day and a half. It was amazing.

Whitcroft recalls that the customer ended up looking like a hero to his people. "That kind of thing can happen and does happen, not regularly, of course, but it sure brings the [customer] back."

VALUE-ADDED SALES STRATEGY 3: TAKE ON YOUR CUSTOMER'S PROBLEM

One form of taking on your customer's problem has been through industry "partnering." We saw it earlier in this book, where, in one example, Wal-Mart and Procter & Gamble are now partnering to keep Pampers stocked on Wal-Mart's shelves. Partnering, in one form or another, can be an effective way to take on your customer's problem and build a long-term relationship with customers.

G&F Industries, a $3-million Sturbridge, Massachusetts, manufacturer of molded plastics, was presented with an opportunity to take on a customer's problem when Bose, the half-billion-dollar-a-year company that makes speakers, also based in Massachusetts, proposed that G&F partner with it by having a full-time person stationed at Bose. This would help Bose save on various aspects of its own operations and would ensure a solid growth pattern for the smaller supplier.

G&F's president, John Argitis, faced a dilemma that is becoming more and more common these days: taking on a customer's problem and making it pay. After thinking it over, and penciling through the projections, Argitis went with it, even though there were risks involved to his company's overall operations.

"This has changed our whole way of doing business," Argitis says, "but I never thought it would work this well. Instead of spending time trying to get new accounts, we concentrate on servicing and pricing. You don't really sell; you look for opportunities." The result of partnering with Bose?

G&F's bottom line has grown 25 to 40 percent per year, and volume of sales has increased from $3 million to $15 million and climbing! In that case, partnering paid off in spades!

How One Power Equipment Distributor Reinvented Its Sales Operation

Coye Consultants, Inc., is a Brevard, North Carolina, power equipment distributor of Toro and Lawn-Boy equipment to independent dealers in the Southeast. The firm does $20 million annually with only 13 employees, 9 of whom are in sales. It distributes Toro and Lawn-Boy lawnmowers and small tractors and other professional grass-cutting equipment. "We help someone do their business better, and they're going to return the favor by buying more product from us, or through us," says Art Coye, president.

Coye has built his company in great measure through value-added services, principally in marketing and promotion, for his dealers. His sales consultants go the extra mile to prepare promotional layouts, advising customers on methods to improve their own advertising and marketing efforts. "They work with dealers and establish missions statements for them," Coye explains, "and often the mission statement can become the core of a dealer's promotional advertising. My consultants try to find what is most unique about that dealership, and then help them to exploit it to the maximum."

One of Coye's own promotional efforts, what he calls an "EduVacation," is offered to his independent dealers, a 3-day event held at the historic Grove Park Inn Resort at Asheville, North Carolina. At such events, dealers are treated to a combination of business seminars and family-style fun. Coye's annual gathering of dealers and their families offers a combination product expo with educational seminars on issues of importance to customers.

Coye adds value in other ways as well. The firm's Senior Dealer Consultants are electronically linked to the home office through the use of Macintosh Powerbooks. Coye keeps the dealers' mastheads and letterheads on a hard drive on a public folder that the Senior Dealer Consultants can download as an E-mail attachment.

"They can download the customized type style for that particular dealership right on the phone lines while they are there, and then use that either in an ad for the newspaper, or for customized hand tags, or for a brochure for an open house, or a print for the dealer right while they're there with him. So that's really where our focus is, doing things for dealers that they can't do for themselves." Coye is a big advocate for new technology: "If you don't get up on the technology curve, you're going to get swept under; that's all there is to it."

In one instance, Coye helped one of his dealers, Vassey Lawn & Garden Centers, with a marketing campaign designed to offset the fact that the dealer was 10 to 25 miles from its prime marketing area. The promotion, "Man Alive—It's Worth the Drive!", was backed up with a $2,000 local television campaign, and resulted in $80,000 in sales over the 2-day event at the dealership.

In a highly competitive industry, Nabisco Biscuit's salespeople were voted number 1 in a survey of over 1,000 retail managers who had plenty of others to choose from. Why? Because Nabisco Biscuit's salespeople are trained to be "extensions of the store," and, as such, they take on their retailer/customers' problems.

At Nabisco, the sales force is responsible for getting the product onto the shelves, certainly, but more important, it's also their jobs to get it *out of the store* and into the people's homes. Nabisco knows that its customers' problems are also its own. In its efforts to win the great cookie wars, the company increased funds for building its sales force and hired 400 merchandisers to handle tasks such as taking care of store displays and placing products on the shelves, thus leaving more time for salespeople to interact with store managers.

Value-Added Selling Strategy 4: Empower the Customer Through Knowledge

Ellet Bros. of Chapin, South Carolina, the largest, publicly owned distributor of sporting goods in the United States, has a secret weapon: Every morning begins with a 45-minute briefing and sales training class that all 143 of its sales associates must attend. That's almost 4 hours of training a week.

These training sessions arm Ellet's sales force with up-to-date information on product and sales, which the telemarketers then pass on to the customers. Ellet knows the value of empowering customers through knowledge, and its dedication to the salesperson's storehouse of information is paying off with greater sales.

"We sell three things," says Joe Murray, president of Ellet Bros., "ourselves, our products, and *information.*" With products ranging from rifles to rubber night crawlers to boogie boards, Ellet distributes to over 18,000 independent sporting goods retailers, most of which are family-owned stores dependent on product information from sales distributors.

Ellet Bros. morning marketing and information sessions might include a manufacturer's representative demonstrating the correct use of a new product, and its goal is providing more information to arm their telemarketers. "If Remington says they're raising prices 5 percent at the end of the month," says Murray, "our sales associates are made aware of this in the morning briefings. We have the ability to contact our entire customer base of 18,000 within 2 days to give them this information."

Contrast this with the traditional sales method where the outside rep may not come around or make any kind of contact for a period of weeks, or even months. Ellet Bros. philosophy has always been to serve the needs of the customer, rather than cater to the biases or preferences of individual salespeople. When the company first pioneered selling by phone nationally in the sporting goods industry, founder Chilton Ellet hired almost all women in what had previously been a man's world of back-slapping good old boys.

Early on, Ellet's founder trained his sales associates to listen, to find out what the customer wanted, and to provide it. Thirty years ago, that wasn't done by traveling *salesmen* (only men sold sporting goods). The traditional method was to push their favorite rifle, fly fishing rod, or whatever products were their personal favorites at the expense of representing the entire product line and serving their customers' needs. As Murray recounts it, sporting goods salesmen of old were attracted—and hired—because they themselves were hobbyists. Their motivation was that they wanted to be around the hunters, fishermen, and consumers of the products in general.

"Our salespeople are not selected because they are sports enthusiasts or hobbyists," Murray says. "They aren't going to get into philosophical discussions of Remington over Winchester. They just want to make the sale and please the customer."

At Ellet Bros., telemarketers are selected by their desire to learn rather than by their experience as hobbyists. Often as not, they're uninformed about the merchandise when they first come on board. An intensive 12-week training course provides them with a depth of knowledge and sales skills that are used to empower the customer to make the best choices.

Empowering the customer through knowledge is the key to Ellet's success. Although it doesn't field a single representative, the firm's positioning is definitely more-for-more. "We're at the high end of pricing," says Murray. Since every distributor has access to the same products, neutralizing Q Factor advantages, it might be assumed that independent retailers would place their orders with the distributor who has the lowest prices. But this isn't the case. Knowledgeable sales associates make the difference.

Still, Ellet Bros. is the largest sporting goods distributor in the country. Ellet's people empower their customers through knowledge—and that's a value that has no price.

Sales force training can't be overestimated. The knowledge received in sessions—whether product specific or industrywide—comes back to you in spades when that salesperson passes on what he or she learned to your customers.

"I've got 11 employees total, and 6 of us are going to Chicago for a 2- day training session," says Bill Whitcroft of Babush Corp., "and it costs a lot of money. It's time away from sales, it's motels, expenses. But I can't afford *not* to have my people get the best training possible. They've got to keep that education going so they're armed with information to pass on to the customer."

For Whitcroft and his team, it's a three-pronged approach: They receive training from the trade association's presenters, they fly down periodically to their manufacturer's Memphis plant, and they have regular in-house brainstorming and information-trading sessions, including a 3-hour formal meeting on the first Monday of every month. "Part of our in-house meeting," Whitcroft says, "is to get current on what everybody is doing. So every proposal in the house always has at least two pairs of eyeballs on it."

Empowering the customer through knowledge has also become the watchword at IBM. In 1990, IBM employed 150,000 salespeople worldwide. By the mid-90s, that number had been reduced to 70,000 and was continuing to dwindle. While part of the decrease was related to IBM's difficulties, it also represents a dramatic remaking of its sales operation. Where IBM had made its mark through an army of salespeople and a "name" that was synonymous with top-of-the-line quality, the new IBM is relying on personnel who are as capable as consultants as they were as salespeople.

Previously, IBM had it "their way," but now the customer, much more knowledgeable than in the past, demands it his or her way. Previously, IBM's sales force focused on selling equipment, but the new customer, corporate or individual, wanted *help* not just the hardware.

One of the horror stories from the "old" era had to do with GTE Corp., one of IBM's leading customers. When GTE announced its intentions to move from the old mainframe computers to a new system utilizing networks of smaller, less-expensive computers, Big Blue's sales representatives tried to discourage it. Instead of going with the customer's needs and selling to that, IBM talked itself out of the sale. GTE went with Hewlett-Packard, much to IBM's chagrin.

IBM's revised sales force has had to create new sales systems to cater to the variety of consumers, corporate and individual. The new IBM strategy involves *accepting the variety of consumer needs* and providing responses tailored to the customer's wishes. Now the customers can avail themselves of services from IBM product specialists, use its telephone marketing services, have a representative come and see them, or never see a salesperson at all.

IBM has refined its sales teams so that each team has a market area, such as financial services, travel, health care, utilities, etc. Its goal is to provide knowledge and services specific to those areas of business, and in so doing, its sales teams are able to design the sales package to the customers' specifications.

In a sense, IBM's consultants also must empower the customer through its knowledge of the equipment and services. Increased training procedures were initiated, including a voluntary 1-year certification program for sales consultants. This special training course includes 3 weeks at Harvard, where the consultants study general business courses, consulting, and one course tailored to the type of industry they're going to be focusing on.

Another change is that IBM's sales consultants aren't limited to recommending the company's products. This has opened the door to further empowering the customer through knowledge, because IBM's sales consultants can educate the customers and offer solutions from a broad array of sources, not only its own. A recent survey showed that about one-third of the equipment IBM now installs is from other sources. Thus the sales consultant has knowledge of a number of systems other than IBM's, and armed with this knowledge and additional sales capabilities, the salesperson is better able to empower customers and their needs.

Value-Added Sales Strategy 5: Manage the Customer's Complexity

When GM's Saturn division was planning its sales approach, senior executives introduced a weeklong seminar for salespeople in which one of the main points involved a "low-key" approach to what has always been a high-gear profession: auto sales. Saturn added value by taking the complexity out of the way cars are sold, a process that normally, in many customers' mind, ranks just above a root canal operation. In place of the leisure-suited, high-pressure salesperson, Saturn offers a low-key, no-haggle service-oriented process designed to create a long-term relationship—and great word-of-mouth promotion.

Instead of the salesperson who'd do everything he or she could short of writing the check, Saturn's sales force adopted a series of new methods *designed to manage out some of the customer's complexity*, including a combination of training sessions that were group encounters, where the salespeople interact with one another as a team, and the "Saturn Cheer," where all the salespeople in a showroom gather together and cheer the new customer as the customer is handed the keys to the car. It's a ritual that brings the customer into the Saturn family, saying, in effect, "We're all in this together." And buyers definitely talk up this part of the sales process; customer satisfaction ratings for Saturn are just behind Lexus and Infiniti, which cost up to 5 times as much as a Saturn.

Saturn saw the customer's complexity and eliminated the hassle. The response to the car and the simplified sales process has been excellent, and now other car dealers have begun to adopt the less-complicated approach.

In today's business environment, a customer's complexity can affect various levels of the operation, and the solutions usually come from many different members of a sales team.

Manco Incorporated, a Westlake, Ohio, distributor of industrial supplies, quickly became aware of the idea of managing its customers' complexities when retailers started asking the firm to manage inventory of the product. Manco's president, Tom Corbo, realized that it was "a burden we *like*; it gives us more control." What Corbo discovered was that value-added selling has many layers to it, and one of those is the need of the salesperson to seek out those opportunities to come up with solutions to the customer's complex problems. Corbo correctly interprets today's selling environment as one that requires teamwork, as opposed to the traditional, old-time methods where the salesperson was a force of one.

"The salesperson doesn't have all the answers and is foolish to pretend to," Corbo observes. Corbo's company, in managing its customer's complexity, might call on as many as 20 different people from its ranks when developing solutions to present to the customer. Manco's ability to solve customers' complex inventory problems has resulted in ongoing relationships with giants such as Wal-Mart and K-Mart, and an annual sales chart well over $80 million.

Managing customer complexity isn't only a business-to-business issue, it's also a way of adding value in the retail sector as well. John Riley, president of Fletcher Music Centers of Clearwater, Florida, knows about that. In an effort to breathe life into a business that had become stagnant, Fletcher analyzed its main customers to such a degree that it came away with new information about their complexities, which in turn enabled it to create a successful sales strategy.

Fletcher's research showed that its main body of customers—retirees—were seeking companionship in their later years. Armed with information about the complexities of senior living and lifestyles, the firm had keyboards and knobs redesigned to make it easier for those with arthritic fingers. It created group classes, bringing customers together for lessons that had a partylike atmosphere and gave the mostly seniors opportunities to meet and socialize with one another.

And Fletcher invested time in its sales associates, convincing them that they and their salespeople were not selling organs: They were selling a balm to the customer's soul, music, and the companionship of others that music brings. Result? Fletcher Music Centers has doubled its sales to $22 million in a market that had been going down for years.

How well do you know your customer's complexity? What can you and your sales team bring to the table to help manage it?

Value-Added Sales Strategy 6: Involve the Customer in Creating Value

"Our real sales tack is that we're offering them an *a la carte* menu," Bill Whitcroft of Babush says. "They can buy engineering only, or engineering and hardware and mechanical installation, or all that with controls, or all that with field wiring, or all that with operator education. How far do you want us to take it?" Whitcroft emphasizes.

Bill Whitcroft uses the analogy of building a house: You can design it yourself or you can hire an architect; you can buy the supplies and then supervise the crew, or hire a general contractor who takes on the responsibilities, etc., and all you do is pay the bills. Whatever is easiest, most efficient for the customer, that's what his company comes up with. And under Babush's system, the sales engineer also supervises the entire project for the client, if requested, from start to finish. This kind of "unbundling" of the services can be a central component of adding value by involving the customer as a partner in the selling process.

Like IBM, which went from a "have it our way" sales approach to a "have it *your* way" tact, Whitcroft has unbundled his offerings to such an extent that it's really almost all *a la carte*. Value-added selling has come to require that the sales team offer a buffet of possibilities where the customer is directly involved in selecting—and thus creating—the value.

Value-Added Sales Strategy 7: Out-customize the Competition

Think about it this way: How many times have you, as a consumer, made a request of a salesperson only to be told, "We don't offer that." What did you do? You probably continued looking around until you discovered a firm that could meet your request.

Customizing is an attitude of trying to meet each customer's needs, even if it's not what you normally do, or what you'd prefer to do because it's easiest for you. It can be one of the most powerful things you can do to build a lasting customer relationship. Customizing the sales of your products and services to fit your customers' needs means first *hearing and sometimes seeing* those needs and then fulfilling them. What happens when new or unusual sales-related requests are made of your company? Certainly you won't be able to accommodate them all, but at least try and meet as many of them as you can. Make it part of your mission to be the business that is willing to customize, willing to meet those off-the-wall requests. The long-term payoff can be surprising.

I once heard of a restaurant that would make anything the customer requested, even if it wasn't on the regular menu. So long as the chef had the ingredients, the rule of the house was, "It may take a little longer, but we can do it for you." Broadcasting this attitude and publicizing the way your sales force is ready to accommodate a customer's unusual request sends an important message to your sales associates: It tells them to be open minded to the need for special requests and allow for creative thinking—in other words, to customize.

Take Kraft General Foods, which dominates grocery store shelves and accounts for 10 percent of the brand names in a typical supermarket. In the early 90s, KGF reorganized its sales force to form "account business teams" that would cater to its key buyers, chains such as Winn-Dixie in the South, Pathmark stores, and over 300 other major buying groups. The teams keep their product specialties, but they cross-pollinate between them in order to *customize* the product mixes between each for their group of customers.

Customization can lead to whole new business ideas, and sometimes even new industries. Federal Express was born because Fred Smith kept getting requests from business people who needed to charter one of his aircraft to get a package to another city in a hurry. When enough of those requests added up, it lit the idea-fuse in Smith's mind, and he customized what became a worldwide enterprise. Customization also has side rewards—the creation of new methods of doing business, which can also have an effect on sales:

Marshall Industries, an El Monte, California, electronics distributor, fills over 3,000 orders a day, packaging them into 1,700 separate boxes. Because many customers have special packaging requirements—from type of packing material to where the label is on the outside of the box—the warehouse keeps a thick manual detailing its customers' requirements. When several customers informed them that they didn't like the peanut packaging material because it made a mess in their warehouses, Marshall responded by researching the field and coming up with a paper packaging material that didn't make the mess and could be obtained at a comparable price.

Marshall customized the solution to the customer's problem. And the firm found that the customization for one customer was applicable to other segments of their market. The result: customer satisfaction. A surprise benefit from its responsiveness was that the new materials required less special handling at the plant, thus saving additional time and money for Marshall.

The result of employing these selling strategies? You sell on value, not price.

A salesperson was in a tough two-way race for a large chunk of business from a major farm equipment manufacturer. The two were the only ones left standing after a battery of other contenders had been eliminated. Finally, after much discussion behind closed doors, Mr. A., our hero, was called in to the head buyer's office and informed that his company would not get the sale because its price was too high.

Mr. A. was just about to accept his company's loss, but as he got up to leave, he noticed the buyer was wearing an expensive brand of boots.

"That's quite a pair of boots you've got there," he said to the buyer. Surprised, the buyer said he appreciated that Mr. A. had noticed his fine taste, and so they exchanged a few words about the hand tooling and calfskin leather and the unique color.

Then Mr. A. had an inspiration. "What made you buy those boots instead of taking any old pair off the shelf?" he inquired with his best Colombo look of concern.

There was a long moment of silence, and then the head buyer began to smile. He realized what Mr. A. was really saying, and within a few minutes, he changed his mind and gave the sale to Mr. A.'s company.

I really like this story because Mr. A. made the head buyer stop and think for a moment: In his own life, something as personal as boots, the buyer went for quality, for added value, and not for price. Mr. A. had brought that home to him, in a very graphic, personal way—and he rescued the sale for his team.

The value-added sales force must educate the customer, and he or she has to do it in the customer's own language. In Mr. A.'s case, the "language" was boots.

A Quick Review

Let's review the seven strategies for adding value to the sales process:

1. *Make the Customer's Life Easier*: Bill Whitcroft at Babush sells them engineering solutions.

2. *Provide Greater Responsiveness*: Michael Dell holds a "customer advocate meeting" with all his employees to review customer complaints.

3. *Take on Your Customer's Problems*: Art Coye's sales consultants roll up their sleeves and tackle the customers' marketing dilemmas.

4. *Empower the Customer Through Knowledge*: Joe Murray at Ellet Bros. has his 143 telemarketers selling *information*. They empower the customer through knowledge, and that adds value, which commands price.

5. *Manage the Customer's Complexity*: GM's Saturn salespeople take the complexity *out* of buying a car, in effect managing the customer's complexity— and win customers in the process.

6. *Involve the Customer in Creating Value*: IBM unbundles its offerings and even adds other companies' products to its menu.

7. *Out-customize the Competition*: Marshall Industries sets out to customize for one customer, and develops a new packaging method that also applies to other customers—and saves itself money in the process.

Review these seven strategies in terms of your own salespeople and sales force as a whole. How can they be applied to your business? Which of these might you have overlooked? Which could be amplified? Salespeople who add value are tremendously important in winning the Value Revolution. But the other people back at the office are important, too, and in the next chapter we'll look at some winning strategies for delivering greater value through all your associates.

10

DELIVERING CUSTOMER VALUE THROUGH PEOPLE

"To get the job done, we have to have the same values."

—Lawrence Bossidy, CEO, Allied Signal

GENERAL ELECTRIC CHAIRMAN JACK WELCH WAS meeting with several hundred employees who had just been laid off. Naturally enough, these people weren't too happy.

"How come I was worthwhile yesterday," one man wanted to know, "but I'm not worthwhile today?"

Welch was sympathetic when he explained: "Look, it's not that you're not worthwhile, but you've just got to understand something. What you were doing is no longer competitive."

As unfortunate as the situation was, Welch did what the marketplace forced him to do: cut people. The message of the Value Revolution is a tough one: The only job security any of us have is by winning in the marketplace. And to win in the marketplace, as we've seen throughout this book, means providing your customers with better and better value that keeps them loyal to you and your offerings. No matter how great your firm's offerings *were* or how great its reputation *was*, what matters is what's happening right now between your customers and your firm.

Your people are, inevitably, a major part of the Value Proposition you offer to customers, and they are vitally important in the delivery of customer value. So in this chapter, we'll examine the role all employees play in creating customer value, and I'll make specific recommendations on things you can do to help everyone on your team understand his or her role in creating value. We'll look at what you owe them, and what you must demand of them to win the Value Revolution.

Winning the Value Revolution

So what's the right way to go? What can you, the CEO, do to make sure that your people—managers, salespeople, staff—fully understand the new realities and unrelenting demands of the Value Revolution? How best to communicate with your associates and spell out exactly what you expect and how they can meet your expectations? Here's a possible speech you might give at the next all-company meeting:

> Good morning, everybody. I've called everyone together to discuss a vital topic: your future employment at this company. The fact is there is today a Value Revolution going on in the global economy and it affects us here at this company. The message of this Value Revolution is that our customers are in the driver's seat. They will not pay for inefficiency in the way we make and deliver our products and services. They will not be loyal to us just because they've done business with us in the past. They will always gravitate to the best relative value as they define it. What worked yesterday cannot be presumed to work today, and what works well today almost assuredly will not satisfy tomorrow. And whether we like this situation or hate it doesn't matter. It's the way things are. So, I want to help you help this company create the success in the marketplace that will ensure job security for all of us. I want to coach you in delivering better value to our customers.

Do you want to ensure you're going to be successful with this company in the future? Are you concerned about your position in the firm? Feeling vulnerable that you might be on the list of people who get cut in the next round of layoffs?

If your answer is Yes to these questions, realize first of all that that's the Value Revolution touching your life. The reality is that there will never be job security at this firm; there will be only the opportunity to create job security by winning in the marketplace. You will be employed by us as long as you add value to the organization. You—not me as CEO—are continuously responsible for finding ways to add that value. In return, you have the right to demand certain things from management: You have the right to the resources you need to perform your job; you have the right to be paid in a way that fairly reflects your contribution; and you have the right to receive the training and retraining necessary to perform your job, which will constantly evolve as we move into the future.

When you get up in the morning and are driving to work, think in terms of how you can add more value today to this organization than you did yesterday. How can you create new value, rather than cost? How can you rethink and reinvent the way you do what you do such that you cut costs and add value? This is the challenge ahead of each of us. Thank you.

What would be the effect if you were to deliver such a message to your people? Do they realize these things already, or have you never taken the time to spell them out? Have you implied job security, thinking that this was the only way to gain their cooperation? The fact is, employees think about their security all the time. While it may not be a topic of conversation, it's in their hearts and minds. And while such a speech may need to be modified, it provides the groundwork on which you can adapt your message.

The rest of this chapter is devoted to looking at what else you can do to manage for greater value, but before we turn to specific suggestions, let's look at several firms that are already doing an excellent job of partnering with their employees to produce excellent customer value.

How Southwest Airlines Delivers Customer Value Through People

Southwest Airlines, as we have seen earlier in this book, is clearly winning the Value Revolution. By providing less of the traditional service customers expect of an airline, Southwest has been able to charge less in the way of fares and has profited consistently for 23 years from this positioning. But plenty of no-frills airlines have had their wings clipped in this tough-as-nails industry, and the vast majority didn't survive. What distinguishes Southwest? In a word, its people: the pilots, ramp agents, flight attendants, mechanics, reservations representatives, baggage handlers, and thousands of others who make this value-creating machine fly each and every day. Much of the credit for this highly motivated work force goes to Southwest CEO Herb Kelleher. Herb cares.

Herb's care is reflected in the time spent selecting, monitoring, and recognizing those who work for this feisty airline. Known as a boss who's willing to listen, he has been known to join 3 a.m. cleanup crews with coffee and donuts. An unpredictable practical jokester, he arm-wrestles co-workers over disputes and is given to spontaneous Elvis impersonations. Other times, Herb can be found flying aboard his own planes introducing himself to customers and chatting, or out on the tarmac interacting with employees, seeing that things are going okay.

When asked why they are motivated to work so hard, employees respond: "You don't want to let Herb down." Southwest enjoys the highest rate of employee retention in the airline industry, with loss rates in some stations of less than 5 percent per year. Southwest is consistently named one of the 10 best places to work.

Result: Southwest associates pass on Kelleher's sense of caring to passengers. A highly cooperative, friendly, productive, and fun-loving work force is evident everywhere. Flight attendants have been known to croon their preflight safety announcements in the melodies of pop tunes and classical favorites ("Please keep your tush on the cush until we have come to a complete stop at the gate"), or to surprise passengers by popping in and out of overhead luggage bins. Passengers are entertained by attendants wearing costumes on holidays.

Company policy strongly supports this "people first" ethic, and it begins in the hiring process. Hiring the right kind of people is so essential that Southwest routinely invites its frequent fliers, who often must take time out from their own jobs, to participate in the selection of flight attendants. If they don't give the thumbs up on a prospective employee, that person doesn't get hired. "We want people who are compassionate, who have positive attitudes, a sense of humor, and, especially in the management ranks, people who are not elitists," explained David Ridley, Southwest's vice-president of marketing. "We are the heaviest union airline; we will work with the unions; they want to get rid of bad attitudes just as much as we do."

Southwest is so sure of its employees that it stands behind them in those rare situations where customers complain. After investigating the complaint, says Ridley, "if we determine that the customer was wrong and [making unreasonable demands], we'll write the person and encourage him to try another airline. It's a real morale booster to our people to know that management won't second-guess their professional judgment. We don't believe the customer is always right."

Encouraging front-line employees to deliver excellent service day in and day out—even for those with the people-loving, patient, and outgoing personalities that Southwest searches so hard to find—is never easy. "Those folks are our customers," says Ridley, explaining how the marketing department team sometimes shows up unexpectedly to greet an incoming flight and goes to work cleaning the plane's interior, which is usually the responsibility of the flight attendants. "In a service environment, if your people aren't delivering good service, it doesn't matter how good your niche is."

Levi Strauss: Pioneering Values-Based Management

What are the values of your firm? At San Francisco-based Levi Strauss, the privately held manufacturer of apparel, the predominant vision is that customer value comes from the values of its employees. That's why one-third of a manager's raise can depend on how well he or she lives up to the company's innovative "aspiration statement," the company's credo that guides its innovative values-based philosophy. They are:

1. *Honesty.* Management must exemplify "directness, openness to influence, commitment to the success of others, and willingness to acknowledge our own contributions to problems." Example: One employee took a

chance and criticized her boss for what she considered heavy-handed behavior. To her surprise, he agreed and changed his act. Says the employee: "I found that 'aspirations' isn't about New Age feel-good, it's about being open and direct. It's about getting rid of hidden agendas."

2. Diversity. Levi's "values a diverse work force (age, sex, ethnic group, sexual orientation, etc.) at all levels of the organization . . . differing points of view will be sought; diversity will be valued and honestly rewarded, not suppressed." Fact: The company has doubled the percentage of minority managers to 36 percent, since Robert Haas became CEO in 1984. Women have climbed from 32 percent of the management ranks to 54 percent in the same period.

3. Recognition. Levi's will provide "greater recognition—both financial and psychic—for individuals and teams that contribute to our success . . . those who create and innovate and those who continually support day-to-day business requirements."

4. High Ethical Standards. Management should epitomize "the stated standards of ethical behavior. We must provide clarity about our expectations and must enforce these standards throughout the corporation." Impact: $40 million of Levi's business has pulled out of China in protest of human rights violations there.

5. Open Communications. Management is committed to being "clear about company, unit, and individual goals and performance. People must know what is expected of them and receive time, honest feedback". . . . Example: Levi's has a "360-degree review process," which requires that an employee be evaluated not just by his or her supervisor but also by subordinates and peers. A typical comment of a just-reviewed associate indicates just how intense, but eye opening, such feedback can be: "I thought I came across as more caring," said one manager. "It upset my self-image." Such in-your-face reviews caused this manager to reevaluate, listen more and be more empathetic.

6. Empowerment. Management must "increase the authority and responsibility of those closest to our products and customers. By actively pushing the responsibility, trust, and recognition into the operations, we can harness and release the capabilities of all our people."

And why would any company go to such extremes to set forth values so difficult to live up to? "We are not doing this because it makes us feel good—although it does—or because it is politically correct," observes Robert Haas. "We are doing it because we believe in the interconnection between liberating the talents of our people and business success."

HOME DEPOT: DELIVERING FRONT-LINE CUSTOMER VALUE

Because a work force committed to delivering value and customer satisfaction is so vital to Home Depot's success, the company hires only two people for every 100 who apply. Unlike many retailers, Home Depot has no part-time positions. Home Depot looks for extroverts who like to deal with people and who already have experience in the construction trades. And it invests heavily in training. All store employees attend product knowledge classes held weekly at each store, which help keep them learning more about all facets of home repair and improvement.

Founders Arthur Blank and Bernard Marcus don't expect the associates to sustain superior front-line service through pep rallies alone. They pay more than they might have to ensure they get the best. Wages typically start at $8 to $10 an hour, well above the retail average. Store managers earn bonuses of 50 percent of their base compensation, and assistant store managers 25 percent if sales and profit goals are hit. Store managers make $40,000 to $100,000 a year or more.

SERVICEMASTER: DELIVERING VALUE THROUGH "SERVICE PARTNERS"

Employees create value when they are empowered to respond to the needs of customers in creative ways. This requires people who are flexible and inventive, who are empathetic to the customer's needs, and who have the training to perform the service proficiently. And yet, how do you deliver these lofty qualities to customers when the type of work you do is mundane, dirty, and unstimulating, and requires that you pay rates that are at the bottom of the pay scale? According to estimates by Professor James Heskett of the Harvard Business School, there are increasing numbers of job-hopping, unskilled "nomads" in the American work force who have no ties or loyalty to any company, nor does any company have such ties to them. One company has found a way to engender loyalty from such ranks.

That company is ServiceMaster, based in Downers Grove, Illinois. The firm first made its mark as a cleaning services firm for hospitals and factories. It diversified in the late 80s, extending its services to other institutions such as schools and nursing homes, as well as providing a variety of residential services including house cleaning (through its Merry Maids unit), fertilizing lawns (TruGreen), and exterminating pests (Terminix). The company's motto seems to be, "We'll do your dirty work for you," leveraging, as we saw in an earlier chapter, the customer's time while providing peace of mind in the process.

To achieve its goal of "helping people grow," ServiceMaster starts with identifying and hiring "service partners" who want to improve their lives and are willing to work hard and make a commitment to the company and its customers. The company uses a 45-question interview called the Perceiver, which identifies people who are positive, committed, and empathetic. Not everyone makes the grade. The Merry Maids subsidiary rejects 9 out of every 10 applicants for entry-level positions.

Once hired, new employees are trained extensively in how to maximize performance in every job category. The five steps in the job skills training process are: (1) Explain the task; (2) the instructor performs the task; (3) the service partner performs the task; (4) the service partner teaches back the skill just learned; and (5) inspection and self-assessment. The training method gives employees a firm grasp of the particular job and pulls them into the process of empowerment right away in their having to teach the task immediately to someone else.

Great attention is given to the distinct parts of each task. The process of polishing a floor, for example, is divided into detailed, 5-minute steps. The manual explaining the proper procedure is 3 inches thick. Floor moppers learn how to stand straight while mopping, and to trace an S pattern on the floor while pulling the mop toward them (the conventional back and forth method can cause back injury and is less efficient).

ServiceMaster personnel continually look for ways of reducing the time and effort required to complete each task and have invented dozens of new techniques and cleaning equipment as a result. The ServiceMaster vacuum cleaner is battery operated, so the operator does not have to waste time dealing with an electrical cord. Cleaning a hospital room is completed in only 20 percent of the time it took 5 years ago, since employees began using a lighter-weight mop, while the company's pump-activated, soap-dispensing sponge has revolutionized wall cleaning. A recent innovation is the Walk Behind Scrubber, a self-propelled device that has reduced by 20 percent the time required to clean vinyl surfaces.

Once specific job skills have been mastered, ServiceMaster's new recruits turn their attention to training in the area of interpersonal skills. The People Development Programs each new hire is exposed to include: diversity awareness, which examines stereotypes and differences in people; change management, aimed at teaching transition skills; and the courtesy ambassador program, which focuses on employee interactions with customers. The aim here is to teach employees to provide courteous, caring, and friendly service and to heighten the awareness of the value of excellent service. The seven-step process for cleaning a hospital room, for example, begins with greeting the patient and ends with asking the patient if he or she needs anything else done. When service workers develop strong communication skills and are able to respond creatively to changing customer demands, this adds depth and dimension to what might otherwise be repetitive work.

Once employees are up and running at ServiceMaster, the learning is just beginning. In fact, continuous learning is a mandate for everyone, not an option. ServiceMaster, whose leaders make no bones about being followers of Jesus Christ, is driven by the desire to use the company as a vehicle for making the world a better place, and developing people, whose lives might otherwise not discover meaning and purpose who push hard to achieve their potential, rather than be treated as "units of production."

Through such avenues as regular team meetings, special training sessions, contracted instruction, and peer teaching, ServiceMaster spreads learning power. The goal: creating "teacher-learners."

"If a manager is too busy to teach," believes ServiceMaster's president William C. Pollard, "he or she is too busy to be a manager. People must constantly try to stretch from what they are to what they can become. Learners must be actively and responsively involved in their learning, growth, and development. Learning new skills and behaviors may be an uncomfortable stretch and might even create tension. But that's part of the process."

Pollard argues that if you want to encourage your employees' growth, you have to take responsibility for creating an open atmosphere for learning. This happens when you encourage and constantly seek to enhance the "gifts and strengths of the individual." In this atmosphere, employees are confident and willing to learn, and they have the highest motivation for doing their very best.

Pollard and other top managers do not run the far-flung company from a glass tower in Downers Grove. Pollard spends considerable time with employees, listening to their suggestions for improvements, and seeing that viable ones get implemented quickly. Managers must spend part of their time "in the shoes" of their workers, so that they do not lose a connection with the often grubby and strenuous realities of the task. This minimizes what the company calls *force stratification*, which is responsible for morale problems in many similar firms.

Employees who perform well can expect to move up rapidly in the organization. ServiceMaster aims to draw 20 percent of its managers from within its own ranks. An effective single-unit manager can soon have supervisory responsibilities for maintenance, custodial tasks, or other workers at more than one facility. Formal recognition programs keep the work from becoming humdrum: Pride Day, the Clean Equipment Program, the Wall of Fame program, and monthly Team Meetings all keep *esprit de corps* high and spread the ServiceMaster spirit.

It sounds pretty good, you might be thinking, but what's the bottom line? In a word, healthy. ServiceMaster reported a net income of $145 million in a recent year on sales of $2.8 billion. Indeed, since reaching its first billion in 1985, the firm has doubled its sales every 4 years. "When people can identify with the company's mission and see something beyond a paycheck," says Pollard," they are motivated to do a better job."

1. Establish a Continuous Value Improvement Process

Rubbermaid, the Wooster, Ohio-based maker of everything from dish drains to garbage cans, is consistently one of the most respected companies in America. When Rubbermaid establishes a "continuous value improvement process," you know they may be onto something. "We wanted to be sure our associates understood that you can bring value to the customer—including internal customers—in all kinds of ways," says George Thompson, vice-president of corporate communications at Rubbermaid.

As Rubbermaid is finding, developing a program that emphasizes customer value rather than just quality or service excellence is a smarter way of targeting what's truly important. Deeply understood, value thinking connects employees with customers in ways that quality programs or reengineering efforts seldom do. The main difference is that quality has as its key emphasis conformance to standards, in other words doing it (whatever it is) with zero defects, at lower costs, for the benefit of the company. Value, too, is doing it right, at lower costs, with zero defects in a way that maximizes customer value. It's a powerful discipline when everyone continually asks: How does what I'm doing right now ultimately add value to our customers? Is it extraneous? Should I be doing it at all? How can I do it better?

The key ingredient of a successful value improvement process is to make sure everyone knows how to measure the value she or he is producing for the firm and understands ways to raise that value in ways that matter to end customers.

Such a program is primarily a communication challenge. If you have already taken steps to rethink and bolster your firm's Value Proposition, now you must let your people know the importance of the value they create for customers. Undertaking a value improvement program begins by instructing your employees—even those who've never come into contact with one of your customers—to understand more about the overall business. Your team needs to know the impact of their work on the value perceptions of customers, whether internal or end customers. And above all, encourage all associates to see that their job security comes from winning in the marketplace.

2. Teach Your Employees How to "Own Their Own Employability"

Intel, the Silicon Valley maker of microprocessors and other complex electronic equipment, has been in the fortunate position of never having to lay off mass numbers of its highly educated work force. But that doesn't mean that the company won't have to in the future, or that individual employees won't be shed because they no longer add value. "We started originally planning careers like Big Brother," says Andrew S.

Grove, Intel's CEO. "But we gave up. It was too complicated and put too much of the onus on us [management]. "

Instead, Grove and other visionary leaders urge that individual employees take responsibility for guiding their own careers and increasing their market value by constant attention. "The only thing you can rely on is your ability to end up where the invisible hand of the economy wants you to be," says Grove. "Our phrase for it is 'owning your own employability.' "

Grove makes a good point. In an ever-changing world, it must be the responsibility of individual employees to continue to learn new skills and to manage change in the unique way of their particular specialty. But to be fair, the employing company owes it to employees to keep them informed with regard to changes that may affect on their individual prospects with the firm. Intel keeps up its side of the bargain with quarterly business updates, in which it outlines the company's recent financial situation, and, twice each year, shares strategic long-range plans.

However you do it, what's important is that you communicate with each new hire what your position is with regard to job security, and your expectations of how each employee might guide his or her career at your firm. Lay it on the table so that there can be no misunderstanding later. Put it in writing. Above all, keep the dialogue going as to what employees should be thinking about with respect to the issue of job security. Here are some suggestions on what employees need to think about, and how you can guide them in this respect:

1. *What's the value-added that my department and I provide to the end customer?* How is this relationship changing in light of the firm's overall financial condition? Is our Value Proposition secure, or are there forces at work in the marketplace that may weaken our position?

2. *What skills will my employees need in the immediate future, and who is encouraging them to learn those skills?* "My employers don't expect me to see 15 years into the future," commented one AT&T engineer we'll call Ned, "but they do expect me to recognize that the box I'm working on now will be a microchip in a year with 10 times as much software, and I'd better be ready."

Ned's engineering projects typically last a year or two. When they end, he must find another project to work on. If he can't find another job within the company within a few months, he must leave. Thus, Ned spends time thinking not just about his current project but also about discovering opportunities that might represent his future. He also thinks about how his skills are developing in relationship to technology that is ever-changing. "What will my role in the project be: electrical engineer, software writer, tester? Will I have a job?"

To stay current, Ned takes advantage of engineering and other courses that the company offers. "Even if my boss says No to covering the costs of such instruction, and even if he won't allow me to take time out to attend classes, it's up to me to find a time when I can take the courses I'll need in the future."

3. *Show employees how to own their own employability.* The employee at a large insurance company, let's call her Jean, comments about her firm's sudden downsizing.

The people who will survive have realized we have to look out for ourselves. If you see a good assignment, you have to go after it. You have to fight for it: Make contacts, talk to people, communicate your interest, show 'em what you bring to the table. If there's a good assignment opening up and I'm not done with my current project, I'll work on the new one at night or on weekends. If I don't do that, I can't complain about not getting new skills.

Gradually, once the shock had worn off, Jean realized that she liked the new, more entrepreneurial atmosphere.

The old days could be obnoxious. You had to kiss up and dress right to get ahead. Now, none of that matters. If you work hard, you'll find a place.

Jean is owning her own employability. Lots of factors go into helping your employees make the transition from the false sense of security they might have wanted to live under to the brave new world that Ned and Jean describe. But like it or hate it, this is what the Value Revolution has wrought. And your employees, if you coach them towards self-empowerment, might just end up feeling like Jean, that there's less politics and everybody knows where they stand.

3. Teach Managers That Serve Internal Customers How to Add Value

Not long ago, I was invited to lead a session on "Unleashing the Innovator in You" for a global firm's marketing communications managers. I learned that the marketing communications managers were demoralized and that there had just been a sizable reassignment of marketing communications managers, and that I would be speaking to the survivors.

What had happened was this: For years, the salaries of these managers had come out of headquarters budget, rather than from the divisions where the managers were individually assigned. The responsibility of marketing communications managers was to work with product managers to create media attention for the various products. The manager for a synthetic product used in ski parkas might, for instance, gain some attention for the fact that a particular Olympic skier wore the parka in her record-breaking race. In other words, the familiar product promotion through free advertising.

But then somebody at corporate headquarters was taking a shower one morning and had a brilliant idea: Hey, instead of us at corporate paying the salaries for these marketing communications managers, let's make the product managers pay for their services out of their budgets. That way there's more accountability. And sure enough, the other folks at headquarters thought that was a pretty nifty idea.

Suddenly the rules got changed. And when headquarters suddenly changed the rules, it forced the product managers to say, "Gee, is Shirley or Bob or Trisha really worth what we're now going to have to pay these people out of our budget, or have they just been blowing a lot of smoke?" The result was that a lot of people didn't make it under the new arrangement and were reassigned or let go. The cold, hard reality was this: When somebody else was paying for these specialists, they were "nice to have around." But when the product managers were asked to support them out of their budgets, their value, in some cases at least, didn't measure up.

As I work with dozens of companies each year I frequently hear such stories. My thought is always that such incidents are merely more examples of the Value Revolution causing reevaluation of the way work gets done. As the CEO, you can help your managers be more proactive about the possibility that they too will suddenly seem more like they're merely adding costs to your company, rather than value. If they're not thinking about such future prospects, they should be. You don't want sitting ducks in your firm.

Any department in a company that doesn't directly serve the external customer needs to reposition itself as a business within a business. As CEO, you can help encourage this process. For clues on how some managers are already reinventing their function in the organization, let's look at what innovative managers are doing to win the Value Revolution.

How Hospital Engineers Are Adding Value

On one recent assignment, I was invited to address the annual meeting of the American Society of Hospital Engineers, the folks who keep hospitals all across the country humming day and night. What I quickly learned was that a lot of hospital engineers are being let go as health care organizations merge and seek to lower costs. It soon became clear to me that the urgent necessity for hospital engineers was to prove their value, and to add more of it—or else.

"If we don't take the challenge that's in front of us, it's called unemployment," observed a past-president of the society. He wasn't exaggerating. And, as he further explained, "You simply had to pick up one of the health care magazines and see that there was a merger and see that the person who sold himself best, who had a better track record, was the person who stayed. The others were out."

Yet what some hospital engineers saw as the crisis of their professional lives, others saw as the opportunity to reinvent their way of doing business and raise the stature of their departments throughout the organization. These innovators asked, what would a value-adding engineering department do that we aren't now doing? How satisfied with our services are our customers? How do expectations of us get defined? What are the specific needs of us of the dietary department? The pediatrics department?

One hospital engineer had this to say: "We got them to tell us what their expectations were of the maintenance department. We asked them to tell us what pieces of equipment were critical to their operation, and how long they felt was a reasonable period when that machine went down before we got it back up." In other words, the threat of having his entire department replaced by an outsourcing firm similar to

ServiceMaster got this engineer thinking along completely different lines. Two seemingly opposing ideas became important and had to be balanced: customer satisfaction and value.

To be maximally responsive to customers would no doubt please the department being served, but if the costs associated with doing so were out of line, the department would be perceived as being too costly, and an outsourcing firm, promising savings, might attack. Producing value, which in this case might be defined as benefits produced divided by the cost to achieve such benefits, is a much more complex equation.

How Training Managers Are Adding Value

Like engineering departments, many training departments—and the managers who run them—face a major challenge in proving the value they add to the organization. In the case of training, it's the value received as a result of the skills they teach.

Often seen as a staff function rather than an activity that correlates directly to the overall Value Proposition, training needs to be justified by objective measurement. It must show how what it does translates to higher quality, increased sales, better service, and greater employee productivity.

Yet even when the time and money are available to evaluate training, the process is often blocked by a lack of measuring data that prove the value added. So when CEOs look around for ways to trim costs, training is often the first to come under the ax. Without a concrete evaluation plan, a training department manager is always a heartbeat away from unemployment.

But training programs do bring tremendous value to organizations, and innovative training managers are figuring out better ways to evaluate not just their quality but also their results in terms of performance and productivity. One of them is John Noonan, training manager at Kraft General Foods. Are sales up? Costs down? Cycle time reduced? Has time been saved? These dollar-value factors, says Noonan, can correlate to the training experience in a proven way if proactive trainers use formulas and techniques that show reasonable evidence, a plausible business case.

How to "tangibalize" the value of training? Noonan advises training professionals to offer courses that teach skills people will use a lot in their jobs and will produce the greatest gains in productivity. By thinking strategically about how to demonstrate value to the organization, and keeping a sharp eye on the productivity of real people in real jobs, Noonan sees the training department repositioning itself as a service company within the larger organization.

By doing so, Noonan believes training managers can bring their departments out of the corporate basement and establish them as essential to the overall value the firm delivers to customers.

Why Human Resource Professionals Can Be Replaced

Listen to Robert Joy, vice-president of human resources global operations at New York City-based Colgate Palmolive. Joy is one of the most respected thinkers in the field of human resources and recently won the coveted HR Executive of the Year award given out by *Human Resources Executive* magazine. Joy believes that most human resource departments have allowed themselves to become transaction-oriented, order-processing units, that, unless they change, are in danger of being either outsourced or automated.

> The only way the function of human resources is going to survive is if it adds value to the business process. The human resource director, to be effective, must go beyond the traditional service mentality, which was so heavily transaction and service oriented. Companies are looking for inefficiencies in organizations, so such routing functions will be taken over by technology or outsourced. The transaction side of the profession will be increasingly automated. But where the human resource professional can add tremendous value is in helping people learn on the job about the change process. We can be the ones to provide others with a road map for success . . . as a human resource person you can see the whole of the organization, so you are in a position to reengineer and streamline the process. To be effective, the HR director must genuinely understand the firm's business plan and the dynamics of the change process as well as any other senior manager.

In short, what we've just seen are various managers reinventing what they do from the standpoint of adding value in new and better ways. Whether your firm is large or small, you can coach your managers toward such reinvention. Once they know what you expect, they'll start gathering ideas when they attend their professional association meetings and they'll start coming back with ideas other leading-edge professionals in their field are implementing to add value. The choice is clear: Internal departments must prove their worth, and improve it at the same time. If this isn't happening at your company, everyone faces a day of reckoning when your customers are suddenly lured away by a competitor with a more attractive Value Proposition.

4. Treat Employees as Customers

Just as you, as "management," must determine the value of each employee, and just as you must attempt to determine the value of each prospective employee, that job candidate you're about to interview is also rating your firm's employment Value Proposition. And when a candidate says, "I don't think I want the job; the price I'd have to pay versus the reward you're offering is out of whack," that's a pretty good indication that you've got a "value veto" on your hands. Today, smart employers are paying attention to their employees' larger concerns.

In the 90s, Americans are working 160 hours longer each year than they did in the 70s. More than 7 million Americans now have a second job, the highest rate in history, according to the Bureau of Labor Statistics. Workers in the service sector and self-employed Americans have greatly lengthened the number of hours spent on the job. As a result of such trends—more single working parents, more single people who've never married, and other factors—employers must be more flexible in the way they view the business day. Americans are spending more work time on personal chores, such as running errands, doing personal business, taking a family member to the doctor. Companies ranging from Southwest Airlines to Steelcase have adapted to the new reality and are treating their employees not as forces to be controlled but as individuals to be accommodated, in order to unleash their skills, talents, and potential. As Jack Welch, chairman of General Electric says:

> If you're not thinking all the time about making every person more valuable, you don't have a chance. What's the alternative? Wasted minds? Uninvolved people? A labor force that's angry or bored? . . . the only way I see to get more productivity is by getting people involved and excited about their jobs. You can't afford to have

anyone walk through a factory gate or into an office who's not giving 120 percent. I don't mean running and sweating, but working smarter. It's a matter of understanding the customer's needs instead of just making something and putting it into a box. It's a matter of seeing the importance of your role in the total process.

I would argue that a satisfied work force is a productive work force. Back when jobs were plentiful and there was no foreign competition, people were satisfied just to hang around. Now people come to work with a different agenda; they want to win against the competition, because they know that the competition is the enemy and that customers are their only source of job security.

Welch is right. And the role of the leader in navigating the firm in the uncharted waters of the Value Revolution has never been more demanding. In the final chapter, we'll now turn our attention to the necessary attributes of the value-adding leader.

C H A P T E R

THE VALUE-ADDING
LEADER

"Of the best leader, when he is gone, they will say: We did it ourselves."

— Chinese proverb

TALKING WITH THE CHIEF EXECUTIVE OF A COMPANY
facing an onslaught of new competition, I happened to ask how all the
changes were affecting him personally. "I sleep like a baby," he said,
"every couple of hours I wake up and cry."

Facing up to the realities and the challenges of the Value Revolution
can be, well, sleep depriving. Realizing that the revolution that is spreading across the economic landscape has set down in your own industry
can be disconcerting. So, in this chapter, we'll turn our attention to the
special requirements that the Value Revolution makes on company leaders. I'll give you the five imperatives of becoming a value-adding leader,
imperatives that you can measure your own leadership style against as
you implement some of the ideas you've gotten from this book.

1. The Value-Adding Leader Champions The Value Vision

When all is said and done, there's only one person in the organization who's responsible for looking at your firm's overall Value Proposition—you. Sure, others on your team have responsibility for a piece of it. And certainly they are aware of it. But you are the only one who can put all the pieces together and determine whether your customers are getting the best value from you. Only you can initiate progress toward rethinking that Value Proposition and innovating improvements.

When John Martin became CEO of Taco Bell, the Mexican fast-food chain was a top-down command and control organization, always seemingly striving for bigger, better, and more complicated procedures in just about everything it undertook. As an organization, Taco Bell believed it knew what the customer wanted without even asking.

Martin changed that focus with a massive "value reengineering" effort. "Throughout the entire process," recalls Martin, "our greatest insight has been our most basic, namely, that everything begins with a simple decision to listen to our customer." Taking its customers' lead, Taco Bell decided to reduce every cost except cost of goods sold. This was the opposite approach of most companies trying to reduce costs. Martin was convinced that if Taco Bell created a better deal for its customers, it would "not have to spend so much to twist people's arm to get them to buy our product." This line of thinking produced a paradigm shift that launched the entire reengineering process. In a few short years, Taco Bell:

- Reorganized human resources, eliminating layers of management and redefining every job in the system.

- Redesigned the operational system to be more innovative and customer focused.

- Reduced kitchen size and increased customer seating areas.

- Started preparing foods centrally in off-site kitchens, then delivering to restaurant locations, saving 15 hours of food preparation per week and allowing employees to focus extra time on customers.

- Introduced TACO, total automation company operation, which brought the company's technology up-to-date.

- Reinvented what an outlet might be, instead of only the traditional site. Taco Bell began showing up in places where people congregate: schools, universities, and even corporate dining centers.

John Martin said he learned many lessons since his journey began with Taco Bell. Among the most important:

- Enhance the things that bring value to the customer and change or eliminate those that do not.

- Expect resistance and be prepared to deal with it. If people are upset, it is a good sign you are doing something significant.

"When your traditional thinkers tell you your goal is farfetched, probably you are onto something big. Second, when they stop telling you it's farfetched, you have probably already lost the war. Each time, I would listen, smile, shake their hand, and thank them for being an important part of Taco Bell's successful past."

- *Everything begins with a simple decision to listen to customers.* "Turn customer value into a key element of your business proposition."

- *Look for synergy in all processes.* "As our value-based marketing strategy drove sales transactions, our efforts at reengineering made sales more profitable and, at the same time, increased customer satisfaction ratings, which we traced on a continual basis."

- *Think big.* "Things really started to happen when we stopped confining ourselves to the goal of becoming the value leader in the quick-service restaurant industry and set our sights on becoming a value leader for all food and meal occasions."

The biggest result of Martin's championing of the value vision was that Taco Bell was among the first to cut prices on popular menu items by 25 percent. By serving the same food for less, they went from a $500-million regional company to a $3-billion global company.

Your vision is the *raison d'être* of the team, unit, organization. It is the mission, philosophy, goals, and shared values as defined by the leader and ratified by the group. It is articulated in response to such questions as: What is the purpose of this team? What are we trying to achieve?

In value-innovating organizations, the vision is not simply to maximize profits. Innovators are primarily motivated by the challenge of turning an idea into reality. Profits are seen as a way of keeping score. Nor does it stop at "We are here to serve the needs of the customers," although customers' needs are most important.

Selling and reselling the team on the vision is one of the leader's most important responsibilities. Here the image of the juggler trying to keep all the balls in the air is particularly appropriate. The ball that is most easily dropped is the one called "delivering best value" —amidst all the pressures and demands of daily business.

2. The Value-Adding Leader Monitors Changes That May Change Customers' Perception of "Best Value"

American Express makes a point to learn 450 things about each cardholder. Unfortunately, its extensive system for finding out what customers are thinking didn't ask enough questions about their changing perception of the card's value, because American Express has been losing customers for the last 5 years.

The value-adding leader looks at how the value of his or her firm's offerings are changing over time. How can you get a jump on the competition with regard to how the world is changing and how your customers' perceptions may be changing as a result? The solution lies in becoming a better trend watcher, so that you are among the first rather than last to spot a new development. I suggest you set up your own "future scan" system to monitor changes, both within your industry and outside it, that may soon have an impact on how you do business.

Component 1: Look for Trends in Your Reading

What newspapers, magazines, newsletters, and trade publications do you read on a regular basis? Stop now and make a list. Then ask yourself: Is this the reading diet of a future-focused executive? Am I getting trivia, noise, and clutter, or am I learning about other pieces of the larger puzzle?

In researching the 1986 book, *Winning the Innovation Game*, coauthored with Dr. Denis Waitley, I personally interviewed over 50 leading American innovators. They had in common one strong attribute: Almost all of them were voracious readers, and they made their reading time count. Here are nine techniques you can put to use right away to get more from your reading:

1. *Read for surprises.* Look for what's different, incongruous, new, worrisome, exciting. Professional social forecasters call this *scanning* and *monitoring.* They scan to monitor trends. The goal is to notice trends before the media does. If you can do that, you know your early-warning system is working effectively. But if you're reading about developments in your field in *Reader's Digest,* you know you're behind—and that means you're vulnerable. So read for what jumps out at you. When you spot something unusual, ask yourself: How can this trend become an opportunity?

2. *Read broadly.* Many executives feel they barely have time to flip through the news weeklies, much less general-interest publications. Be forewarned: Lack of broad information can hurt you. My recommendation is that business leaders subscribe to at least a dozen magazines and newspapers, even if you don't read them all as they come in. Save them. When you're taking a flight or have a block of free time, whittle away at the stack. Even if you only skim them, you'll pick up a wealth of information, and you'll notice connections and start seeing patterns of change emerge.

3. *Read for different points of view.* One executive I know told me he reads everything from *The Wall Street Journal* to matchbook covers for the variety of inputs. Accept the free literature you're offered; send off for those sample issues of new publications; and constantly reinvigorate your reading materials. You never know where a new idea may come from.

Buckminster Fuller, the great inventor, supposedly always bought the top right-hand magazine when he visited a newsstand, no matter what magazine it was. Once his purchase turned out to be a nature magazine carrying an article about the structure of the eye of a housefly. Fuller read that article, thought about the fly's eye, and came up with a nifty little invention he called the *geodesic dome.*

4. *Read for the wheat and skip the chaff.* There's plenty that you can safely skip. Celebrity profiles, crime reports, the latest scandal—these stories won't help you spot opportunities. Spend your time reading feature stories, where you'll often find the most valuable information.

For example, features are often found on the far-right and far-left columns of *The Wall Street Journal* and other major newspapers. Your local paper may not carry feature stories on current issues and trends. If not, you must rely on magazines or subscribe to a national newspaper. Also, if your local newspaper is short on wheat and long on chaff, be sure you subscribe to one of the news weeklies, such as *Time*, *Newsweek*, or *US News & World Report*.

5. *Read up on at least one new subject every week.* It might be a new technological or scientific breakthrough or an emerging political or social issue. Make it a point to read a long in-depth article on the subject, even if you aren't particularly interested. You may be wondering what this has to do with trend spotting. Remember, the more you know and understand about the other pieces of the puzzle, the less likely something will blindside you.

6. *Read the local newspapers when you travel.* You'll find amazing tidbits plus local insights and viewpoints. You can also compare business climates and spot new opportunities in regional markets.

7. *Subscribe to newsletters and trend reports.* Some are very expensive—the *Yankelovich Monitor* runs $15,000 a year. But if you keep your eyes open, you'll discover excellent trend leaders for your industry. By subscribing, you earn the right to call the editor on occasion to check out your hunches or to bounce around ideas. My current favorite newsletter is *Kami's Strategic Assumptions*. In addition, some local banks publish trend reports and are happy to put you on their mailing lists. These reports are like vitamin supplements for your regular information diet.

8. *Read the nonfiction bestsellers.* Develop a list of titles gleaned from periodicals, newspapers, and radio interviews. Keep your list active and you'll soon develop your own network of "book news."

9. *Read your mail.* Or more to the point, scan your mail, especially your junk mail, for patterns of change, for information on who's doing what and why. Look for what's different about the direct mail you're receiving this year as opposed to last. The mail, if you look at it as an opportunity spotter, becomes one more window on the world.

Component 2: Connect with People

People are the second resource of your future scan system: the people surrounding you, the members of your trade association or society, your associates, your sales team, your golf buddies, your family, in short the people you depend on for ideas and insights.

The first question to ask is: Are there opportunity spotters among these folks? Are there leading-edge thinkers? People who are looking at and thinking about the big picture, as you are? Do they spur you to think more deeply about current events, new inventions, the latest developments in your field? The people in your life have a tremendous influence on how you think, and what you think about. They can be great motivators to try new ideas out yourself, to dig deeper, to experiment with new possibilities and ways of doing business, or they can reinforce a false sense of security that the world is not changing rapidly and therefore you don't need to change either.

Evaluate your current circle of contacts. Identify how many change agents there are among your acquaintances. If they can't help you keep abreast, take action immediately. Make it a point to expand your circle of friends; mastermind groups and professional associations. Attend conventions and trade shows. Take along your business card. When you meet people whose ideas interest you, establish contact. Send them a note when you get back to the office, and cement the contact with a follow-up phone call.

Another way to meet new people in your profession who are leading-edge thinkers is to volunteer to do a panel with your trade association or professional society. Suggest that the topic be "industry trends." Then, invite several of the sharpest people in your industry to appear on the panel with you. During the course of preparing for the panel, you'll find the interactions with these people to be especially educational. Also, you can call others in your industry and ask questions on a wide variety of topics. Of course officially you're just preparing for the panel, being a good volunteer. But you're also asking questions that can give you awesome insights into what you should be doing next with your business, and where others are finding success.

In short, you may find that you've been overlooking one of the greatest trend-spotting teams you've got: your associates. Your salespeople are out in the field every day, listening to and keeping tabs on an ever-changing market. How are you "incentivizing" them to share this information and their insights with you in a systematic fashion?

Utilize the knowledge within your employee group of what are the unmet needs in the marketplace, especially with regard to your service development efforts. Anytime they spot a development that they think has the potential of being a trend, make sure they are encouraged to document it and inform you.

To keep such reports coming, you'll need to show appreciation in some form or fashion, even if it's a quick e-mail word of thanks or public acknowledgment at a sales meeting. Communicating to one and all how important trend watching is to the success of the company is vitally important and so often overlooked.

The time you spend with others can widen your base of information if you learn to ask the right questions. Make people the cornerstone of your early-warning system.

Component 3: Observe Your Own Changing Habits and Lifestyles

The third part of your early-warning system is self-observation. The greatest opportunity spotters are self-observant. They listen to their intuition. Intuition plays a crucial role in spotting trends. But you must be sensitive to the signals. You must be willing to respond when your internal early-warning system sends notice that something important is happening.

Self-observation also helps by letting you "see the world as if you are the whole market." You look at your own needs, likes, and dislikes, and apply them to your business. Imagine yourself as a customer of your own company. Then ask: What would I want that isn't presently available? What do I like? What turns me off? By asking yourself such questions, you stay tuned in to customers. Ask the questions often enough, and you'll begin to anticipate what customers will want next.

COMPONENT 4: CHALLENGE YOUR ASSUMPTIONS

Chances are, you're a specialist in some field. That specialty is your comfort zone. Staying in that comfort zone can be dangerous to you, your career, and your organization. Markets and customers are changing faster every day. Some of the biggest assumptions we make turn out to have major flaws. A good friend of mine brought this point home after his Dallas-based real estate investment syndicate was forced into bankruptcy after the tax law changes of 1986.

"We all began to think the bonanza days would go on forever, despite the tremendous overbuilding of office complexes." he told me. "And then the balloon burst." What does "everybody know" to be true in *your* industry? It could turn out to be a house of cards.

3. THE VALUE-ADDING LEADER HELPS CREATE SHARED VALUES

The global economy of the 90s has legitimized layoffs, made a formerly full-time, permanent work force into a part-time, contingency work force, where insecurity reigns. While no company can offer "lifetime employment security" any longer, what can employees legitimately expect from you? My suggestion is that you spell these things out, the social contract, so to speak. What can you promise your associates? What conditions do they seek that you might want to communicate openly with them?

One of them is trust. Trust is enormously powerful in a firm, and its absence can be devastating to morale and productivity. People won't give their best unless they believe they'll be treated fairly, unless they trust your fairness, trust the boss, and unless there's no cronyism and everybody has a real shot at proving themselves. The only way to create that kind of trust is to take the time to decide what your values are and then walk the talk. And keep walking it, over time, even when sticking to those values is difficult.

Just as today's consumers are more sophisticated, so are today's employees. If you don't consistently live up to the "shared values" you post on the bulletin board by the water cooler, they'll quickly see it. You can count on their seeing just about everything; even the stuff that is "secret" and you don't think they "see," they will "feel." So that's the stark choice, and it isn't easy. But in the long run, as the companies we've examined in this book surely prove, it's worth it.

Perhaps the biggest value of all, the one most yearned for in this era of tumult, is a sense of belonging, a sense of community, whether to a church, social group, softball team, or company. Here's why:

- One in five American children are born into poverty.
- For two out of three children under the age of 18, either both parents or the only parent works outside the home.
- Unwed mothers account for one in four births in America.
- Seven out of 10 children experience the trauma of being "under new management" at least once in childhood.

"The value system is being torn apart," warns industrial psychologist Dee Soder, president of Endymion corporation, a counselor to top executives. "Your stockbroker has just been thrown into jail, and your priest is being accused of child abuse. Where do you go for a source of values?"

The standout leaders in times of tumultuous change have always been those who genuinely believe in the values they espouse and have the courage to back them up with consistent action. While such firms are few and far between, what is striking is how well they do both in the marketplace and in meeting the needs of their workers. From Levi Strauss to ServiceMaster to Federal Express to Wal-Mart, they instill in associates the self-respect that comes from service to others, of giving value and in turn receiving value.

4. The Value-Adding Leader Masters New Technologies

One of the more significant changes of the past decade—and one that will relentlessly shape the next decade—is the explosion of technological innovation. That explosion increased expectations. People expect products to become faster, cheaper, more powerful, and more reliable and maintenance-free. They expect software to become easier to use. And it company A can't deliver, they'll go to company B. If a U.S.A-based supplier can't deliver, they'll find one in Brazil or Singapore that can.

To give the customer the same as you gave him yesterday is to give him less. Which is why the role of technology has become so vitally important. It has been called the "great enabler," and it is. For those firms that are pushing back the envelope in using new technology, there is a clear and consistent pattern: They tend to do better on the bottom line than do those that merely wait for all the bugs to be ironed out.

Today technology is driving change in other ways as well: It can change industries, alter long-standing relationships, and create new forms of competition overnight. Consider the retailer-manufacturer relationship, for example. Prior to the introduction of scanners (computer systems that record every purchase) in the past decade, retailers relied on manufacturers to tell them how each product was performing.

Today, they can do this themselves. The balance of power is shifting. Many retailers now make manufacturers pay to keep new or underperforming products on shelves. Since they know exactly what's selling and what is not, retailers are quick to replace slow movers with competing brands. This shift occurred over 5 short years, changing decades-old traditions. Many manufacturers were caught off-guard. In the coming decade, there will be other firms that fail because they failed to adapt new technology that kept them from improving their value equations. The trick is not to be one of them.

To lead the field, you must continually use technology as a strategic weapon. In a moment, we'll take a look at ways you can make technology part of your battle plan. But first, let's look at companies that have used technology to produce greater customer value.

Winners on the Techno-Edge Battlefront

Rarely is the demise of a business blamed directly on "failure to implement new technology." Instead, reports say the business filed for bankruptcy because it "did not control costs," or "overpriced its merchandise," or "took on too much debt." But often the insiders know that the business went under because the competition had a technological advantage that was at the heart of the problem.

To lead the field, you must continually use technology as a strategic weapon. Value Innovators use technology to revolutionize how they serve customers, find new ones, and lower costs. Conventional wisdom holds that technology-based advantages are difficult to maintain. Yet the Value Innovator companies we've looked at demonstrate that the creative use of a technology (in each case, the computer) has provided and will continue to provide an advantage.

You can develop your company's next techno-edge. The critical question becomes: What's the next step in your evolution? How can you create competitive advantage from technology? Don't leave technology to chance. Develop a systematic plan for finding and exploiting new developments.

Whether you are division head of a large manufacturing concern, president of an independent bank, or the owner of a multistate service company, your industry has a techno-edge. Some company somewhere in your industry is the state of the art, technologically speaking. Make it your business to know what others in your industry are doing with new technologies to give them an edge. Businesses that discover and use new technologies before the rest of the pack are worth watching. They could provide a blueprint of your firm's future. Here are some tactics you can use to stay ahead of the pack:

- Start a new-technology file. Ask colleagues to contribute interesting articles, ideas, and suggestions that might apply to your business.

- Attend at least two trade shows a year and pay particular attention to new technology. Or assign at least one person as your "technology scout," with the responsibility of reporting back to the rest of the team.

- Subscribe to at least one industry newsletter. Call the editor at least once a year to ask about his or her favorite new ideas.

- Meet every 6 months with your top team for the sole purpose of reviewing technological developments and plans.

- Brainstorm ways to adapt new ideas. Ask: What is our techno-edge right now? What do we want it to be in the future? List the technologies the competition uses. Are these ideas you can adapt?

5. The Value-Adding Leader Stresses Continuous Learning

The leader's task is to create an environment that allows knowledgeable workers to learn at a rate that is greater than others in their industry. They must be encouraged to learn on their own, by enrolling in classes and seminars outside the company that pertain to their own professional development in sales or accounting or in being the best receptionist possible. They must be encouraged to see that learning from each other is mutually beneficial to all, not to believe as some do that when a manager shares expertise freely, it means that he or she loses his or her perceived value.

A Final Message

There is a revolution spreading across the economic landscape, and it demands entirely new leadership skills. It first of all demands that we understand its dimensions; that at root, it is a change in the relationship between buyers and sellers. As we have seen, buyers are becoming more demanding and less loyal because they have so many more choices for satisfying their demands than they did previously. And thus, they are refusing to pay for things they once accepted without question, negotiating harder for the absolute best deal.

And there is little doubt that they will continue to substitute or clone generic products for those that do not offer a unique difference, a "unique Value Proposition," as some call it. It is clear that the trend is toward bypassing middlemen who add no unique value, as consumers and contractors, small dealers, and independent businesses shop at warehouse clubs for goods they once purchased through distributors.

Perhaps the biggest driving force of change—the Information Highway—has yet to develop to the point where its impact can be speculated about, much less measured. But there is an inevitability about this new shopping center; it, like the Value Revolution already underway, will leave no business untouched.

But this exciting, volatile new world need not unsettle us, not so long as we continue to stay on top of, and be proactive about, adding value to our products, services, and ways of doing business. These changes can be our opportunity.

NOTES

PAGE
NO.

CHAPTER 1: THE VALUE REVOLUTION

2 American Express's dilemma outlined in "Less-Than-Fantastic Plastic," *Business Week*, Nov. 9, 1992, and updated with AmEx official data provided by Ron Stovall.

2 BPIA figures courtesy of the association's research department.

2 Warehouse club growth information from J. M. Degan & Co. and "Wearhouse Clubs Feed Frenzy for Value," *Los Angeles Times*, Sep. 27, 1993.

7 Information on Sam's Clubs from "Why Sam's Wants Businesses to Join the Club," *Business Week*, June 27, 1994.

7 Private-label insights from "Private Label Nightmare: Big Name Marketers Are Being Stalked by Strong, High-Quality Store Brands," *Advertising Age*, Apr. 12, 1993.

8 "Private label is here. . . ." CEO David Glass quoted in "And the Winner Is Still . . . Wal-Mart" *Fortune*, May 2, 1994.

8 "We have become enlightened consumers. . . ." Robert Weinbaum's quote is from "The Verdict: Guilty of Overcharging," *BusinessWeek*, Sep. 6, 1993.

9 "This market is getting much pickier. . . . " Steven Brill's quote is from "Slump Hits Elite Firms, Survey Shows," *The Wall Street Journal*, June 29, 1993.

9 "We're fighting for our existence as an industry. . . ." Quote is from "The Layoff Industry Learns that the Ax Can Be a Real Grind," *The Wall Street Journal*, Nov. 28, 1994. Additional information from Association of Outplacement Professionals.

10 "Bargain Hunting Catches on in Japan," *The Wall Street Journal*, May 19, 1992.

12 "We Americans have gotten into the discount mindset. . . ." Professor Dale Achabal's quote is from an author interview.

12 "You are already sharply aware. . . ." Quote is from "The Tough New Consumer," *Fortune* special issue, Autumn/Winter 1993.

227

12   "Consumers in the 90s are taking the time. . . ." From *Grey Matter*, privately circulated publication of Grey Advertising.

13   "Holy cow, I'm not going to live forever. . . ." John Parikhal's quote is from an author interview.

14   Merrill Lynch study of Boomer consumers from "Living for Today: Boomers Awake to Discover Unpleasant Truth: They Haven't Saved Nearly Enough," *The Wall Street Journal*, Dec. 9, 1994.

15   "It is possible for banks to die and still have vibrant economy. . . ." Edward Furash was quoted in "Are Banks Obsolete," *Time*, June 28, 1993.

16   "Our firm is made up of computers. . . ." Walter Forbes was quoted in "Fall of the Mall," by Grechen Morgenson, *Forbes*, May 24, 1993.

22   Wallace Co. filing for Chapter 11 from "Quality: How to Make It Pay," *BusinessWeek*, Aug. 8, 1994.

23   The story of how AT&T discovered the limits of customer satisfaction and the supremacy of overall value is from *Managing Customer Value*, by Bradley T. Gale.

PAGE   CHAPTER 2: RETHINKING YOUR VALUE PROPOSITION
NO.

31   Information on Singer Sewing Machine Co. from *Managing the Future*, by Robert B. Tucker.

35   Marlboro's pricing move discussed in "New Price Move by Philip Morris Intensifies War," *The Wall Street Journal*, July 21, 1993.

41   Saatchi study summarized in an author interview with Saatchi's Myra Stark.

45   GM's value pricing strategy examined in "Value Pricing Drives GM Sales," *Los Angeles Times*, Oct. 11, 1994.

46   Procter & Gamble's rethinking efforts are reported on in "P&G Hits Back," *BusinessWeek*, July 1993.

48   Information on Lloyd Mandel Levayah Funerals from "Value pricing comes to funerals," *USA Today*, July 14, 1993.

49   Boise Cascade's pricing innovation from author interviews with company officials.

Page No.	**Chapter 3: Becoming a Value Innovator**

52   The value-adding shoeshine man story is told with permission of Dr. Barry Asmus.

53   "There's nothing wrong with serving a lousy cup of coffee. . . ." Truett Cathy's quote from "P>E," Delta Sky, July 1992.

54   "Nobody was really performing a service. . . ." George Orban's quote is from an interview with the author.

57   "In a service environment. . . ." Southwest Airlines' Dave Ridley's quote is from a presentation he made at the "Designing, Developing & Delivering Outstanding Service Value" conference, New Orleans, Dec. 1994, sponsored by the Institute for International Research.

60   For more on how Wegmans wins with more-for-more, see "As big as Kodak is in Rochester, it still isn't Wegmans," The Wall Street Journal, Dec. 27, 1994.

64   "We priced our program less than competitors. . . ." Jimmy Calano's quote is from an author interview.

66   Michael Porter's book is Competitive Strategy, published by Free Press.

67   "Discount brokerage used to be faceless. . . ." Jeffrey Lyons quote is from Advertising Age, Oct. 3, 1994.

69   "Anybody can build a cheap hotel. . . ." Robert Hazard's quote is from an author interview.

70   "Home Depot caters to the do-it-yourselfer. . . ." Bernard Marcus's quote is from "Companies That Serve You Best," Fortune, May 31, 1993.

71   "What allows us to be both a discounter and a full-service retailer. . . ." Richard Sharp's quote is from an interview with the author.

Page No.	**Chapter 4: Seven Powerful Strategies for Adding Value**

75   "[Intuition] is some kind of internal extrapolation. . . ." Robert Giamo's quote is from an author interview. See also Winning the Innovation Game," by Waitley and Tucker.

PAGE NO.	CHAPTER 6: CUSTOMER LOYALTY AND VALUE

119   "... added value as part of the product is expected." Mava Heffler's quote is from "Credit Cards Up Ante for Incentives," *Advertising Age*, Sep. 12, 1994.

125   Information on Sauder is from "Key Market Study," *Sales and Marketing Management*, date unavailable.

126   "We don't know their political opinions. ..." Jim Frain's quote is from "Retailers Trying Harder to Please Regular Customers," *The Wall Street Journal*, May 5, 1994.

127   "We find that they do come in at all hours. ..." Blacks Industrial's Rolly Johnson's quote is from an interview with the author.

128   "We are trying to think faster than competitors. ..." Robert Stoltz's quote is from an interview with the author.

131   Carlene Thissen's prediction is quoted in "Loyalty: Check It Out," *Los Angeles Times*, July 8, 1994.

132   "An island of excellence in a sea of mediocrity. ..." Christopher Hart's quote is from "More Firms Pledge Guaranteed Service," *The Wall Street Journal*, July 17, 1991.

PAGE NO.	CHAPTER 7: MARKETING AND COMMUNICATING VALUE

138   For more information on The Body Shop, see "Beyond the Body Shop Brouhaha," *Utne Reader*, Jan./Feb. 1995.

142   "I'll grant that steel makes a good railroad tie. ..." David Reynolds's quote is from "Aluminum Producers, Aggressive and Agile, Outfight Steelmakers," *The Wall Street Journal*, July 1, 1992.

143   "This company's offices were absolutely beautiful. ..." Robert Kohlhepp's quote is from an interview with research assistant Darcy Ellington for the author.

152   "Our philosophy was, if you built a better product. ..." Hillary Keeney's quote is from "Pella: Moving Up by Downscaling," *Fortune*, Aug. 9, 1993.

PAGE
NO.

CHAPTER 8: Adding Value to Products

161 "When the AIDs crisis hit. . . ." Quote is from "Condoms join march to value," *Advertising Age*, Mar. 14, 1994.

162 For more on the changing value equation in med-tech, see "It's New, It's Improved. Who needs it?" *Business Week*, June 6, 1994.

164 "It was like a contest to see how many gadgets you could get. . . ." David Humphrey's quote is from "RV Mania: Buyers Are Back and Not in the Mood for Chandeliers," *Los Angeles Times*, Aug. 27, 1994.

166 "Today's products are far too complex to follow this path. . . ." Manuel Diaz of Hewlett-Packard made this statement at the "Value Marketing" symposium sponsored by The Conference Board.

168 Information on Tallon supplied by the company.

PAGE
NO.

CHAPTER 9: Value-Added Selling

177 "With very few exceptions, there is no legitimacy to detailing. . . ." Francis Crosson's quote is from "Managed Health Care Jeopardizes Outlook for Drug Detailers," *The Wall Street Journal*, Sep. 10, 1993.

181 "I haven't hidden the talent under a green eye shade. . . ." Bill Whitcroft's comments are from an interview with the author.

184 "They work with dealers. . . ." Art Coye's comments are from an interview with the author.

186 "We sell three things. . . ." Joe Murray's comments are from an interview with the author.

190 "The salesperson doesn't have all the answers. . . ." Tom Corbo's quote is from *Inc.* June 1993.

PAGE
NO.

CHAPTER 10: Delivering Customer Value Through People

199 "We want people who are compassionate. . . ." Southwest Airlines' Dave Ridley's quote is from a presentation he made at the "Designing, Developing & Delivering Outstanding Service Value" conference, New Orleans, Dec. 1994, sponsored by the Institute for International Research.

201 "We are not doing this because it makes us feel good. . . ." Levi Strauss CEO Robert Haas's quote is from "Managing by Values," *Business Week,* Aug. 1, 1994.

203 "If a manager is too busy to teach. . . ." William Pollard's quote is from "ServiceMaster Puts Faith in Consumer Biz," *Crain's Chicago Business,* May 16, 1994.

204 "We wanted to be sure our associates understood. . . ." Rubbermaid's George Thompson was interviewed by the author.

206 ". . .own your own employability" Andrew Grove, CEO of Intel, was quoted in "Managing Your Career," *The Wall Street Journal,* Nov. 15, 1994.

210 For more information on John Noonan's ideas about measuring the value of training, see "How to Escape Corporate America's Basement," by John Noonan, *Training Magazine,* Dec. 1993.

211 "The only way the function of human resources is going to survive. . . ." Robert Joy's quote is from an interview with the author.

212 "If you're not thinking all the time about making every person more valuable. . . ." Jack Welch's comments are from the book *Control Your Destiny or Someone Else Will,* by Noel Tichy, who interviewed Mr. Welch.

PAGE NO.   CHAPTER 11: HE VALUE-ADDING LEADER

216 "When your traditional thinkers tell you your goal is farfetched . . . ." Taco Bell's John Martin was quoted in *Reengineering the Corporation* by Michael Hammer and James Champy.

223 "The value system is being torn apart. . . ." Psychologist Dee Soder's quote is from "How Will We Live with the Tumult?" *Fortune,* Dec. 13, 1993.

INDEX

ABOUT THE AUTHOR

ROBERT B. TUCKER is one of America's leading authorities on profiting from change through innovation. Founder and president of The Innovation Resource, a research and executive development firm, Tucker has brought his practical, results-oriented presentations to literally thousands of managers, trade associations, and companies throughout the United States and abroad.

His book, *Managing the Future*, identified the 10 Driving Forces of Change, and was translated into over 10 languages. His acclaimed book, *Winning the Innovation Game*, coauthored with Dr. Denis Waitley, was the first to identify the traits of leading innovators and to demonstrate that all of us can become more innovative by mastering some surprisingly simple skills. In addition, he is the author/narrator of *How to Profit from Today's Rapid Changes*, a Simon and Schuster audio program, *Innovative Secrets of Success*, and *Breakthrough Thinking: Strategies for Winning Big in Business*, all audio formatted.

To find out how a customized presentation on *Winning the Value Revolution* can add value to your next meeting, or to request information about our various audio and video learning systems, contact:

Marketing Director
The Innovation Resource
PO Box 30930
Santa Barbara, CA 93130

Telephone: (805) 682-1012
Fax: (805) 862-8960
Compuserve 74454,1406